New Orleans

Bethany Ewald Bultman
Photography by Richard Sexton

Compass American Guides
An Imprint of Fodor's Travel Publications, Inc.

New Orleans

Copyright © 1996 Fodor's Travel Publications, Inc.
Maps Copyright © 1996 Fodor's Travel Publications, Inc.

LIBRARY OF CONGRESS CATALOGING-IN-PUBLICATION DATA
Bultman, Bethany Ewald
New Orleans/by Bethany Ewald Bultman; photography by Richard Sexton—2nd Ed.
  p. cm. – (Compass American Guides)
  Includes bibliographical references and index
  ISBN 1-878867-86-5
  1. New Orleans (La.) — Guidebooks. I. Sexton, Richard.
  II. Title. III. Series: Compass American Guides (series)
  F379.N53B85 1996   95-21811
  917.63'350463—dc20   CIP

Editors: Kit Duane, Julia Dillon   Designers: Christopher Burt, David Hurst
Managing Editor: Kit Duane   Map Design: Eureka Cartography
Photo Editor: Christopher Burt
Compass American Guides, 5332 College Avenue, Suite 201, Oakland, CA 94618
Production house: Twin Age Ltd., Hong Kong
Printed in China
10 9 8 7 6 5 4 3 2 1

COMPASS AMERICAN GUIDES gratefully acknowledges the following institutions and individuals: Photographs ©Richard Sexton, except as noted. Michael P. Smith, pp. 67, 83, 145, 183, 194, 201-207, 210-212, 219, 231, 246; Historic New Orleans Collection, pp. 15, 27, 30-31, 32, 35, 40, 41, 45, 46, 48, 49, 51, 58, 61, 62, 69-71, 77, 89, 104, 121, 139, 141, 144, 149, 150, 153, 174, 223, 224; Syndey Byrd, pp. 18, 19, 163, 170-171, 175, 177, 181, 196; Porché West, p. 23; Underwood Archives, pp. 53, 55; The Louisiana State Museum, p. 65; Hogan Jazz Archive, Tulane University, pp. 73, 189, 191, 192, 198; Sharon Dinkins Collection, Inc., 59462 Neslo Rd., Slidell, LA 70460, pp. 78, 221, 234; Eric Lassing, Art Resource/NY, p. 120; The Maryland Historical Society, p. 186; Ann Deseran for her gumbo recipe; Dan Duane for his piece on Audubon; Bernard Guste of Antoine's for his alligator story; Sara Deseran for her meticulous fact-checking; Kelly Mays for line editing; Howard Tilton Memorial Library at Tulane University for access to Helen d'Aquin Allain's memoirs; Kit Duane for Louis Henderson's memoirs; Alice Dillon for help on voodoo and Mardi Gras Indian sections.

To my parents, who first shared New Orleans with me.
To my husband and sons who make living here such a joy.

C O N T E N T S

Maps

Literary Extracts

Topical Essays

New Orleans is famous for its lush, secluded gardens.

NEW ORLEANS FACTS

BASICS: CITY OF NEW ORLEANS

Name derivation	for French regent Philippe, Duc d'Orleans
Founded	1718
Designated capital of Louisiana	1722
Incorporated	1805
Area	199 square miles of dry land
Elevation	city ground elevation runs from 5 feet (1.5 m) below sea level to 17 feet (5.1 m) above
Visitors	approximately 10 million each year
Population	1,238,816 Metro Statistical Area (1990) 496,958 New Orleans proper

POPULATION 1740 TO 1990

ETHNIC COMPOSITION

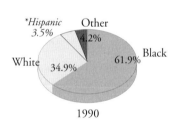

1990

by 1850 New Orleans became the fourth most populous city in the U.S.A.

*Population of Hispanic origin is an ethnic grouping and not additive to the population racial groupings

WEATHER: RECORD HIGHS AND LOWS

Hottest Day Aug 22, 1980	Coldest Day Feb 13, 1899	Strongest wind Aug 17, 1969	Heaviest rain May 8, 1995	Heaviest snow Feb 14-15, 1895

ATHLETICS

The New Orleans Saints football team is
the city's only major league sports team

NOTABLE STRUCTURES

Oldest surviving building is the Ursuline Convent
built between 1749 and 1753

Tallest building in New Orleans
is One Shell Square at 697 feet
(219 m) and 51 floors

The Louisiana Superdome in New Orleans has the longest
roof span in the world with a diameter of 680 feet (207 m)

WATER FACTS

• Almost half of New Orleans total 363.5-square-mile (931-sq-km) area is water.

• Lake Pontchartrain is 621 square miles (1590 sq km) in size but nowhere more
than 15 feet (4.5 m) deep.

• The Mississippi River is at its widest and deepest in New Orleans at 212 feet
(64 m) deep and 2200 feet (661 m) wide.

• Average annual rainfall is 60 inches (152 cm) making New Orleans the wettest
major city in the United States.

LAKE

KENNER

Canal #1
41st St

Elmwood Canal
Duncan Canal

W Esplanade Ave

Kawanee Ave

Clearview
Suburban Canal

Metairie

Lake Pontchartrain Causeway

Veterans Hwy
Veterans Memorial Blvd

New Orleans
International
Airport

Williams Blvd
Roosevelt Blvd

Westgate Ave

Lafreniere
Park

W Napoleon Ave

Oaklawn Dr
Bonnabel Blvd

Canal #4

David Dr
Airline Park Blvd

Transcontinental Dr

Pkwy

Cleary Ave

Severn Ave

Blvd

Metairie Rd

Ridgewood Dr

49

Canal #5
W Metairie Ave

Terminal

Louisiana State
Railroad Museum

Airline Hwy

61

Causeway

Airline Hwy

LaBarre Rd

Amelia Earhart

Little Farms Ave

Hickory Ave

Clearview Pkwy

Central Ave Hwy

90

Iris Ave
Monticello St

Jefferson Hwy

S Kenner Rd

River Rd

River Rd

Jefferson

River
River Rd

Carrollton

Colonial Club Dr

Dr

HARAHAN

18

48

N

W   E

S

Mississippi River

Huey P. Long
Bridge

541

90

Bridge City Ave
(Old Spanish Trail)

18

Bridge
City

River Rd

Zoological
Garden

Walnut S

NEW
ORLEANS

0   0.5   1
mile

90

Lapallo Blvd

West Bank Expwy

Main Canal

Louisiana St

WESTWEGO

18

BUS
90

PONTCHARTRAIN

City Yacht Harbor

New Orleans Lakefront Airport

Lakeshore Dr

Terminal

Hayne Blvd

47

Read Blvd

Morrison Rd

Spring Lake

Lake Willow

Lake Kenilworth

10

University of New Orleans

LC Simon Dr

Pontchartrain Park

Congress Dr

Dowman Rd

Inner Harbor Navigation

Menteur

Hwy

90

Robert E Lee Blvd

Outfall Canal

Mirabeau

St Bernard St

Elysian Fields Ave

Ave

Franklin Ave

Press Dr

Chef

Almonaster Ave

West End Blvd

Pontchartrain Blvd

Harrison Ave

Orleans Ave

Paris Ave

London Ave

London Ave Canal

City Park

Bayou St. John

Ave

Dillard University

Blvd

Gentilly

Canal

Gulf Outlet Canal

Intercoastal Waterway

610

Alvar St

DeSaix Blvd

New Orleans Museum of Art

Fairgrounds and Race Track

St Bernard Ave

Florida

10

Ave

Main Outfall Canal

Longue Vue House & Gardens

10

Orleans Ave

Esplanade Ave

Ave

Ave

Almonaster Ave

Louisa St

Expwy

61

Jefferson Davis Pkwy

Tulane Ave

Broad Ave

N Claiborne Ave

Franklin Ave

Poland St

N

Claiborne Ave

St Claude Ave

39

46

Ave S

Louis Armstrong Park

Royal St

Claiborne

French Quarter

Civic Center

Canal St

Poydras St

Algiers

Mississippi River

Arabi

Louisiana Superdome

Louisiana St

LaSalle St

New Orleans Convention & Exhibition Center

Newton St

Gen Meyer Ave

Chalmette National Historic Park

Tulane University

Calhoun St

Ave

Napoleon Ave

Jackson Ave

BUS 90

Greater New Orleans Bridge

Franklin St

Gen de Gaulle Dr

Audubon Park

St Charles Ave

Magazine St

MacArthur Blvd

Woodlawn Dr

Tchoupitoulas St

GRETNA

River Rd

4th St

18

Whitney Ave

Holmes Blvd

Brechtel Park

Intracoastal Waterway

4th St

Ames Blvd

Barataria Blvd

Destrehan Ave

Peters Rd

West Bank Expwy

Manhattan Blvd

23

Belle Chasse Hwy

Harvey Canal

Carol Sue Ave

Terry Pkwy

Behrman Hwy

45

ACKNOWLEDGMENTS

MY HEARTFELT THANKS to Kit Duane, Julia Dillon, and Tobias Steed of Compass for making the research, writing, and editing of this book such a pleasurable process; to photographer and friend, Richard Sexton, for his faith and support; to my assistant, Evelyn Feagin for the stacks of notes she had to decipher; and to my son Gwyther for the hours he donated to log information into the computer. Thanks also to my patient agent John Ware, my versatile husband, Johann, my clever little chef Tristan and the hours and hours that Zachary Richard, Maria Maldaur, and The Neville Brothers spent singing to keep me awake and working.

I'm also grateful for the invaluable support and assistance of Syndey Byrd, Jason Berry, Inez Douglas, Gwen Carter, Chief Larry Bannock, Charmaine Neville, Jessie Smallwood, Vaughn Banting, Lucy Burnett, Julie Smith, Dorian and Kell Bennett, Marguerite Oestricher, Leah Chase, Miki DeJean, Chef Kevin Graham, Michael Llewelyn, Bernard Guste, Macon Riddle, Roxy Wright, and Mari Kornhauser.

To those gracious guardians of New Orleans's historic treasures and present resources who have given so tirelessly of their time, I also owe my deep appreciation. They are: John Magill, Elsa Schneider, and Pamela Arceneaux at the Historic New Orleans Collection; the Special Collections and the Hogan Jazz Archives at Tulane University; the late Ulysses Ricard at the Amistad Research Center; Beverly Gianna and Anthony Leggio, Jr. of the Greater New Orleans Tourist and Convention Commission; Sue Ellen Lewis at the Louisiana Office of Tourism; Simone Rathle-Enlow; Britton Trice of the Garden District Bookshop; Marsha Underwood of the New Orleans Jazz & Heritage Foundation; and Ann Belkov of the National Park Service for her invaluable research data on jazz.

Many thanks to those who helped in the fact-checking process, especially Dr. Bruce Boyd Raeburn of the Hogan Jazz Archives, Lucy Core, the staff of the Louisiana Collection of the New Orleans Public Library, the Louisiana Landmarks Society, Ann Masson of the Gallier House Museum, the Preservation Resource Center, Dr. Fred Steilow of the Amistad Research Collection, David Johnson of the Louisiana Endowment for the Humanities, and Dr. Alfred Lemmon of the Historic New Orleans Collection.

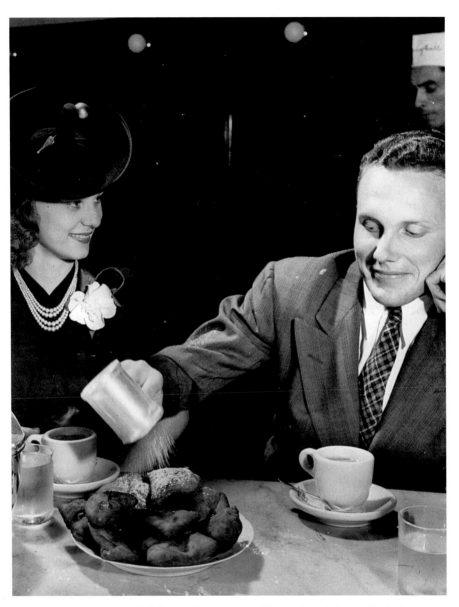

Eating beignets at Café du Monde in the 1940s. (Historic New Orleans Collection)

Citizens' Bank of Louisiana

Will pay **TEN DOLLARS** *to the bearer on demand New Orleans.* 186

CASHIER.   PRESIDENT.

INTRODUCTION

THE NAME NEW ORLEANS invariably conjures up the succulent aroma of sweet olive, the syncopation of jazz and ceiling fans, and the vision of black-haired, magnolia-fleshed damsels fanning themselves as they sit in white wicker chairs on lacy wrought-iron verandas. La Nouvelle Orleans was the original Dixie, named in the mid-nineteenth century by the hell-raising Kentucky flatboatmen who traded their merchandise in the city for the *dix* or $10 paper tender minted in New Orleans. Though geographically Southern (Rhett Butler brought Scarlett O'Hara to New Orleans for their honeymoon), it is not a garden-variety Southern city in the sense of Richmond, Memphis, Savannah, or Montgomery. It is more of a Caribbean port city, anchored in the continental United States by what often seems a mere socio-geographical accident.

An hour before dawn, the French Quarter becomes mantled in timelessness. The shimmer of streetlights is reflected on cobbled sidewalks dampened by gentle mist. The cries of a trumpet commingle with a few bluesy chords from Luther Kent's finale in the dying hours. On the swollen Mississippi, giant tankers quietly slip down the river towards the open mouth of the Gulf. For a few moments the dull roar of their engines is drowned out by the clanging bell of the riverfront street-car, which beckons a handful of the night shift from a late-night restaurant. They have stopped to savor conversation, thick chicory-laced coffee, and *beignets* (New Orleans' famous doughnuts) en route to their beds Uptown. A few blocks down-river, at the 200-year-old French Market, the produce vendors lean against the dull green fender of a Ford pick-up as they sing along with Fats Domino on the radio.

New Orleans is an archipelago of ethnicity. Tuning in to WWOZ, the New Orleans Jazz & Heritage Foundation jazz station; sucking the spicy juice from the head of a crawfish at an open-air seafood joint; taking a ride on the Algiers ferry at dawn: these are a few of the things that locals and visitors savor as they enjoy this twinkle in the eye of the old Protestant American South. The sensuous and exotic street names of Elysian Fields, Bourbon, Erato, and Desire bespeak a society that is not unsympathetic to the weaknesses of the flesh. William Faulkner once said of the city that it is "a place created for and by voluptuousness, the abashness and un-abashed senses."

The term "Dixie" originated from the "dix" note ($10) minted in New Orleans.

Culture in New Orleans spews from the ground up and is carried away to intoxicate the rest of the world. The city's sultry environs have served as the fertile foundation for the backstreet movers and shakers whose thunder is heard in the worlds of music and food. It is the hometown of a potpourri of celebrities whose talents were fostered in any number of the city's ethno-cultural enclaves: from the queen of gospel Mahalia Jackson, to the darling of New York cafe society, Harry Connick, Jr.; from international opera star Marguerite Piazza to diet guru Richard Simmons; from R&B legend Fats Domino to Emmy Award-winning actor John Larroquette.

New Orleanians prefer to see themselves as part of a festival of cultures. There are more facets to the city's multi-culturalism than there are varieties of hot sauce in a local grocery store. New Orleans is a place where people from all walks of life smile or nod when they pass strangers on the street. People encountering each other on a public bus or streetcar more than three times may feel like they're close enough friends to share a grandmother's recipe for bread pudding.

The ambiance and magic of New Orleans is impossible to appreciate at a fast clip. It is a city that gladly relinquishes its secrets to those who take the time to

Fats Domino (above) and Kid Thomas Valentine (right), legendary New Orleans musicians. (Syndey Byrd)

wander. For those who have only a short time between meetings, parades, concerts, or meals, the best thing to do would be to see one area thoroughly, preferably on foot. New Orleans is a loosely connected amalgam of neighborhoods, many of which still have their own curbside vegetable wagons, at least three snowball stands, 10 or so corner bars, a half-dozen combination po-boy sandwich/grocery stores, and a smattering of folks who pass the day stoop-sitting and visitin' with all those who pass and savor the aroma that drifts out of their kitchens.

In the older residential districts from Faubourg Marigny to the Irish Channel, each street is a visual delight as one shotgun-style house gives way to another. Some are weathered down to the bare cypress boards, others shine with color as vividly as Easter eggs. Houses that are essentially wood-frame shoeboxes have been tarted up with ornamental scrolls, brackets, shutters, hanging ferns, the occasional balustrade, and porch swings whose creaking chains and rusty springs attest to three generations of "swingers."

It's possible to spend an entire week in the French Quarter, another wandering through the Garden District and browsing through the antique and junk shops along Magazine Street, and a third enjoying the Uptown area, Audubon Park, and the zoo. The problem is that stepping into any of these areas is much like falling into visual quicksand for the aficionado of architecture and local culture. New Orleans is a city that never quite gives up all of her mysteries. Each trip to a certain street provides just one more layer in a multifaceted and often contradictory paradise of funk and splendor.

New Orleans is fueled by diversity. Its neighborhoods are a Crayola box of bright, intense, ethnic influences. On any Friday, old-line businessmen gather at noon at Galatoire's to dip their crusty French bread in the butter sauce just as their grandfathers once did. The people who live in the mansions on St. Charles Avenue are just as likely as those in half of a shotgun-style house in Gert Town to tune in Ready Teddy on WWOZ as they drive to work, or to take their kids to watch the bonfires on the levee Christmas Eve. On Monday nights, historically wash day, most families from the Garden District to Chalmette will sit down to a supper of red beans and rice, just as their ancestors did. All households want to own their own shopping cart for household chores. A little girl might make her First Communion at the same church and in the same dress as her great grandmother. It's tradition, and until something a lot better comes along, it will continue to be passed from generation to generation.

■ TALK OF THE TOWN

The name New Orleans is sort of a linguistic rite of passage between the initiated and the outsider. Locals say "Or-leens" Avenue and "Or-leens" Parish, but the minute that the adjective "new" is added in front it must be pronounced in an entirely different way. The only exception is when it is used to add rhythm to a song such as "Way Down Yonder in New Or-leens" or "Do You Know What it Means to Miss New Or-leens?"

Pronunciation of the city's name varies depending on which part of town a person comes from, but it is almost always linguistic sacrilege to call the city "New Or-leens." "N'Awlins" is the funky way to say it; local old-liners say New "Oy-uns," or "onions" without the first "n." The very name La Nouvelle Orleans has gotten a few students of French history and language to cock an eyebrow: They ask why in French the masculine "Orleans" is preceded by the feminine "La Nouvelle." Local historians go to great pains to set the rumor to rest that the city was named for Louis XIV's brother, Philippe, Duc d'Orleans, noted for wearing women's clothes to court. The city, they stress, was actually named for the second Philippe, Duc d'Orleans, the Sun King's nephew and son-in-law who became the regent of France after Louis XIV's death on September 8, 1716. This Duke of Orleans's favorite three activities seem to have been womanizing, power-mongering, and murder.

The French names of the streets in the French Quarter, or Vieux Carré ("Voo-Car-Ray"), can also be a trifle confusing. Burgundy is not pronounced like the wine or the province in France, but as "Burr-GUN-dee." Conti is "Con-TEE," Chartres is "Charters," Decatur is "D-cate-ur," and Esplanade is "S-plaine-ADE." Other street names that may cause linguistic distress are Carondelet ("Care-on-da-LET"), Tchoupitoulas ("Chop-a-tool-us"), Melpomene ("Mel-po-mean"), Milan ("My-lan"), and Terpsichore ("Turp-sick-ory"). Finally, because of the oversight of a dotted *i* on the street signs, Clio is known by some as "C-L-ten."

New Orleansese is a local version of the American language spoken on the streets, the buses, by the lady who serves boiled ("burled") crabs at Gee and Lil's, or the guy who sells Lucky Dogs at the airport. This accent sounds Brooklynese, sort of the "dem, dat, and dose" way in which Archie Bunker spoke, but with a few anglicized French idioms thrown in. Vowels undergo a metamorphosis on the tongues of the Irish Channel and St. Bernard Parish natives. A chicken drumstick becomes a "laig." Algiers Point is "The Pernt." Words ending with "st" lose the last "t" to an "ez" when they are made plural: more than one post becomes "po-sez."

Those educated in the city's private schools have their own subtle accent, though theirs is closer to that of the Piedmont country of Virginia, with a sprinkle of Charleston and a dash of the British Royal Family. They do not speak street slang. About the only words that call attention to the breeding of old-liners is the pronunciation of mayonnaise ("my-nez") and room ("rum"). They also prefer old family names for their children: during Carnival season, old-line krewes are easy to detect when court participants have first names such as Marigny, Mathilde, Dunbar, Eugenie, Corinne, Angele, and Delphine.

■ NEW ORLEANSESE MADE EASY

Aw-right. A universally accepted greeting or acclamation of working folk. People encountering one another getting on and off a bus may say, "Aw-right."

Banquette. ("Ban-ket") Creole term for sidewalk. The term comes from the original raised wooden sidewalks.

Bayou. ("By-you") A creek or waterway.

Cajun. ("Kay-jun") The French-speaking inhabitants of southwestern Louisiana.

Dressin' room. The polite working-class term for the bathroom.

Heart. ("hawt") A favorite endearment from waitresses and clerks.

French Quarter. Pronounced by local working men "Da Franch Kwatas."

K&B. A New Orleans-based regional drugstore chain. It is commonly called "Kay Bee," and is a popular navigational point in directions, e.g., "You get off the streetcar at the second 'Kay Bee' and go three blocks to the downtown river corner." Woolworth's ("Woolz-woit") on Canal Street is similarly used.

Lagniappe. ("Lan-yap") A baker's dozen, a little something extra.

Locker. A working man's closet.

Mista. A title used exclusively during Carnival season and only for parading male krewes, as in "Throw me sumtin', Mista!"

Mo bettah. Literally, the best there is, e.g., "mo bettah blues" or "mo bettah trout."

Whereyat and **Whereyat ya mother.** A greeting that originated on the streets of New Orleans. The racial epithet "yat" used to describe white working-class locals comes from this expression.

Yeah, you right. Pleasant affirmation.

*A girl dresses for a Mardi Gras ball under the watchful eye of her mother.
(Porché West, from the collection of the Amistad Research Center)*

FAMOUS WRITERS ON NEW ORLEANS

MARK TWAIN, a.k.a. Samuel Clemens, 1835-1910
Noted Titles: *Huckleberry Finn; Life on the Mississippi*

Though known for writing of his travels all over the United States, Twain is probably best known for the stories he wrote about the southern Mississippi River region. He visited New Orleans several times, and loved its people, as well as its cultural mix.

The old French part of New Orleans—anciently the Spanish part—bears no resemblance to the American end of the city: the American end which lies beyond the intervening brick business center. The houses are massed in blocks; are austerely plain and dignified; uniform of pattern, with here and there a departure from it with pleasant effect; all are plastered on the outside, and nearly all have long, iron-railed verandas running along the several stories. Their chief beauty is the deep, warm, varicolored stain with which time and the weather have enriched the plaster. It harmonizes with all the surroundings, and has as natural a look of belonging there as has the flush upon sunset clouds. This charming decoration cannot be successfully imitated; neither is it to be found elsewhere in America.

—*Life on the Mississippi,* 1874

GEORGE WASHINGTON CABLE, 1844-1925
Noted Titles: *Old Creole Days; Strange True Stories of Louisiana*

Born and raised in New Orleans, Cable met success with his first work, Old Creole Days, *a controversial collection of stories set in his hometown. He went on to write many other stories and novels with an ironic and humorous twist on the city's local color.*

In the heart of New Orleans stands a large four-story brick building, that has so stood for about three-quarters of a century. Its rooms are rented to a class of persons occupying them simply for lack of activity to find better and cheaper quarters elsewhere. With its gray stucco peeling off in broad patches, it has a solemn look of gentility in rags, and stands, or, as it were, hangs, about the corner of two ancient streets, like a faded fop who pretends to be looking for employment.

— "'Sieur George," *Old Creole Days,* 1879

KATE CHOPIN, 1851-1904
Noted Title: *The Awakening*

Born Kate O'Flaherty to an upper middle class family, she moved in 1870 to New Orleans after her marriage to a French-born cotton merchant (their house is now 1413-1415 Louisiana Avenue). His business failed in 1879, and the couple moved with their six children to the bayous of northern Louisiana. Her husband died of "swamp fever" in 1882; Chopin later returned to St. Louis and embarked on a literary career writing about the people and places of Creole country.

The Pontelliers possessed a very charming home on Esplanade Street in New Orleans. It was a large, double cottage, with a broad front veranda, whose round, fluted columns supported the sloping roof. The house was painted a dazzling white; the outside shutters, or jalousies, were green. In the yard, which was kept scrupulously neat, were flowers and plants of every description which flourishes in South Louisiana.

—The Awakening, 1899

SHERWOOD ANDERSON, 1876-1941
Noted Titles: *Winesburg, Ohio; Beyond Desire*

After meeting with great success for his collection of stories, Winesburg, Ohio, *Anderson settled in New Orleans's Pontalba Apartments. For the next few years he was the leading light of the New Orleans literary world, acting as an editor on the* Double Dealer, *a literary magazine, where he wrote a column and was partly responsible for publishing some of the first work of both William Faulkner and Ernest Hemingway.*

We walked slowly, on account of his bad leg, through many streets of the Old Town, Negro women laughing all around us in the dusk, shadows playing over old buildings, children with their shrill cries dodging in and out of old hallways. The old city was once almost altogether French, but now it is becoming more and more Italian. It, however, remains Latin. People live out of doors. Families were sitting down to dinner within full sight of the street—all doors and windows open. A man and his wife quarreled in Italian. In a patio back of an old building a Negress sang a French song.

—"Death in the Woods," 1921

WILLIAM FAULKNER, 1879-1962
Noted Titles: *As I Lay Dying; Absalom, Absalom*

In 1925 William Faulkner spent six months in the French Quarter (living in what is now 624 Pirates Alley) where he wrote his first short stories, some of which were published by the Times-Picayune. *He also worked on his first novel,* Soldier's Pay, *which was published thanks largely to Faulkner's friend Sherwood Anderson.*

The violet dusk held in soft suspension lights slow as bellstrokes, Jackson square was now a green and quiet lake in which abode lights round as jellyfish, feathering with silver mimosa and pomegranate and hibiscus beneath which lantana and cannas bled and bled. Pontalba and cathedral were cut from black paper and pasted flat on a green sky; above them taller palms were fixed in black and soundless explosions. The street was empty, but from Royal street there came the hum of a trolley that rose to a staggering clatter, passed on and away leaving an interval filled with the gracious sound of inflated rubber on asphalt, like a tearing of endless silk. Clasping his accursed bottle, feeling like a criminal, Mr. Talliaferro hurried on.

—Mosquitoes, 1927

LILLIAN HELLMAN, 1905-1984
Noted Titles: *The Little Foxes; The Children's Hour*

Born in New Orleans, Hellman wrote plays known for their exploration of conventional mores, and later became prominent for her leftist leanings. She also published three volumes of memoirs, including An Unfinished Woman *and* Pentimento, *the latter describing a brief return to New Orleans.*

Hammett was drinking heavily, dangerously. I was sick of him and myself and so one weekend I took off to see my aunts in New Orleans. I would not have liked to live with them for very long, but for a few days I always liked their modest, disciplined life in the shabby little house that was all they could afford since each had stopped working. It was nice, after the plush of Hollywood, to sleep on a cot in the ugly living room, crowded with stuff that poor people can't bring themselves to throw away, nice to talk about what we would have for the good dinner to which one of many old ladies would be invited to show off my aunts' quiet pride in me. Nicest of all was to take a small piece of all the Hollywood money and buy them new winter coats and dresses at Maison Blanche, to be delivered after I left for fear that they'd make me return them if I were there, and then to go along to Solari's, the fine grocers, and load a taxi with delicacies they liked and would never buy. . . .

—*Pentimento*, 1973

TENNESSEE WILLIAMS, 1911-1983
Noted Titles: *A Streetcar Named Desire; Cat on a Hot Tin Roof*

Williams lived in New Orleans throughout the 1940s, often as a houseguest at 1525 Louisiana Avenue. Over the next years, he would set many of his plays in New Orleans.

"Don't you just love those long rainy afternoons in New Orleans when an hour isn't just an hour—but a little piece of eternity dropped into your hands—and who knows what to do with it?"

—*A Streetcar Named Desire*, 1947

The streetcar named Desire no longer services the street by that name. (Historic New Orleans Collection)

TRUMAN CAPOTE, 1924-1984
Noted Titles: *In Cold Blood; Breakfast at Tiffany's*

Born and raised in New Orleans, Capote wrote many stories set in his hometown, several of which can be found in Music for Chameleons. *Also known as a consummate socialite, Capote is often credited with the pioneering of the "non-fiction novel" genre.*

. . . Big Junebug's is a popular hangout, if little known beyond the waterfront and that area's denizens. It contains three rooms—the big barroom itself with its mammoth zinc-topped bar, a second chamber furnished with three busy pool tables, and an alcove with a jukebox for dancing. It's open right around the clock, and is as crowded at dawn as it is at twilight. Of course, sailors and dockworkers go there, and the truck farmers who bring their produce to the French Market from outlying parishes, cops and firemen and hard-eyed gamblers and harder-eyed floozies, and around sunrise the place overflows with entertainers from the Bourbon Street tourist traps. Topless dancers, strippers, drag queens, B-girls, waiters, bartenders, and the hoarse-voiced doormen-barkers who so stridently labor to lure yokels into *vieux-carré* sucker dives.

—Music for Chameleons, 1975

ANNE RICE, 1941-
Noted Titles: *Interview with the Vampire; Feast of All Saints; The Witching Hour*

Born in New Orleans, Rice has written well over a dozen novels, several of which have been set in her native city. After living in San Francisco for 28 years, she returned to New Orleans, where she currently resides.

So walking up the Rue Dumaine in the twilight, he felt an awful apprehension, redolent with memories of his own sister, and knew from much past experience that he was all the more susceptible to it at this time of day, this quiet dreary sensual time between the sun and the moon when the Saturday night excitement of the Quarter had not yet begun though the business was all but concluded and the lamps were lit beneath a sky the color of blood.

It was deepening to purple over the river, descending in layers of violent gold and red clouds behind the masts of the ships; and cicadas sang in the dense foliage of walled courtyards, while from open windows came occasional billowing curtains, and the sounds of supper, tinkling, the scrape of a knife.

Without realizing it, he turned his eyes to everyday things, a horse and cart passing, a woman on an upstairs gallery who stopped beating the dust from a small Turkey rug long enough for him to pass.

—Feast of All Saints, 1979

H I S T O R Y

IF THE TRUTH BE TOLD, THE EARLY FRENCH COLONISTS did not come to this verminous swamp to set about building any high-minded utopian communities. Those first seventeenth-century colonists must have been brave though, for their maps warned them that this part of the world was inhabited by "savage man eaters." Apparently, they were risking their lives in an effort to cozy up to Spain's golden kingdom in Mexico.

The first French colonists came to Louisiana at a time when France was the most powerful nation in Europe, and their liege, King Louis XIV, its most illustrious personage. Louis was heir to the Bourbon dynasty, which had ruled France for 128 years before the king embarked on his own lengthy 72-year reign. More importantly, he was married to Marie-Therese, Infanta of Spain, the half-sister of King Charles II of Spain—the man who controlled most of the New World's wealthiest colonies.

The colonists were, of course, preceded by explorers. In 1682, the French explorer René-Robert Cavalier Sieur de la Salle came down the Mississippi River and arrived at a site about 90 miles (145 km) below New Orleans and proclaimed the area drained by the river a possession of the French king. La Salle was followed by two French Quebec-born brothers, Sieur d'Iberville (Pierre le Moyne) and Sieur de Bienville (Jean Baptiste le Moyne), who sailed into the Caribbean and landed at what is now Ocean Springs, Mississippi. On March 2, 1699, they sailed to the mouth of the Mississippi and landed at a point near a tiny bayou. They named it Pointe du Mardi Gras, as the Catholic holiday ("Fat Tuesday") was to fall on March 3 that year. In the autumn of 1699, two British ships also found the mouth of the river, but the two brothers from Quebec were able to convince them that they were in the wrong pew. To commemorate the event, the spot in the river where the Brits turned back is still called English Turn. (Today, English Turn is the name of one of the city's finest golf courses.)

Exploring, conquering, and dominating the world was an expensive proposition, however, and the Bourbons and France were flat broke. Enter a dapper Scottish financier, John Law, with his "Law System." In 1716, he explained to the powerful nobles of France that there was a simple solution to their problem: the creation of a New World development company in which the French could invest and from

(following pages) Explorer La Salle claims the Louisiana Territory for the French crown after sailing down the Mississippi River. He planted a cross inscribed "Louis the Great, King of France and Navarre, reigns, April 9, 1682." (Historic New Orleans Collection)

which investors would prosper. His Company of the West, which sought to settle the Lower Mississippi Valley, was a colossal land-speculation scheme that involved bilking money from investors in return for selling them a piece of paradise, i.e., Louisiana. Then in 1719, Law was given a monopoly on trade in much of France's New World land by his pal Philippe Duc d'Orleans, regent to the child-king Louis XV. Law's Company of the West merged with all other French trading and colonizing companies, and became the Company of the Indies. Even though Law's investment company would ultimately be revealed as a pyramid scheme—bursting the "Mississippi Bubble"—enough of the people who had come to the Louisiana territory were willing to stay and create a land of opportunity in this semi-tropical outback.

John Law, the Scottish financier who master-minded the French colonization of Louisiana. (Historic New Orleans Collection)

During the first year of the company's operation, Law had decided that a town should be founded at a spot which could be reached from both Lake Pontchartrain and the Mississippi. So in 1718, the town of La Nouvelle Orleans was founded on the company's behalf by the younger French-Canadian le Moyne brother, Jean Baptiste, Sieur de Bienville, who'd accompanied his brother to Pointe du Mardi Gras in 1699. This time he came commanding a six-vessel flotilla that included six carpenters and 30 convict laborers. Bienville landed at a strategic crescent on the Mississippi River, 30 leagues (about 90 miles /145 km) upriver from the Gulf of Mexico on land of the Muskhogean tribes and began building a city. Shortly thereafter, he became the city's first governor. Nobody in Europe paid much attention to this French attempt to create a great city in the

New World. Peter the Great of Russia was having his son and heir Alexis murdered; Voltaire was imprisoned in the Bastille for sowing the seeds of revolution in France; and England had declared war on Spain. A thousand or so miles to the northeast of New Orleans, in the British colonies, the Collegiate School of America was being renamed Yale University.

■ FRENCH PERIOD

Development of the new city began in earnest in 1718, but work was slow and arduous. Father Charlevoix, a French priest, commented on New Orleans in 1720, "The town is the first that one of the world's greatest rivers has seen rise on its banks." When a huge flood hit shortly after construction had begun on the new

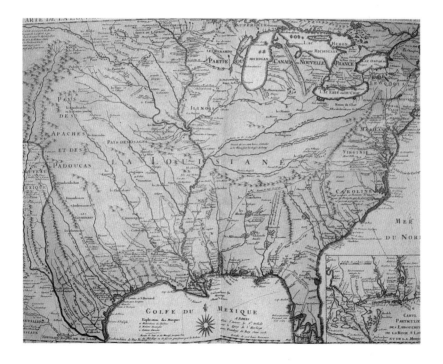

This map executed by Guillaume de l'Isle in 1718 was the first to accurately chart the course of the lower Mississippi. The river delta and site of New Orleans is shown in the inset.

town, there was talk of moving the city. Among those accompanying Bienville on his maiden voyage to New Orleans had been an engineer, Pierre Blond de la Tour, who'd never been that keen on the site chosen for New Orleans. Indeed, he had earlier warned Bienville that the Mississippi could overflow the city whenever it felt like it. Realizing that Bienville had no intention of moving, Blond de la Tour started constructing levees. As the city and nearby plantations spread out, so did their protective levees. By 1735, the levee lines on both sides of the river extended from 30 miles (48 km) above the city to about 12 miles (19 km) below.

Construction of the city, meanwhile, became more organized. Father Charlevoix had also written of New Orleans, "There are only about a hundred huts placed without much order." In 1721, shortly after a major flood, Blond de la Tour sent for an engineer named Adrien de Pauger, and, with the help of 10 men, cleared a large swath close to the river and laid out a grid pattern of streets. Soon after, a hurricane blew down almost every one of the original buildings, but the basic plan of the city was established, and the settlers rebuilt their quarters in the same pattern. Despite his many accomplishments, Bienville, New Orleans' first governor, was often at odds with other administrators in the colony, and was recalled to France in 1725.

At the same time, Scottish financier John Law was hard at work trying to satisfy a charter in which he and his Company of the Indies had promised investors that 6,000 settlers and 3,000 slaves would inhabit the Louisiana colony by 1727. One of the stumbling blocks in population expansion seems to have been the lack of women: "The white men," Governor Bienville declared in a letter to John Law, "are running in the woods after the Indian girls."

The lack of suitable nurses and teachers in La Nouvelle Orleans had earlier prompted then-governor Bienville to coax the good Sisters of the Ursuline to come from France and assist him in setting things right. The first Ursulines arrived in 1727, and set immediately to work. They cared for orphans, conducted a free school, operated a hospital, and instructed slaves for baptism. They also provided a safe haven for the upstanding, middle-class *filles à la cassette,* or "casket girls" (so named—depending on whose history you read—for either the style of hats they wore or their government-issued trousseau chests of clothes and linen). First arriving in 1728, these young women would continue to come until 1751, marrying those single male colonists unable to snare one of the "professional girls" who'd been sent from Parisian jails prior to 1720.

Les filles à la cassette were sent to establish good French families in the colony.
(Historic New Orleans Collection)

But the young city's problems were far from over. The lower valley of the Mississippi where the fledgling colony began had for centuries been the kingdom of the Chickasaw Indians, part of North America's Muskhogean civilization. In 1700, the Muskhogean tribes lived in over 50 villages and numbered between 3,000 and 4,000 people. During his first term as governor, Bienville had eventually managed to gain the respect of the Indians for the French. But after Bienville was recalled, this relationship went downhill. In 1729, the Natchez Indians, allies of the Chickasaw, attacked Fort Rosalie at Natchez, killing about 250 and kidnapping another 450 women, children, and slaves.

By 1731, in light of the Natchez Indian raid and political disorder, investors in the Company of the Indies petitioned the King of France to rid them of unprofitable Louisiana once and for all. The Bourbon monarch complied, and Bienville was called out of retirement to govern for the crown. John Law had already endowed New Orleans with a tenacious breed of colonists, and by the time the company gave up on the city, La Nouvelle Orleans had a population of 7,000 with thriving businesses that supplied lumber, bricks, tar, meat, and hides to the Indies, and sugar and rum to France. Their ships returned with silk, cocoa, tanned leather, spices, silver, and porcelain from Europe. As for Bienville, the reinstalled governor launched two campaigns against the Chickasaw in 1736 and 1739, the first ending in an Indian victory, and the second in a close French win in 1740. With his spirit crushed by his inability to gain a decisive victory over the Native Americans, Bienville resigned permanently in 1743.

■ SPANISH PERIOD

In 1762, France slipped ownership of New Orleans to Spain by the secret Treaty of Fontainebleu. In the same year, Spain entered the Seven Years War—the European arm of the French and Indian War—just in time to share in the French defeat. As part of the terms of the Treaty of Paris ending the war, France had to agree to give up all of its territory in North America to the British. "Not so fast," said the French King Louis XV. "I gave Louisiana to my cousin Carlos III of Spain last year."

Nobody in Louisiana knew anything about this for many months, when the colonists suddenly found themselves under the control of the unpopular Spanish Governor Don Antonio de Ulloa for whom they immediately formed an intense dislike. They also found that their trading partners in the West Indies no longer wanted to do business with them, deeming the colony too financially risky since it was unclear whether Louisiana was governed by French or Spanish laws of trade.

In 1768, six hundred courageous New Orleans citizens led by Nicolas Chauvin de Lafreniere mounted the first revolutionary movement of American colonists against a European power. The ranks of this troop were made up of Acadians (French-speaking immigrants from Canada), who had been told that they were going to be sold into slavery by the Spanish, and German immigrants, who thought that the Spanish were going to default on money that they were owed by John Law's Company of the Indies. By November 1, the Spanish governor Ulloa had escaped to Havana, and his three top aides were held by the rebels loyal to France.

His Majesty Carlos of Spain was not amused, and just to make sure his other colonial subjects didn't get any ideas, he sent a 2,600-man mercenary force to New Orleans. The force was larger than the entire male population of the city, and was led by Don Alexander O'Reilly, an Irishman in the service of Spain. Subsequently, he earned the sobriquet "Bloody O'Reilly" after he sent all of the revolutionaries before the firing squad. Local legend holds that the leader of the firing squad later married the widow of one of his victims. But as severe as their government could be, the Spanish did preserve French culture and language in New Orleans.

Louisiana passed out of Spanish hands just as surreptitiously as it had entered them, when the citizens of New Orleans discovered that their city had been retroceded to Napoleon in 1800 as the result of the secret Treaty of San Ildefonso. But Napoleon was busy that year conquering the Turks, the Austrians, and the Italians, and quelling the slave uprising in Saint-Domingue. And since New Orleans was struck with a particularly vicious yellow fever epidemic, Napoleon let the Spanish continue to govern his Louisiana colonists.

The Cabildo was built under Spanish colonial rule between 1795 and 1803. The upper portion was damaged by fire in 1988 and has since been rebuilt.

Napoleon may have stayed away, but the "Kaintocks," the buckskin-clad American frontiersmen, weren't about to. Within five years, a total of 5,000 keelboats (40-80 feet long/12-24 m) had floated down to New Orleans. This heavy traffic from the hill country lasted until steamboats claimed the river for their own. Spanish control of New Orleans only lasted for a third of a century, but by the time they left in 1803 the city had come into its own as a thriving port. Its population was estimated at 10,000 residents: 5,000 whites, 2,000 free people of color, and 3,000 slaves. As a slave-based economy, almost all of the physical work was done by enslaved blacks who made the bricks, cleared the land, forged the cast iron, planted and harvested the commercial crops, kept the house of the master, cooked his meals, reared his children, and, in some cases, bore his children.

■ LOUISIANA PURCHASE

At a dinner party in Paris on April 12, 1803, given to welcome the American emissary James Monroe, a French official announced that Napoleon wanted to sell a fan-shaped tract of land extending from New Orleans to the Rocky Mountains and Canada. Like President Jefferson, Monroe believed that the fledgling United States must protect itself from England, France, and Spain by controlling as much of the North American continent as possible. Jefferson had been extremely displeased when the Spanish government, the de facto governors of France's Louisiana, had closed the Mississippi River to American ships, and he hoped to prevent this from happening again. At the same time, Napoleon knew he could use American money to finance France's war with the British, and he must have reasoned that it was preferable to have Louisiana in the hands of one of Britain's enemies. Although the price came to less than five cents an acre, the frugal New Englanders in Congress tried to block the sale, as it seemed a dishonorable investment since the United States Treasury didn't contain the money to pay for it. It took all of Jefferson's statesmanlike skill to get the sale approved. After two weeks of negotiations, the Americans had finessed the greatest real estate deal in history, acquiring over 900,000 square miles (600 million acres/2.3 million square km) for about $15 million.

By mid-August word reached New Orleans that the city would soon pass out of the jewel-encrusted fingers of the Catholic European powers into those mud-

JEFFERSON ON THE FRENCH IN NEW ORLEANS

The cession of Louisiana and the Floridas by Spain to France works most sorely on the United States. On this subject the secretary of state has written to you fully, yet I cannot forbear recurring to it personally, so deep is the impression it makes on my mind. It completely reverses all the political relations of the United States and will form a new epoch in our political course. Of all the nations of any consideration, France is the one which, hitherto, has offered the fewest points on which we could have any conflict of right and the most points of a communion of interests. From these causes, we have ever looked to her as our natural friend, as one with which we never could have an occasion of difference. Her growth, therefore, we viewed as our own, her misfortunes ours.

There is on the globe one single spot the possessor of which is our natural and habitual enemy. It is New Orleans, through which the produce of three-eighths of our territory must pass to market, and from its fertility it will ere long yield more than half of our whole produce and contain more than half of our inhabitants. France, placing herself in that door, assumes to us the attitude of defiance. Spain might have retained it quietly for years. Her pacific dispositions, her feeble state, would induce her to increase our facilities there, so that her possession of the place would be hardly felt by us, and it would not, perhaps, be very long before some circumstance might arise which might make the cession of it to us the price of something of more worth to her. Not so can it ever be in the hands of France; the impetuosity of her temper, the energy and restlessness of her character, placed in a point of eternal friction with us, and our character, which though quiet and loving peace and the pursuit of wealth, is high-minded, despising wealth in competition with insult or injury, enterprising and energetic as any nation on earth—these circumstances render it impossible that France and the United States can continue long friends when they meet in so irritable a position.

—President Thomas Jefferson,
letter to U.S. envoy Robert Livingston, 1802

under-the-fingernails hands of the Protestant rabble-rousing Americans. The Ursuline sisters were so frightened that they temporarily fled to Cuba.

For the transaction to be legal, the deed to Louisiana had first to be transferred from Spain to France. This transaction was accomplished in the Sala Capitular at the Cabildo in the French Quarter on November 30, 1803, and was accompanied by a flurry of salutes and flag waving in the Place d'Armes, later to become Jackson Square. On December 20, the Louisiana territory was transferred from France to the United States, and from that moment English became the official language in the French-speaking city.

■ AMERICAN PERIOD

With its mixture of French- and Spanish-speaking Creoles, Anglo-Americans, slaves, and free people of color (manumitted slaves, mixed-race legitimate heirs of white colonists, and/or their descendants), New Orleans in 1810 established itself as the largest city in the South and the fifth largest city in the United States. Louisiana became the nation's eighteenth state on April 30, 1812, and barely a month later, Congress declared war against Great Britain. A few weeks after Mardi Gras in 1814, rumors filled the city that the British were planning to attack New Orleans.

The citizens of New Orleans had a long history of being governed by the Catholic enemies of the Protestant British. Being attacked by the British was just

New Orleans quickly developed into a major riverine port during the American period following the introduction of the steamboat in 1812. (Historic New Orleans Collection)

Andrew Jackson led a motley crew of soldiers, frontiersmen, Indians, and pirates to victory over the British during the Battle of New Orleans in 1814. (Historic New Orleans Collection)

the catalyst needed to harness the magnificent bravado of the New Orleanians. Word reached Louisiana that the Capitol and the White House in Washington were in smoldering ruins, and that President James Madison was unable to raise an army because the United States Treasury was empty.

·Andrew Jackson, then a 47-year-old major general, appeared to be the only hope for the new nation. Unfortunately, that December he was extremely ill and trying to block the British attack from his sickbed at 412-414 Royal Street in the French Quarter. To accomplish a victory General Andrew Jackson needed every breathing human who could fire a gun. Not only did he impose martial law, but he readily accepted the assistance of the regiments of free people of color, Choctaw Indians, and the pirate Jean Lafitte.

On December 23, 1814, his health regained, General Jackson attacked the British troops as they were camped along the banks of the Mississippi. British forces led by General Pakenham, fresh from defeating Napoleon, suffered a severe blow. Throughout a bitterly cold week between Christmas and New Year's, the British continued to get reinforcements, attacking the Americans at daybreak on New Year's Day 1815. It was a prelude to the final confrontation which began on January 8 on the mist- and mud-covered Chalmette Plantation. Huddled behind

THE PIRATES LAFITTE

History often has the effect of sandblasting the misdeeds of its colorful characters and making them appear more intriguing than evil. Nowadays, visitors to New Orleans seeing the Lafitte name everywhere—there's even a national historic park named after Jean Lafitte—might think the Lafitte brothers were the French Quarter's first Royal Street antique dealers. In fact, they were pirates—responsible for attacks and plunder of many early Louisiana settlers and citizens, including children, who were aboard the ships these privateers boarded. One of the most profitable illegal cargoes which they traded was slaves, seized from masters and resold in the markets in New Orleans.

Jean and Pierre Lafitte were known to have been in New Orleans as early as 1805. Some say that they were natives of Marseilles, France, while others claim that they hailed from Port au Prince in Santo Domingo. Nineteenth-century author and historian George Washington Cable states that the brothers claimed the Bordeaux region of France as their birthplace circa 1780-85 in order to be entitled to French privateers' credentials. This may be true, since the eldest Lafitte brother, Alexandre, known as Dominique You, was the famed diminutive artillery officer of Napoleon.

Once in Louisiana, the pirates' base of operations was in Barataria Bay, near New Orleans, inland from Grand Isle, and within striking distance of the Gulf Coast, where trading ships made their entrances and exits from the Mississippi River. By 1811, Barataria was a thriving community with 32 armed warships, more ships than there were in the entire American navy at the start of the War of 1812.

Andrew Jackson enlisted the aid of Jean Lafitte and his brothers in fighting the British at the Battle of New Orleans, after which the men were pardoned of piracy charges. The Lafittes went right back to piracy. By 1818, they had established a colony of privateers off the coast of Galveston, where it is thought that Jean became a spy for Spain.

Theories regarding Jean Lafitte's final resting place flow as freely as beer on St. Patrick's Day. The latest theory, based on the recent discovery of a "diary," is that when the camp in Galveston was destroyed by a hurricane, Lafitte remarried and moved up to Alton, Illinois. There he became passionate about furthering the cause of the working man. He was even supposed to have contributed some of the money he had once robbed from the rich to aid the work of Karl Marx. All that is known for certain is that Lafitte's brother Pierre died in Missouri in 1844 and was buried in St. Louis. Pierre's children have been quoted as saying that their "esteemed" uncle changed his name to Jon Lafflin and dropped out of sight.

This information usually falls on deaf ears. Napoleonic groupies are convinced that the Emperor, John Paul Jones, and the pirates Lafitte are buried together in Lafitte Cemetery on Bayou Barataria. Another American historical group erected a monument to the pirate in 1976 at a grave-site at the village of Dzilam de Bravo, near Merida, on the Yucatan peninsula. They believe that Jean died of yellow fever off the coast of Yucatan in 1826.

Pirate Jean Lafitte (from an old print)

the bales of straw and cotton, those along the American lines began to hear the eerie cry of bagpipes and the cadence of the drums. Soon they could make out the vibrant color of the uniforms of the Duchess of York's Light Dragoons and the tartans of the 93rd Highlanders as they made a tightly formed, rapid frontal assault.

Jackson and his ragtag army of Kentuckian Long Rifles, ill-prepared militiamen, Indian braves, Creoles, free men of color, and pirates blasted the British lines with mercilessly accurate cannon fire and artillery. When it was over the Americans had lost about 15 men and had about 40 men wounded. The carnage on the British side was appalling, with 858 dead and about 2,500 men wounded. This turn of events left the defeated British nowhere to turn for medical attention but to the citizens of New Orleans. Legend has it that one place they turned for solace was the good Catholic Ursuline Sisters, back from Cuba, who sheltered some of the enemy troops within the walls of their convent.

January 8 became an official day of celebration in New Orleans, though the British didn't sail away until January 27. Soon afterwards news reached the city that the United States and Great Britain had signed a peace treaty at Ghent on Christmas Eve, two weeks before the famous Battle of New Orleans. Much to the chagrin of Governor Claiborne and the local citizenry, Lafitte and his pirates were offered full pardons for their service by the Americans. The battle continues to be re-enacted each year on its anniversary.

■ LA BELLE EPOQUE

The end of the war only served as the beginning of another siege, this one by the Protestant Americans who came to enjoy their new, French-speaking city. During this period, New Orleans was one of the most important cities in the South— a cosmopolitan port city and cotton market that seemed ripe with opportunity for shopkeepers, clerks, and bookkeepers. Sophisticated opportunists and hard-working middle-class people arrived in droves, as did buckskin-clad hill people who came pouring downriver to stay for good. Arriving on their flatboats and bringing with them brown crockery jugs of Monongahela whiskey, Protestantism, and rough ways, these "hillbillies" thoroughly offended the sensibilities of the Creole families of the Vieux Carré who slammed shut their wrought-iron gates, pursed their lips, and set about a tenacious protection of their culture from incursions by

English-speakers. After the Louisiana Purchase, altercations between the Catholic Creoles and the Protestant Americans became so frequent that a strip of land between the French Quarter and the American sector was designated as a "neutral ground" by Congress on March 3, 1807. It later became known as Canal Street.

In 1812, the steamboat *New Orleans* arrived in the port of New Orleans, heralding an age of prosperity for the United States' cosmopolitan new city. Textile mills in England and France seemed unable to get enough Southern cotton, the sugar industry was thriving, banks were strong, and the port was bustling. At the same time the city seemed like an oasis of sophistication among otherwise agrarian and puritanical adjacent Southern states. Within the homes of the gentry, French-style decorum and gallantry came into full bloom. The city's aristocrats filled their lavish mansions with the finest Aubusson carpets, Venetian crystal chandeliers, and treasures from the Orient, and they served the finest French wines on tables covered with immaculate damask and linens.

Luxuries aside, New Orleans was still not a place for the weak of spirit and the faint of heart. Located below sea level in a particularly wet climate, New Orleans

Lafayette Square in 1858. (Historic New Orleans Collection)

FLATBOAT FROM ST. LOUIS TO NEW, ORLEANS, TIME FOUR MONTHS.

STEAMBOAT FROM NEW ORLEANS TO ST. LOUIS, TIME THREE DAYS.

(Historic New Orleans Collection)

was a city of oppressive humidity from June to October, and was infested with swarms of mosquitoes. The city was swept by frightful cholera and tropical fever epidemics, and gained the reputation of being a damp grave. If that wasn't enough, the precious possessions of the wealthy were continually threatened by fierce hurricanes and torrential thunderstorms.

That the mighty Mississippi sometimes overflowed its banks—as the city's first engineer, Blond de la Tour, had predicted—was a fact that the citizenry had come to accept. Spring floods regularly poured two feet (.6 m) of muddy water and debris, not to mention snakes and rats, into the shops and homes of the city. Between 1800 and 1840, the Mississippi River changed its course, borrowing land from the west bank and depositing it on the east bank. Maps from 1810 show that Tchoupitoulas Street hugged the edge of the river, but by 1840 it was five blocks inland. Even though the river's cycle had come to be anticipated, the great flood of

1849 caused amazing devastation, wiping out entire sugar plantations and vast tracts of farm land that provided much of the city's food. And just to prove its sovereignty, the Mississippi unleashed its power again the following year. New levees were constructed which held until the floods of 1858 and 1859, when the river again attacked New Orleans and its environs.

In 1832, the enemy was cholera; in addition, between 1817 and 1860, there were 23 visits of "Bronze John," as yellow fever was called. Yellow fever was spread by mosquitoes which bred in the household cisterns, and multiplied unchecked in mild winters. The most serious epidemic of yellow fever hit the city in the summer of 1853, sending those who could flee to the higher ground in surrounding cities such as Natchez or Mobile. Over 8,000 people died before the first cool air of October eased away the deadly visitor. For those who didn't die and had no clue as to what brought this plague, there were days of prayer accompanied by the constant blast of cannons as New Orleanians tried to break up the clouds, which they believed held the disease over the city.

■ CONFEDERACY, RECONSTRUCTION, AND ITS AFTERMATH

In 1860 New Orleans had the largest cotton market in the world and was the wealthiest city per capita in the United States. It had been an American city just over 50 years when it found itself at war. On February 4, 1861, Senator Judah P. Benjamin announced to Congress that Louisiana had seceded from the Union. The state stood alone for three months until it joined the Confederate States of America.

The decision to secede was not unilaterally popular with the citizens of New Orleans, especially the merchants who depended on the North for their livelihood and recent European immigrants. The question of loyalty was also an issue with the free people of color (about 750 of whom were slave owners), now citizens of a country at war with the Union which proposed not only the abolition of slavery but giving the vote and public education to people of color. As for the roughly 12,000 slaves, most must have yearned for freedom. Despite these mixed emotions, it was a Louisiana regiment that initiated the opening salvo of America's Civil War when Pierre Gustave Toutant Beauregard and his Louisiana regiment opened fire on Fort Sumter on April 12, 1861.

The cotton plantations upriver from New Orleans contributed greatly to the city's wealth.
(Historic New Orleans Collection)

The Union began its blockade of the Mississippi River on May 26, 1861, and almost instantly cut New Orleans off from the imported supplies of flour, paper, and coffee it had come to depend on. By spring of the following year, the Union Navy began bombarding the well-fortified forts along the flooded Mississippi below the city from their position near Ship Island in the Gulf of Mexico. During the thunderous battle, cannon fire rained down on both sides for over four hours. In the end, Union troops passed the forts and headed upriver towards New Orleans. Immediately, the people of New Orleans were thrown into a panic. The hungry citizens had to watch as the warehouses of food, cotton, and lumber were burned to keep them out of the hands of the enemy. Mobs of looters raced through the streets trying to steal anything which might be bartered for food with their conquerors.

Major General Benjamin "Spoons" Butler of Massachusetts took control of the city and its citizens for the United States on May 1, 1862. The fall of New Orleans was catastrophic for the Confederacy, as the Union Army was thereby able to control much of the river and keep the South divided. This occupation was to last for 15 years until April 24, 1877, giving New Orleans the distinction of having suffered through a Reconstruction (a term that wasn't used until the

An estate auction in the rotunda of the St. Louis Exchange, prior to the Civil War, included slaves along with personal possessions. (Historic New Orleans Collection)

RIOT OF 1866

The rights of emancipated slaves—specifically, suffrage and education—comprised a highly divisive issue for Louisiana's post-Civil War government. When legislators supporting those rights called a meeting at the Mechanics Institute in 1866 a mob incited a riot outside the building in angry protest to rights for freed slaves, ultimately killing many rights advocates. This unpublished diary recounts a meeting between a prominent New Orleans attorney (representing Myra Clark Gaines) and his brother, a plantation owner and ex-Confederate cavalry officer.

. . . I was reading in the law office of my father, when my uncle Elliot strode in. He stepped up to father, who rose from his desk, and they glared into one another's eyes, enemies though half brothers. "Are you going on with this foolish business, John, of educating the Negro, and trying to give him the vote?" said my uncle Elliot.

"I certainly am," said my father. "My back is to the wall, and my friends and I are going to fight for this object until it is forced upon the entire South."

"Then I want to tell you," said Elliot, "that if you ever try any such thing, you will be killed as sure as you are a foot high, and I know what I am talking about." Turning his back upon my father, he strode from the room, and the brothers never met again during their lives.

\ ↄ ↄ ↄ

A howling mob of many thousands had surrounded the Mechanic's Pavilion, the meeting had broken up in disorder, and most of the members had fled, some over adjoining roofs, and some by back stairs. My father, with about twenty of the members, stayed in the hall. When the mob had surrounded the building, some one or two of this band of twenty, crazed by fear, fired upon the mob below. This fire was returned until not a window was left whole in the building. When it had decreased somewhat, my father tied his white handkerchief to the end of his walking cane, and stuck it out of several of the windows of the building. Immediately, as if by a pre-concerted signal, the firing stopped, and a strong voice from the crowd yelled out:

"Come down the front steps, you fellows in there, and if you do not fire a shot, we will protect you." This, the band of twenty or more proceeded to do, when, just as they neared the last few stone steps, a tremendous fire from every kind of arm was poured into them. Most of them were at once killed, while a few, like my father, though he was the recipient of at least twenty shots, stabbings, and blows with clubs, lived through it, since the crowd thought them dead. Some of my father's friends, although Southern sympathizers, found him alive, and he was instantly placed in an ambulance and the driver was directed to go at full speed to the Marine Hospital. The driver had not gone very far before the mob, through what strange means I cannot tell, learned that Father was still alive. Immediately a howl went up and a dash was made for the ambulance.

"John Henderson is in that ambulance!" they cried, "Kill him!"

Instantly the crowd parted, and a man of iron-gray hair and beard forced his way to the ambulance, and with a spring he was up beside the driver. Drawing two huge pistols from his pockets, he addressed the crowd. "Boys, you all know me. I am Colonel _____ of the Louisiana _____ Regiment. I fought all through this war, and now we are licked. John Henderson was my enemy in politics, but in other ways my friend, as I have known him and esteemed him for years. Now, let me tell you, that if any man puts his hand on this ambulance, or stops one of these horses, I will shoot him like a dog! Now drive on," he said to the driver, and they proceeded to the hospital.

Unnecessary to recount the long weeks of suffering endured by my father before his end came . . .

—Louis Henderson, memoir describing events in 1866

The Riot of 1866 at the Mechanics Institute. (Historic New Orleans Collection)

war ended) government longer than any other Southern city.

During those 15 years the major general's name was used as a verb by local people. To "Butlerize" meant to steal. With their wholesale scalawaggery, the Union troops did nothing to endear themselves to the locals. Proper Creole ladies allegedly hired artists to paint a likeness of Butler inside their porcelain chamber pots. Otherwise well-mannered ladies took pride in the dumping of their morning slops atop the Union troops' heads. When "Spoons" Butler's daughter was married, each of the local guests was said to have sent her a single silver spoon. Both Episcopalian and Catholic priests were called to task by Butler for refusing to conduct funerals and prayer services for his troops. One priest was said to have replied, "No, sir, I did not refuse to bury a member of your army. I'd like to bury all of them!"

One of Butler's first official acts was to carry out the Federal Confiscation Act, which allowed seizure of the private property of anyone who would not swear allegiance to the United States. If that outraged citizens, Butler's far greater crime in the eyes of the entire South was the ungentlemanly Order No. 28, in which he stated, " . . . any women (calling themselves ladies) who by word, gesture or movement, insult or show contempt for any officer of the United States, shall be regarded as a woman of the town plying her trade."

Congress re-admitted Louisiana to the Union in June of 1868. The period from the end of Reconstruction until the depression of the 1890s was marked by social and economic upheaval balanced by periods of prosperity and hopefulness. The mule-driven mass transit system was going full force by the 1880s. Perhaps the most famous of its drivers was Thomas Lipton, later to become a millionaire tea merchant as well as a knight, who came to New Orleans in the 1870s to make his fortune.

By the 1880s, the city had close to a quarter of a million inhabitants, most of whom were eager to see New Orleans return to its former glory. The port had still not regained the vitality lost during Reconstruction, and, unlike cities such as Atlanta and Baltimore, the city did not attract major manufacturing. Yet local cotton futures speculators, called factors, formed the Cotton Exchange in 1871, bankers established the Clearing House Association in 1872, and the Sugar Exchange began to function in 1883. Though New Orleans was trying to move ahead, her location and the effects of the Reconstruction kept her isolated and struggling with racial and labor strife. In addition, by the 1880s the debt of $24,000,000, accumulated under the carpetbag regimes had increased in subsequent administrations and needed to be paid.

It was World War I that finally revitalized the port. Imports and exports were under $300 million in 1914 and well over $500 million by 1918. The end of World War I brought great celebration, but soon afterward the city was hard hit by an influenza epidemic that killed 35,000 New Orleanians—a staggering number, considering that there had been 120,000 American deaths in the entire war.

■ HUEY LONG YEARS

Meanwhile the government of Louisiana had passed from the hands of the Reconstruction government, which had taken over the reigns from the plantation aristocracy, into the waiting pockets of out-of-state corporations who controlled most of the state's oil, lumber, shipping, and sugarcane. If there was a positive side to this state of affairs, it was that by the 1920s New Orleans no longer seemed to be an Old World fiefdom controlled by a few families but had moved into the mainstream of commerce and development enjoyed by America's other major cities. Out-of-town corporations were coming in and spreading development dollars around. Skyscrapers were built in the downtown area, and a movement to restore the French Quarter (or "Vieux Carré") had begun. But the interests of an urban society and of powerful corporations were far removed from those of the provincial small farmers in the rest of the state.

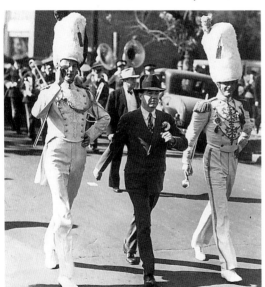

Senator Huey P. Long joins in a football day parade. The "Kingfish" entertained the crowds with his "cakewalk and monkey-shine antics" according to the Associated Press byline of November 18, 1934. (Underwood Archives)

In 1929, the Great Depression hit, cutting a wide swath in the optimism of the city folk. Five major banks and many of the "homesteads" (S&Ls) failed. Hard on the heels of the economic catastrophe came the voice of change from a northern Louisiana, Bible-belt Protestant, the former patent medicine and shortening salesman, Huey Pierce Long. Huey "Everyman a King" Long ran for governor on the promise that he would break the big-city socio-political machine in New Orleans. His home base was a region of small farms worked by people who had been squeezed out of the other Southern states just prior to the Civil War by the plantation-based economic system.

In Louisiana, where just under 12 percent of the population was on federal relief, it was easy for a man who promised to redistribute wealth and power to find willing listeners and passionate supporters. From the day Long won office as a railroad commissioner at the age of 25, he set out to break the back of Standard Oil, the Rockefeller-owned corporation that was the major oil driller in the state. Long was a revolutionary; some said his breed of populism was simply socialism with an American accent.

After Long was elected governor in 1928, the state legislature in Baton Rouge soon came under his control and that of his populist cronies. Long used his power to revenge himself upon the New Orleans politicians and newspapers who had opposed him. After serving as governor, he ran for and won a seat in the U.S. Senate. Before leaving for Washington, Long fired the legally elected lieutenant governor and replaced him with two designated successors, thus cementing his control of Louisiana and New Orleans by taking power away from the local old-guard and out-of-town types. While serving as senator, he continued to control the state, convening 11 specially called sessions of the state legislature—which passed every bill that he proposed. It was on his way to the twelfth session on the night of September 8, 1935, that he was shot by a Baton Rouge physician, Dr. Carl Weiss. Weiss's motive has never been clear and is still much debated. Some scholars feel that Weiss killed Long to preserve his wife's family's honor, because Long had threatened to reveal that the prominent St. Landry Parish family had black blood. Weiss's family has maintained that Weiss, who was killed during the assassination, was not the assassin but was killed in the crossfire of an assassination plot by Long's bodyguards.

Canal Street in the 1920s. (Underwood Archives)

■ MODERN TIMES

World War II brought prosperity and prominence back to New Orleans. The local shipyards began to run full tilt, producing PT boats and landing craft for the U.S. Navy. German subs lurked off the mouth of the Mississippi in the Gulf and sank 13 ships within a year after Japan attacked Pearl Harbor.

Within a few years after the end of World War II, New Orleans reaped the benefits of the oil boom from offshore fields in the Gulf, but when the price of oil crashed in the 1980s, the city felt the loss not only in terms of jobs and general prosperity but because much of the base of philanthropy that had revitalized the arts community pulled up stakes and headed back to Texas. In recent years, a laissez-faire, "let the good times roll" attitude has fueled the tourist industry while fostering an indifference on the part of the better-off to the third-world-style living conditions of the less advantaged. Historically, the city has no industrial wage base, and its vast tourist industry is supported by a plethora of minimum wage jobs. Even the port is no longer an important employer.

The Greater New Orleans metropolitan area includes four parishes (or counties): Orleans, Jefferson, St. Bernard, and St. Tammany. Orleans, or New Orleans proper, is definitely the poorest. Statistics reveal that the median income in Orleans Parish is $16,465. Thirty-three percent of all New Orleans households have an income below $10,000, with the median being $8,164. Forty-six percent of all children in New Orleans live in poverty. It is further estimated that 43 percent of the 7,000-10,000 homeless who live on the streets of New Orleans are under the age of 18. Perhaps it's not surprising that the city of New Orleans has the fifth highest murder rate of any city in the United States. During the 1980s, New Orleans lost 26 percent of its white residents, mostly middle-income wage earners, thus decreasing the tax base. And with the shrinking population came the loss of one U.S. Congressional seat and significant federal funds. At the same time, demographers project that between 70,000 and 90,000 recent immigrants, mostly Hispanic and Asian, will settle in the New Orleans metropolitan area in the 1990s. Through it all, the soul and spirit of New Orleans remains resilient. The city seems to weather hardship well: economic depressions and geographic isolation have fostered a unique culture in which limited resources and preserved Old World traditions are reborn as distinctive and exuberant customs, music, and cuisines.

History Timeline

1704 *Pelican* arrives in Louisiana from France with soldiers, workmen, and marriageable women.

1717 Scottish financier John Law and his Company of the West (later, Company of the Indies) receive the charter for control of Louisiana for 25 years from the French government.

1718 Sieur de Bienville selects townsite on the Mississippi and names it New Orleans in honor of Philippe Duc d'Orléans, the regent of France. Population: 68.

1765 France asks Spain to assume control of Louisiana.

1777 Spanish governor Bernardo de Galvez demonstrates his partisanship for the American side of the revolution by seizing 11 richly laden English ships on the Mississippi.

1803 Colonial Prefect Pierre Laussat announces the transfer of Louisiana from Spain back to France. James Monroe, representing the United States, concludes the purchase of Louisiana from France for $15,000,000.

1812 Louisiana is admitted to the Union.

1813 U.S. dragoons capture the pirate Lafitte. Legal prosecution begins in the United States District Court in New Orleans but no conviction obtained.

1815 American troops and local supporters defeat British at Chalmette.

1834 Napoleon's death mask is presented in New Orleans by his former physician.

1861 Louisiana secedes from the United States.

1861 New Orleans blockaded by the Union Army.

1873 The first through train service to Chicago from New Orleans begins.

1896 Louisiana Supreme Court makes the first decision on "separate but equal doctrine" in "Plessy vs. Ferguson." They held for "separate."

1904 Fifty automobiles are in operation in New Orleans.

1909 The last epidemic of yellow fever.

1928 Inauguration of Huey P. Long as governor.

1930 Huey P. Long joins the U.S. Senate.

1956 Federal judge orders desegregation of public schools.

1969 The trial of New Orleans businessman Clay Shaw begins. He is charged by District Attorney Jim Garrison with being a conspirator in the assassination of President Kennedy. He is acquitted.

1977 First black mayor of New Orleans since the Reconstruction, Ernest N. "Dutch" Morial, is elected.

P E O P L E

THE TRADITIONAL CREOLE AND CAJUN CATHOLIC cultures of the southern part of Louisiana survived purely through the dogged chauvinism of their practitioners. Television delivers homogenized white-bread America to their doorsteps. They say "no thanks," continuing instead to revel in their brand of French heritage. That heritage is reflected in the names that they bear from birth, their special affinity to certain over-the-edge heroes such as the pirate Jean Lafitte, and the careful preservation of the social, culinary, and musical rituals of their ancestors.

■ FRENCH AND CREOLES

In the early days of New Orleans, the French Company of the Indies needed to colo-

Philippe, Duc d'Orleans, after whom the city of New Orleans was named. (Historic New Orleans Collection)

nize the territory, so they accepted just about any able-bodied "volunteers." The combination of the violence of the elements and Louisiana's remoteness pretty much insured that few decent folk would want to get near New Orleans. Among the few eager French immigrants were those from debtors' prisons and the houses of correction, including 88 "working girls" who were given the choice of incarceration or a one-way ticket to matrimonial bliss with a Louisiana colonist. In 1720, the regent of France, Philippe, Duc d'Orleans put a stop to the practice of flushing forth the unsavory elements of France into his New World colony. Perhaps it is a coincidence, but it is almost impossible to find any modern citizen of New Orleans who claims an ancestor who came to Louisiana prior to 1727.

One of the city's preeminent cultures is Creole, though it is one of the most

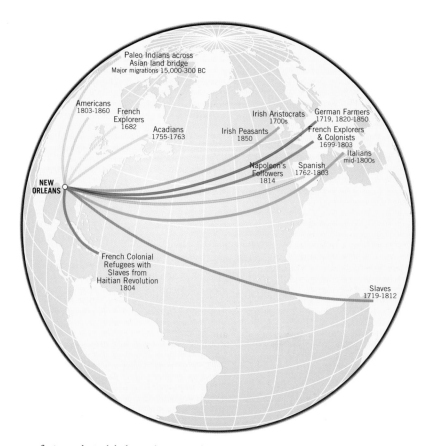

Paleo Indians across
Asian land bridge
Major migrations 15,000-300 BC

Americans
1803-1860

French
Explorers
1682

Acadians
1755-1763

Irish Peasants
1850

Irish Aristocrats
1700s

German Farmers
1719, 1820-1850

French Explorers
& Colonists
1699-1803

Italians
mid-1800s

Napoleon's
Followers
1814

Spanish
1762-1803

NEW
ORLEANS

French Colonial
Refugees with
Slaves from
Haitian Revolution
1804

Slaves
1719-1812

confusing ethnic labels in the United States. Two distinct groups claim the label "Creole" for themselves. White Creoles use the word to describe themselves as people of European colonial parentage. They are very proud descendants of old "aristocratic" families who trace their ancestry back to French and Spanish colonists who came to Louisiana. The other group who lay claim to the title are "mulattos," "quadroons," and "octoroons"—light-skinned African-American Catholics bearing many of the same French and Spanish surnames as white Creoles, and tracing their lineage back to some of the same ancestors.

Both groups agree that the origin of the word is *criollo,* a Spanish term which had been used in the West Indies to refer to a person of European descent born in New World colonies. The intent of the noun was to differentiate anyone of Old

World stock born in the New World from both recent immigrants and Africans. The noted Louisiana historian Charles Gayarré reports that when the first child of French parents was born in Louisiana, Governor Bienville sent a dispatch to the French government to announce the fact. A document of March 4, 1731, proves that the French government paid a bounty to Claude Jousset de la Loire, the infant son of a Canadian trader.

By 1790, the city had a population of 8,000 souls, including "Creoles, free people of color, and slaves." European New Orleanians wanted to distinguish themselves from the Americans after 1803. Similarly, it is thought that French-speaking free people of color adopted the Creole label after the Union army occupation in the 1860s as a means of differentiating themselves from the English-speaking former slaves who were pouring into the occupied city. Interestingly, while slavery existed in New Orleans until the 1860s, most Seventh Ward Creole-of-color families had been free people since the late 1700s.

Both sets of Creoles cling to their history as tenaciously as powdered sugar sticks to beignets. There is an old local riddle, "What do the Creoles have in common with the Chinese?" The answer is that they both eat a lot of rice and worship their ancestors. Creoles, of either group, take great pride in their European heritage, despite the fact that France never showed much support for its emigrés. Perhaps this had to do with the fact that every time things "hit the wall" in France, many of the old guard packed up their pedigrees and pretensions and high-tailed it to Louisiana. Among white Creoles, the most popular ancestors are the members of the nobility who still had their heads after the French Revolution. From the sound of most local family histories, these nobles were as numerous and as prodigious breeders as the casket girls.

At the dawn of the nineteenth century, a time of social and political upheaval throughout much of the world, another group of French-speaking refugees arrived who were to have a major social impact on the city—those fleeing from Toussaint L'Overture's slave revolution against the French settlers in Saint-Domingue (Haiti). Many cane planters packed up their households and fled to Louisiana. One of the new emigrés was John James Audubon, the famous naturalist painter, whose mother—alleged by some to have been a Creole of color—had been killed in the revolution. Another was James Pitot, who from 1804 to 1805 served as the second mayor of the city under American rule. His country home at 1440 Moss Street, built circa 1780 and purchased by Pitot in 1810, is now a museum home on Bayou St. John, where it was moved in the 1960s.

Portrait of Dr. Hardin, a Creole of color in 1895. (Historic New Orleans Collection)

The next group of Frenchmen to leave their imprint on the city were the followers of Napoleon. When Napoleon was exiled to the island of Elba in 1814, many of his dejected soldiers sought passage to the newly American New Orleans. Among these refugees was Napoleon's trusted aide from the Battle of Waterloo, General Charles Lallemand. Evidently many of the soldiers had come to Louisiana to prepare for Napoleon's victorious return. (One legend has it that Jean Lafitte did rescue Napoleon, but that the emperor had a heart attack off the coast of Mexico and was buried in the pirate enclave later called Lafitte in Louisiana.)

Another of Napoleon's exiled lieutenants, Pierre Benjamin Buisson, designed the second New Orleans Customhouse and served as the surveyor for the Village of Lafayette, later known as the Garden District. He is given credit for naming Napoleon Avenue and for affixing the names of Napoleon's victories on Milan, Austerlitz, Marengo, and Constantinople streets in the Uptown section, an American part of the city.

By the time Napoleon ended up at St. Helena, Dominique You (also spelled Youx), the brother of pirate Jean Lafitte, had been persuaded to lead an expedition to free the former French emperor and bring him to Louisiana. The Napoleon House, the bar that stands at the corner of Chartres and St. Louis in the French

New Orleans waterfront during the antebellum period. (Historic New Orleans Collection)

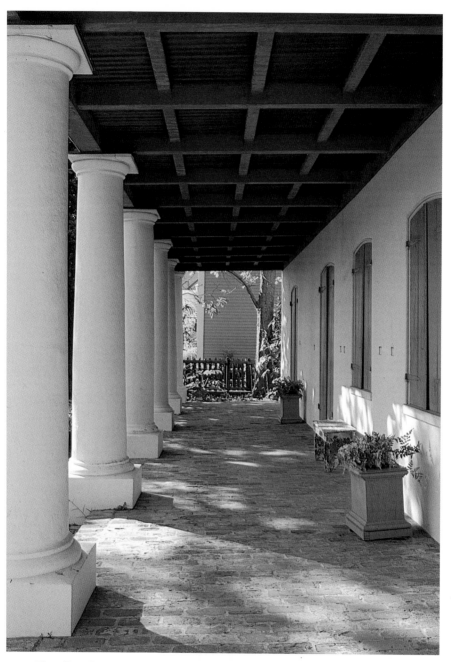

The gallery of Pitot House, 1440 Moss Street in Bayou St. John. Built circa 1780, the house was purchased in 1810 by James Pitot, the second mayor of the city under American rule.

Quarter, was the home of Mayor Nicholas Girod, who offered it as a residence for the great Bonaparte. Napoleon did not live long enough to be rescued, but Napoleon's personal physician, Dr. C. F. Antommarchi, did move from St. Helena into Girod's house and here practiced medicine for the next 13 years. In 1834, Antommarchi gave one of Napoleon's three bronze death masks to the Louisiana State Museum's Cabildo (the other two are in Paris), and it is now in the collection of the Louisiana State Museum. On December 20, 1821, an elaborate Grand Mass honoring Napoleon was celebrated in a black-draped St. Louis Cathedral.

■ CAJUNS

The term "Cajun" comes from the name "Acadian," Acadia being the name of the French Canadian colony founded in 1604 by Samuel de Champlain and now called Nova Scotia. Champlain was joined in 1632 by 300 settlers from Poitou who were fleeing religious persecution in France. The Acadians lived in relative isolation for over 100 years until the French and Indian War in 1754, after which the British demanded that these French-speaking people pledge allegiance to England and renounce their Catholic religion. When the Acadians refused, they were rounded up, separated from family and household members, and deported with the few possessions they could carry. Some were sent as indentured servants to the American colonies; others were sent back to France; some were sent to concentration camps in England; and a few managed to hide and remain in Nova Scotia.

The Acadians would have remained a people divided had not the Spanish invited them to relocate to Louisiana. As the Acadians were Catholic and staunch enemies of the British, they were considered ideal Louisiana settlers. By 1763, the first Acadians had begun to burrow deep into the southern Louisiana swamps, adapting quickly to both the open prairies and the bayous—land of alligators, poisonous snakes, and bountiful fresh foods. It was a place of primordial beauty, and the Cajuns dug in like crawfish, spending more time with the Indians than with the uppity Creoles. They learned to build canoe-like cypress *pirogues* that were light enough to skim on dew. Their raised cottages were built along lazy, meandering bayous tangled with palmettos and moss-draped cypress, where "Dutch nightingales" (frogs) croaked an antiphonal opera and moccasins and alligators slithered from one spot of dry land to the other.

Cajuns were isolated from the urban French in New Orleans, and their language retained much of the seventeenth-century France their ancestors had left. Although both speaking versions of French, the Creoles and Cajuns probably have no common ancestry. The immigrants from Wales, Scotland, Germany, and Spain who moved into southwestern Louisiana soon fell into the Cajun ways, gallicizing their surnames and learning to, in the words of the famous Cajun song, *"Laissez Le Bon Temps Rouler"* ("Let the Good Times Roll").

The Cajun homeland lies to the southwest of New Orleans, in the area around the city of Lafayette and between Baton Rouge on the east and Lake Charles on the west. Today the descendants of the original Acadians are thought to number close to three-quarters of a million.

Paul Prudhomme, America's most famous chef and the man who put Cajun food on the international map, serves up Cajun-style cuisine from his restaurant,

A palmetto house, late 1890s—a typical Cajun trapper's shack. (The Louisiana State Museum)

Nathan and the Zydeco Cha-chas. Zydeco music combines African blues and R&B with traditional Cajun dance music.

K-Paul's, in the French Quarter. Two Cajun dance clubs thrive in the Warehouse District, where people from all over the world can learn to line dance or two-step to the chinka-chinka beat of a live Cajun French band. Zydeco music, a combination of blues and Cajun music, is regularly featured at many of the city's most popular jazz clubs (see "MUSIC"). The New Orleans Jazz & Heritage Festival, during the last weekend in April and the first in May, provides a glorious taste of Cajun music, food, and crafts. Three Lafayette-based festivals (a three-hour drive from New Orleans) that are popular with lovers of Cajun culture are the *Festival International de Louisiane* in mid to late April, the *Cajun Heartland State Fair* in early to late May, and the *Fêtes des Acadiens* in mid-August.

■ AMERICAN INDIANS

One of the country's earliest large Native American communities, constructed approximately 2,700 years ago, can be found in the northeastern part of the state near Monroe (a five-hour drive from New Orleans), at Poverty Point. This ancient

Blessing of the shrimp fleet. Many Louisiana shrimpers are of Cajun descent. (Michael P. Smith)

Native American city is remarkable not only for its size—an estimated 5,000 people lived here—but also for the fact that it was erected between 800 and 600 B.C., at the beginning of the American Neolithic Age. The village at Poverty Point represents the earliest record of the southward movement of Hopewell Civilization.

The ancient community sustained itself in a fixed location, though it remains a mystery how they managed this, since the site predates any evidence of the domestication of animals or the planting of crops. The site is dominated by a mammoth eagle-shaped mound, 600 feet (183 m) long and 70 feet (21 m) high, the second tallest Indian mound in North America. Close by is another mound that measures 600 feet (183 m) by 55 feet (17 m). Archaeologists marvel at the fact that the Indians had to dig the earth with sticks and that they transported over a half-million tons of dirt in baskets.

This civilization seems to have been overtaken about 1,000 years ago by a group of Indians who moved north from Mexico, bringing with them agricultural techniques and more efficient weaponry. Most of the tribes who lived in permanent fortified villages on navigable waterways around Marksville, Louisiana, wove baskets and made a wide variety of pottery. It is estimated that at that time there were 13,000 Indians in the entire land area that was to become the state of Louisiana.

By the time the French colonists arrived, Indians in southern Louisiana spoke versions of three different languages: Tunican, Caddoan, and Muskhogean. The Acalopisas, the Chitimachas, the Tunicas, and the Bayougoulas taught the earliest colonists the survival and food-gathering skills that saved their lives. But sadly, while the Indians showed them how and where to grow crops and procure meat, fish, skins, and timber, the legacy of the white man was disease, particularly smallpox, which reportedly wiped out entire villages.

Today the 283-acre Chitimacha Reservation on Bayou Teche in the St. Mary Parish (south Louisiana) is less than a two-hour drive from New Orleans. The intricately patterned Chitimacha baskets are included in museum exhibitions around the world. Due to the shortage of mature five-year-old swamp cane, these baskets now sell for about $20 per square inch (5.25 square cm) and are smaller in scale than the ones of a generation ago. Also there are fewer weavers who have mastered the difficult and time-consuming craft. By the early 1990s, there were only six weavers skilled in making the traditional black, red, and ochre motifs such as the "alligator entrails," "worm tracks," and "blackbird eyes." Many of the elders have predicted that with the arrival of gambling establishments on the Indian reservations, all of the ancient skills will be lost to a younger generation who may prefer to become roulette operators and bingo callers. Nowadays an Indian Powwow is held in early May at the Tchefuncte Campground in Folsom, about an hour from New Orleans.

■ AFRICANS

On nights when a breeze pushes the pungent smells and the sounds of metal against metal from the holds of football-field-sized ships docked along the wharves, the heart of downtown begins to feel like Pireaus or Istanbul. But then those two port cities don't have the soul of black New Orleans. The evocative rhythm that dominates the sounds of the city and the pace that resonates from its streets puts New Orleans in ethno-cultural harmony with Rio or Dakar. Since the mid-eighteenth century the evolving culture of African Americans has been a driving force of the city.

The first Africans who came to Louisiana were brought in 1719 from the Senegambia region (near Senegal) by French slavers. Recent research shows that between 1719 and 1731 the French Company of the Indies brought in 7,000 slaves. In 1727, the *Code Noir*, a set of regulations for the treatment of slaves, made Louisiana a less oppressive place for blacks to live than in some areas dominated by the British. Though the importation of slaves was outlawed in the United States in 1808, New Orleans was not exempted from this law until 1812. Slavery continued for another sixty-odd years, and local slave auctions were well attended. By 1860, there were some 12 small, year-round slave auction houses, in addition to

Photographs of former slave children, such as this one of three New Orleanian children, were used by the North during Reconstruction to promote the idea that education should be given to former slaves. (Historic New Orleans Collection)

grander affairs conducted in late winter and early spring—ironically the season of Lent. At these events, New Orleans auctioneers would dress the slaves up in European clothes, hoping to make the Africans look less fearsome. Slave auction sites included the Cabildo, the St. Louis and the St. Charles hotels, and Maspero's Exchange, now a cafe on Chartres Street.

Records show that as early as 1805, the *Place Congo* or Congo Square (now known as Louis Armstrong Park) was a grassy plain on the edge of the swamps at the far side of the French Quarter where *gens de couleur libre* (free blacks) and slaves would congregate. It became a place where African rituals and ceremonies were kept alive and where disparate peoples from a variety of tribal groups found a cultural bond in their improvised music. The immigration of the *gens de couleur libre*, slaves, and former slaves from Haiti in the early nineteenth century served to infuse other African tribal traditions into those of the Louisiana slaves, many of whom were by then third-generation Louisianians.

An account of 1853 describes the *bamboula*, a dance performed by the blacks: "The head rests on the breast or is thrown back upon the shoulders, the eyes closed, or glaring, while the arms, amid cries, and shouts, and sharp ejaculations, float upon the air, or keep time . . . to music which is seemingly eternal."

Not all of the African Americans living in Louisiana were slaves. There are reports from the 1720s of free blacks, often former slaves who moved to Louisiana from the Caribbean. Between 1763 and 1803, the numbers of free people of color increased from 99 to 1,355, partially due to immigrants from the Indies, and partially due to the number of light-skinned mixed Euro-African citizens.

Dancing the bamboula, as depicted in an old print. (Historic New Orleans Collection)

Between 1840 and 1860, the census reported over 7,500 free people of color. By the time of the Civil War, many blacks in Louisiana were 20 generations removed from Africa and 10 from slavery. Additionally many a Frenchman left property to his mixed-race offspring. The initials F.P.C. (Free Person of Color) came to be used after the name of a person of mixed race who might be mistaken for being white and therefore try to assert his civil rights. Oppressive as this was, however, New Orleans afforded free blacks more rights than any other American city north or south, allowing African Americans to own property and to seek justice through the judicial system.

President Abraham Lincoln's Emancipation Proclamation of January 1, 1863, freed slaves in all of the areas of the United States that were in rebellion. By a peculiar stroke of bad luck, slavery was to last in New Orleans longer than in any other part of the United States, as the city was under federal control. Slavery was allowed to continue for almost a year by federal occupation forces. From this period on, one segment of black culture was to be permanently set off from the other by a sociocultural Hadrian's Wall. Uneducated, poor, often darker-skinned, and raised on English-speaking plantations, these recently freed slaves were ostracized by Creoles and free people of color and American slaves tended to move into an area known as "back-a-town" (Mahalia Jackson and Louis Armstrong were from this area).

Plantation life. (Historic New Orleans Collection)

Reconstruction proved to be a time of great discord for the people of the "third race." The *gens de couleur libre*, many of whom had owned slaves themselves, lived in relative seclusion and some prosperity in the Seventh Ward downtown, the site of Bernard de Marigny's estate in the 1800s. (Today, its Corpus Christi Catholic parish is the largest predominantly black Catholic parish in the United States.) Many of the wealthiest among them were French-speaking professionals who educated their children in France. Also among them were master craftsmen and the fathers of jazz. Yet after Reconstruction, they found themselves stripped of all of the freedoms and dignity that they had once enjoyed. Consequently, some migrated to Latin America or Europe; and some moved into uptown neighborhoods, married recent immigrants, and permanently crossed from black to white. In many contemporary Creole-of-color families, some members will have white as the race marked on their birth certificates, while a sibling will be categorized as black, depending on the opinion of the mother's doctor. (In the 1920s Huey Long stated that you could feed all the pure white people in the city with one cup of beans and rice and still have some left over.)

Ethnic strife is well known in New Orleans. After ugly riots in 1866, the Louisiana Constitution was passed in 1868, insuring rights for blacks that included enfranchisement and the prohibition of segregation in schools and in public spaces. By the end of Reconstruction in 1876, 45 percent of the black population was registered to vote, and by 1897, this figure increased to 95 percent. But the enforcement of Louisiana's infamous grandfather clause and "Jim Crow" laws reduced the percentage to less than 10 percent the following year, and to one percent by 1901.

U.S.A. Convention Planners and Heritage Tours at 1212 St. Charles Avenue, 592-0560, offers black heritage tours of the city. The four-hour bus tour leaves from local hotels twice daily and covers everything from Zulu and other black social aid and pleasure clubs to the Sisters of the Holy Family, a nineteenth-century order of black nuns; and from the Neighborhood Gallery, an artists' cooperative, to the Amistad Research Center at Tulane University, the nation's largest black archive and an invaluable research resource. The Black Heritage Festival at the Audubon Zoo, held the second weekend in March, is a nice way for the entire family to get a history lesson and have fun. And each year, from late April into early May, the New Orleans Jazz & Heritage Festival spotlights the extraordinary contribution of the black community to New Orleans and to music.

GROWING UP IN NEW ORLEANS

I'm always wondering if it would have been best in my life if I'd stayed like I was in New Orleans, having a ball. I was very much contented just to be around and play with the old timers. And the money I made—I lived off of it. I wonder if I would have enjoyed that better than all this big mucky-muck traveling all over the world. . . .

But man I sure had a ball there growing up in New Orleans as a kid. We were poor and everything like that, but music was all around you. Music kept you rolling.

When I was about four or five, still wearing dresses, I lived with my mother in Jane's Alley in a place called Brick Row—a lot of cement, rented rooms sort of like a motel. And right in the middle of that on Perdido Street was the Funky Butt Hall— old, beat up, big cracks in the wall. On Saturday nights, Mama couldn't find us 'cause we wanted to hear that music. Before the dance the band would play out front about a half hour. And us little kids would all do little dances. If I ever heard Buddy Bolden play the cornet, I figure that's when.

—Louis Armstrong, "Growing Up in New Orleans," *Life* magazine, 1966

Louis Armstrong sponsored the "Secret 9" baseball team in 1931.
(The Hogan Jazz Archive, Tulane University)

■ SPANIARDS

The Spaniards were, in a manner of speaking, the state's first white tourists. Hernando de Soto first arrived on the western coast of Florida in 1539, and in the years that followed he explored as far as Arkansas in a fruitless search for silver and gold. While Castilian rule of Louisiana lasted a mere 34 years (1769-1803), the city was nevertheless wedged in between, and profoundly and permanently influenced by, flourishing Spanish settlements in Texas, Florida, and the Caribbean.

Spanish rule was greeted by more than a little "unpleasantness" from French settlers and required military force to quell the unrest. Spanish officials must have seen that their only hope was to marry the problem, and Governor Luis de Unzaga obliged by marrying Mlle. St. Maxent, and a few years later, the third governor, Don Bernardo de Galvez, wed the brilliant Felicie d'Estrehan—a particularly popular first lady of Louisiana.

During his eight-year administration, from 1777 to 1785, Galvez supplied the American frontiersmen with weapons to use against the British, and seized any British ships he could get his hands on. This was of great assistance to the American Revolutionary army. In September of 1779, Galvez captured Baton Rouge and Natchez; in 1780 he took Mobile; and in 1781 he overtook Pensacola. This is why the Daughters of the American Revolution (the DAR) will admit members who trace their ancestry back to those who fought with Galvez.

The fourth governor, Miro, did his marital duty to the locals by taking as his bride the extremely wealthy Celeste Elenore Elizabeth Macarty, daughter of one of the city's premiere Irish Creole families. (The family's original name was Macarthey-Mactaig, an Irish family who had fled Ireland for France to escape the tyranny of the British.) Mlle. Macarty's father and uncle had come to New Orleans in 1731 as part of a French marine detachment. Bienville honored both men by making them *Chevaliers de Saint Louis*, and assisted them in gaining large land grants.

One of the most interesting enclaves of Spaniards is the *Islenos* who came to Louisiana over 215 years ago from the Canary Islands, a Spanish colony off the northwestern coast of Africa. Today close to 500 of the group who live in St. Bernard Parish (one of the four parishes that make up metropolitan New Orleans) still speak their eighteenth-century Creole Spanish, in an area where 25 percent of the 67,000 residents are of Isleno descent. They live in the communities of Delacroix Island and Reggio and make their living as fishermen and trappers.

Casamento's, an Italian-owned restaurant in operation since 1918.

Since 1976, when the group formed the Spanish Heritage and Cultural Society of St. Bernard, they have actively sought to keep the Spanish heritage of Louisiana alive. The Islenos Museum (1357 Bayou Road, St. Bernard Village, 682-0862) is free and affords an intriguing look at photographs and artifacts reflecting the culture that traces its origins to the Canary Islands.

Spanish architectural heritage is highly visible in the French Quarter, and many streets bear the names of the Spanish governors—Galvez, Gayoso, and Miro. The Latin influence has been reactivated in a new form by the many prominent Cubans who came to the city in the 1960s, and by communities of people from Nicaragua, Honduras, and Guatemala who've come since. Spanish-language movie theaters, Latin restaurants, and Latin dance clubs can be seen on parts of Magazine Street. The Carnival Latino, held along the riverfront late in June, offers a taste of many of the Latin cultures that are prevalent in the city today. The Honduran Independence Day Festival, held at the French Market on the second weekend in September, fills the area with the sights and sounds of Latin America.

■ GERMANS

In the eighteenth century, it became crucial to the survival of the fledgling colony that John Law's Company of the Indies find enough sturdy immigrant farmers to grow something for French settlers to eat. Toward this end, the company inundated southern Germany and Switzerland with handbills promoting Louisiana as a "paradise." The first large German-speaking Catholic groups arrived in November 1719 on the vessel *Les Deux Freres*. The last great eighteenth-century German-speaking migration started out two years later with over 1,000 Germans. No sooner had the four ships left the French port than an epidemic of cholera broke out.

Once they arrived they were in for more bad news; they soon realized that New Orleans, the "Paris of the New World," was in reality the capital of mildew and malaria, and far from an idyllic place to farm. When John Law's pyramid scheme failed in France, he fled to Italy, leaving the German farmers stranded in the soggy French-speaking Louisiana colony. Law had promised the Germans money and land, but they were still waiting for both when they learned that their new homeland had been given to the Spanish. The Germans pulled out of New Orleans and found dry land to farm 25 miles (40 km) upriver in an area that became known as the *Côte des Allemands,* or the German coast.

The German farmers did their job well, supplying the city with an abundance of fresh produce. Surnames such as Schexnaider and Hymel (pronounced "Hee-mel," the Francophone version of Himmel) are still prominent in the suburban communities of Jefferson Parish. Other Germans intermarried with the French or simply found that it was easier to adapt their names to the language of the region.

Not only were the Germans excellent farmers, but they also soon gained a reputation for being among the finest bakers of French bread and pastries. Even today most of the top local bakeries bear Swiss and German names, and much of the French bread for local po-boys comes in paper wrappers printed with the name Leidenheimer. The Germans also built many impressive churches, and introduced commercially brewed beer.

In the middle of the nineteenth century and at a time when New Orleans still enjoyed a reputation as an Old World European-style city with New World possibilities, political upheaval in Europe brought yet another wave of Germans to

New Orleans enjoyed a reputation as an Old World, European-style city with New World possibilities. (Historic New Orleans Collection)

Louisiana. Between 1820 and 1850, more than 50,000 Germans passed into the United States from the port of New Orleans. By 1870, an estimated 17,000 people spoke German as their principal language. This wave of immigrants was proud of its Teutonic heritage. Moving into commerce and banking alongside Americans, these newly arrived Germans seemed to have managed to straddle the fence between the old French social strata and newly moneyed Americans. Many of them settled

German settlers were brought to Louisiana to grow wheat and became the city's preeminent bakers. (Sharon Dinkins Collection)

alongside the Creoles in Faubourg Marigny, which would be nicknamed "Little Saxony" by the end of the nineteenth century.

By the early twentieth century, New Orleans' German diaspora was sharing its vibrant musical tradition with other New Orleanians: German oompah bands found appreciative audiences when they played outdoors in the city's parks and plazas. Their use of instruments and upbeat tempos would later influence New Orleans' famous marching bands.

Many people in town trot out their German heritage during Oktoberfest. One of the nicest of these autumn celebrations is the Oktoberfest de l'Acadian celebrated at the Ormond Plantation in Destrehan (about 30 minutes from the French Quarter) on the third weekend in October. There are also celebrations at Deutsches-Haus (200 South Galvez, 522-3014) every Saturday in October.

■ IRISH

From its founding, New Orleans proved an attractive destination for enterprising Irish Catholic grandees who loathed the British. Many found their way to New Orleans through military service with the French and Spanish. Once there, they tended to marry into Creole families, and/or adapt their own last names accordingly. The builder of the Gallier House, now a museum house in the French Quarter, was a Mr. Gallagher. Records show that he changed his name before his arrival in the French-speaking colony. The Galliers, the father and the son of Ravensdale, Ireland, are responsible for some of the city's finest architectural treasures, including Gallier Hall, the original city hall, and St. Patrick's Church on Camp Street, as well as many of the city's finest private residences.

The experiences of the old-line, eighteenth-century Irish Creoles (known as "lace-curtain Irish") upon their arrival in New Orleans, and those of the mid-nineteenth-century potato famine immigrants who followed them were as different as a chestnut horse and a horse chestnut. In the years after the 1845 potato blight, hundreds of thousands of starving Irish poured through the Port of New Orleans, arriving in a city where every section of dry land had already been claimed, where housing was scarce, and where menial labor was usually done by slaves. The new arrivals couldn't afford passage north or west; so they were trapped in a city where they were unneeded.

In 1860, New Orleans had about 175,000 inhabitants, 40 percent of whom were foreign-born. Of this number 24,000 were Irish. Potato famine-era Irish could be hired for next to nothing and were often assigned to tasks considered too dangerous for a valuable slave or servant. One of these

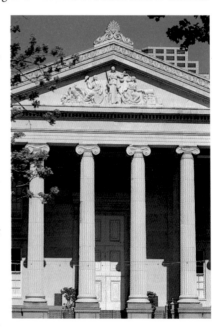

Gallier Hall, New Orleans's former city hall.

tasks was to dig the city's canals. Fortunately, the Irish being a hearty lot, many of them managed to survive not only a brutal work load and yellow fever, but also the injustices dished out by both Creoles and Americans. The first statue ever erected in honor of a woman in the United States was dedicated to an illiterate Irish peasant, Margaret Haughery, credited with caring for hundreds of Irish children orphaned after one of the yellow fever epidemics. Her statue stands in a small park at Camp and Prytania with an inscription that simply reads "Margaret."

Another lasting memorial to Irish women and men are the festivities of March 17. All hardship is forgotten when St. Patrick's Day rolls around, though the festivities often start the weekend before in the 1100 block of Decatur Street in the French Quarter. Here the Decatur Street Marching Club leads a parade that includes other festive groups, such as Joe's Jungle Marching Club, the Kazoozie Floozies, and the Pipes and Drums of New Orleans. Just about everybody in town dons green and takes to the streets to enjoy the party. Some suspect that there may be a papal dispensation allowing Catholics to break their Lenten abstinence to celebrate St. Patty's Day with gusto.

And yes, there are many parades. The weekend following St. Pat's, there's even an Irish-Italian parade in the suburbs that features Pete Fountain's Half-Fast Walking Club. At these parades float-riders throw cabbages and potatoes, as well as

---

IRISH CHANNEL

*J*ody's bar didn't cater to just anyone that happened to drop by to get a drink or lay a bet. It was the oldest neighborhood bar in the Irish Channel section of New Orleans, and its regular customers included second- and third-generation drinkers from many walks of life. Descendants of Creole blue bloods mingled easily with house painters and deliverymen stopping by for a quick one on their route.

Jody ran a notoriously tight ship. No one but Jody himself had ever answered the telephone that sat beneath a framed copy of The Auburn Creed, and no woman, no matter what her tale of woe, had ever managed to get him to call a man to the phone.

"Not here," he would answer curtly, "haven't seen him." And Jody would hang up without offering to take a message. If a woman wanted a man at Jody's she had to come look for him in person.

—Ellen Gilchrist, *In the Land of Dreamy Dreams,* 1981

doubloons and plastic necklaces (usually recycled Mardi Gras jewels), to the crowds; and green and white paper carnations are traded for a kiss. At noon on St. Patrick's Day, businessmen in pinstripe suits and emerald green derbies can be seen jaunting down Camp Street for mass at St. Patrick's. The street outside Parasol's, a bar in the Irish Channel, is filled to overflowing with folks eager for a mug of green beer. While most of the beer served in local pubs is green, those desperate for a more conventional brew can usually find it at Molly's At the Market in the French Quarter, near the beginning of the parade route. Another Irish-friendly enclave is O'Flaherty's Irish Pub at 524 Toulouse Street, which often hosts live concerts by musicians who favor the ceili, fiddle, and whistle over the electric guitar and the saxophone.

■ ITALIANS

Throughout the eighteenth century Italians were attracted to New Orleans's Latin/ Catholic culture and mild climate. As with the Irish, many aristocratic Italians made their way to Louisiana in the service of the French and Spanish governments. Enrico Tonti was part of the La Salle expedition that discovered the mouth of the Mississippi in 1682. Famed Confederate General Pierre Gustave Toutant Beauregard was the son of Helene Judith de Reggio, of the family of the Duke of Reggio, part of the House of Este. (Another Reggio descendent is married to Senator Edward Kennedy.)

Many other Italians came later, part of the last large wave of immigrants to come to New Orleans in the nineteenth century, most of them arriving from Sicily. By 1890, there were 15,000 Italians living in the city. Many moved into the crumbling French Quarter, which had fallen out of favor with Creole families.

One powerful group among these immigrants came from the village of Contessa Entellina in Sicily. In 1886, these Sicilians founded the Contessa Entellina Society, one of the oldest Italian-American organizations still in existence in the United States. Each fall their descendants hold a Mass of Thanksgiving at St. Louis Cathedral to commemorate their coming to America.

The late-coming Italians were treated just a shade worse than the Irish and a tiny bit better than blacks. But like the Irish and blacks, they too survived. One notable Italian was Joseph Vaccaro, who rose from being a door-to-door fruit peddler to founding the company that would later become Standard Fruit and Steamship Company. A second notable immigrant was Mother Frances Xavier Cabrini, the first American citizen to be canonized by the Catholic Church. Mother Cabrini came to New Orleans in 1892 as a missionary to the French Quarter, which was by then 90 percent Italian. Within her lifetime she established 67 different institutions to aid recent immigrants to the city, including orphanages, hospitals, and day-care centers, as well as St. Mary's Italian Church, which served as the focal point in the lives of French Quarter residents.

During the 1970s, four of New Orlean's seven city councilmen, as well as the mayor and the chief of police, were of Italian heritage. Today a visit to the vegetable stalls in the French Market, to the Italian grocery stores near Jackson Square on Decatur Street, or to one of the many Italian ice cream shops will confirm that Italian culture continues to thrive in New Orleans.

The American-Italian Renaissance Foundation Museum, at 537 St. Peters in the Warehouse District, 891-1904, is a treasury of artifacts and historical documents reflecting the struggles and resourcefulness of Italian immigrants.

The Italian community still pays homage to St. Joseph—the patron saint honored as the protector of the family—for delivering the Sicilians from famine in the early 1800s. On St. Joseph's Day, March 19—the day the Creoles called "La Mi-Carême," the middle of Lent—the Italian community gives the city yet another reason to celebrate. On this day, many Italian-American New Orleanians bake and bag several thousand cookies to give away; others cook up gallons of fava beans, the food that saved their nineteenth-century ancestors from starvation in Sicily. These dishes and dozens of other meatless Sicilian delicacies are prepared, including stuffed artichokes and mirlitons, pasta Milanese, *baccala* (codfish), *sfingi* (an eggplant and olive oil dish), a magnificent array of decorative breads, and pastries and cakes such as dolci and cuccidati. Once prepared, the food is set on special St. Joseph altars around the city. After each altar has been blessed by a priest, it is opened to the public for viewing and sampling. Afterwards, the foods that have been displayed are served to the poor.

Ads in the *Times-Picayune* classified section invite the public to partake at St. Joseph altars in homes, churches, and businesses. The St. Joseph's Church at 1802 Tulane Avenue presents one of the largest outdoor altars in the world.

St. Joseph's Day also brings yet another parade to the streets of New Orleans. On the Saturday nearest to March 19, the French Quarter fills with thousands of

A St. Joseph's Day altar, an Italian tradition. (Michael P. Smith)

PEOPLE TIMELINE

1704 An epidemic of yellow fever kills more than 35 people, a blow to the struggling colony.

1706 Sieur d'Iberville, one of New Orleans's founders, dies of yellow fever at Havana where his duties in the war against England had taken him. One of his missions had been to find a source of bread for the colonists as wheat would not grow near swampy New Orleans.

1719 Two hundred and fifty Germans arrive.

1720 The first shipment of slaves arrives in Louisiana.

1728 The first of the *filles à la cassette* arrive in December. These were the first women of good character to be sent as wives to the colonists.

1739 Governor Sieur de Bienville makes a second attack on the Chickasaw.

1764 The first Acadian immigrants to Louisiana, four families, arrived from New York.

1809 Nearly 6,000 refugees who had fled from the slave insurrection in Santo Domingo to Cuba, arrive in New Orleans after being driven out of Cuba by the Spanish.

1825 The American Revolutionary war hero, the Marquis de Lafayette, visits New Orleans.

1835 Sam Houston plots the Texas Revolution with the Freemasons at 833 Ursuline in the French Quarter.

1836 The longest court trial in history, the Myra Clark Gaines case begins. It will not end until 1891. (Her lawyer, John Henderson, is described on pages 50-51.)

1850 Large migration of Irish arrives due to the potato famine that began in Ireland in 1845.

1878 The last great yellow fever epidemic. The cost of ice rises from $16 a ton to $60 a ton.

1884 New Orleans erects the first statue in America honoring a woman. She is Margaret Haughery who cares for the Irish poor.

1890s Large migration of French-speaking Lebanese merchants arrives.

1894 Carville, the only leprosarium on the U.S. mainland, is founded.

1903 A large gypsy camp is established at St. Louis and Scott streets.

1910 Louisiana native Edward Douglass White is appointed Chief Justice of the U.S. Supreme Court.

1976 New Orleans native Mrs. Anne L. Armstrong becomes the second woman to be named to a major embassy by the United States when she is appointed the American Ambassador to Great Britain.

1990s Large numbers of Hispanic and Asian immigrants arrive in New Orleans.

members of the Italian-American marching clubs. Horse-drawn buggies and marching bands accompany floats, each of which depicts a different Italian province. Those in the parade trade red, white, and green carnations for kisses and throw fava beans and doubloons.

The other important Italian festival not to be missed is the Festa D'Italia, held in early October at Poydras near the river.

While New Orleans maintains its traditional connections to the Old World, the greatest post-World War II migrations to the city have come from Cuba, Latin America, and Vietnam. Each of these new groups has brought along its native culture to a place that continues to nurture ethnic communities; and each new group has established its own native-language churches (usually Catholic), as well as its own festivals. While these immigrants have brought altogether new cultural riches, their arrival has also ensured that New Orleans remains what it has always been—a uniquely exciting, multi-cultural, multi-ethnic city, where a world of traditions are honored and preserved, yet intermingled with an unrivaled exuberance.

FRENCH QUARTER
V I E U X   C A R R É

SPRAWLING, SULTRY, SEDUCTIVE, AND AGELESS, the original neighborhood that was New Orleans still exists as the French Quarter just where Sieur de Bienville, its French founder, left it when his 30 convicted salt smugglers first hacked down razor-sharp palmetto thickets to clear a spot for a few ramshackle houses. An area only 4,000 feet (1,219 m) long and 1,800 feet (549 m) wide, the Quarter remains both the heartland of old New Orleans and its most progressive neighborhood. As the decades pass, Jackson Square—the old town square that faces the river—continues to be vitally alive with new generations of neighborhood children playing ball, lovers having a lunch-time smooch over a muffuletta, pigeons looking for handouts, and itinerant artists sketching the passersby. The neighborhood remains part residential and part commercial. Bourbon Street clubs still serve as a finishing school for local musicians, and strip joints and gay dance clubs co-exist with T-shirt shops on carefully maintained pedestrian walkways. Not far from all this ebullience and sleaze, expensive antiques are sold from posh shops. Also within the borders of the old city are a thriving public elementary school, an A&P, numerous bakeries, and praline and perfume shops. Above all this exuberance, contradiction, and energy looms the new city of New Orleans—20 or so office and hotel towers that poke up in the uneven pattern of a child's toothy smile. On one side are the twin bridges that span the Mississippi River. The other side of the skyline is dominated by a gigantic aluminum soufflé, the 128,000-cubic-yard Louisiana Superdome.

The first step to establishing a relationship with old New Orleans is to stay in one of the small hotels or guest houses operated in one of the older neighborhoods —places such as the Soniat House, the Lafitte Guest House, the Hotel Maison de Ville, and the La Mothe House in the French Quarter; the Columns or the Josephine in the area near St. Charles; or the Parkview near Audubon Park. The second step involves food and drink—meals at Antoine's, the oldest restaurant in America; sandwiches at Uglesich, one of the oldest neighborhood po-boy places; and drinks at the Napoleon House and Lafitte's Blacksmith Shop.

Next to taking a guided walking tour (see "PRACTICAL INFORMATION"), a fine way to get the feel of the architecture of the French Quarter is to take a carriage

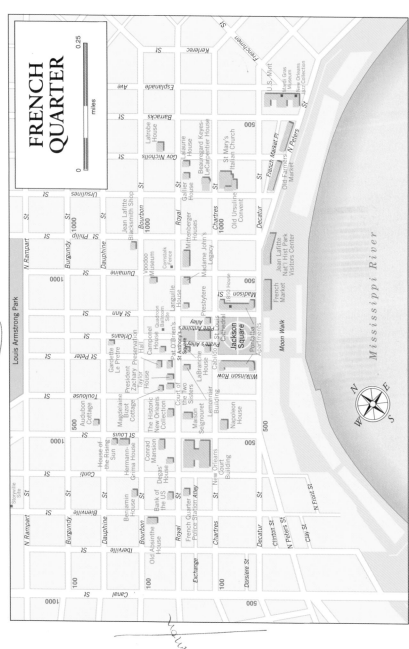

FRENCH QUARTER

miles

0   0.25

Louis Armstrong Park

Mississippi River

N Rampart St
Burgundy St
Dauphine St
Bourbon St
Royal St
Chartres St
Decatur St

Ursulines St
St Philip St
Dumaine St
St Ann St
Orleans St
St Peter St
Toulouse St
St Louis St
Conti St
Bienville St
Iberville St
Canal St

Kerlerec St
Esplanade Ave
Barracks St
Gov Nicholas St

Bourbon 1000
Chartres 1000

Frenchmen St

U.S. Mint
Mardi Gras Museum
New Orleans Jazz Collection

French Market Pl
N Peters St
Old Farmers Market

Jean Lafitte Blacksmith Shop
Latrobe House
Lalaurie House
Beauregard Keyes-LeCarpentier House
St Mary's Italian Church
Galier House
Mittenberger Houses
Voodoo Museum
Cornstalk Fence
Madame John's Legacy
Languille House
1850 House
Old Ursuline Convent
Jean Lafitte Nat'l Hist Park Visitors Center
French Market
Presbytere
St Louis Cathedral
Pere Antoine's Alley
St Anthony's Square
Pirate's Alley
Jackson Square
Pontalba Apartments
Moon Walk
Quadroon Ballroom Site
Campanel House
Pat O'Brien's
Gardette Le Pretre
President Zachary Taylor House
LaBranche House
Cabildo
Wilkinson Row
Lemonnier Building
Court of the Two Sisters
Maison Seignouret
The Historic New Orleans Collection
Magdelaine Bizot Cottage
Audubon Cottage
House of the Rising Sun
Hermann-Grima House
Conrad Mansion
Degas' House
Napoleon House
New Orleans Court Building
Bank of the US
Benjamin House
Old Absinthe House
French Quarter Police Station
Exchange Alley
Storyville Site

N Front St
Clinton St
N Peters St
Clay St
Dorsiere St

French Quarter Police Station Alley

Madison St
1000
500
100
1000
500
100

N   W   E   S

ride—that is if you can stand being seen in a carriage displaying advertisements for the Wax Museum and pulled by a mule sporting diapers and a straw hat festooned with plastic flowers. (If this sounds like too much, you might consider wearing a mask. Passersby will not give you a second glance, because in the Quarter there are always a few hard-core partyers who celebrate Mardi Gras year round.) It is preferable to make this half-hour excursion at dusk, when the streets are less crowded and a dreamy lassitude settles over the old city. A few of the drivers who give tours will even point out the balcony in the 1000 block of Royal from which "The King" sang in *King Creole*. But listener beware: these drivers are not licensed guides, and their monologues tend to be more folksy than accurate. One group of local preservationists was horrified to overhear a carriage driver referring to Spanish moss as "Mardi grasses." The point is to sit back and enjoy studying the buildings of the French Quarter from the second floor on up.

■ EARLY HISTORY

In 1721, the governor of New Orleans sent for a French engineer named Adrien de Pauger to create a grid of European-style streets and a grand public square on the ramshackle outpost. Of course, this entailed convincing the crusty settlers that their new city would be more aesthetically pleasing if they knocked their homes down and reconstructed them in an orderly fashion. A document dated September 5, 1722, describes how Pauger and a man named Traverse got into a violent fistfight over the engineer's scheme. Nevertheless, Pauger's 66-square-block network of streets was soon established.

But the French sense of civilized orderliness and the well-considered architecture of the buildings that soon graced New Orleans eventually proved no match for the natural disasters that continually plagued the city. On March 21, 1788, a fire began at the Spanish paymaster's house on Chartres and Toulouse streets that destroyed all but a tiny portion of the fledgling colonial city. When the city was rebuilt, the (by-now) Spanish governor, Baron Francisco Luis Hector de Carondelet, initiated many improvements, adding the first streetlights—80 oil lamps suspended from poles on street corners—and a drainage canal along Carondelet Street; editing the city's first newspaper; and encouraging the establishment of a theater. Then in 1793 and 1794, the newly improved city was struck by three hurricanes;

and in 1794 another terrible fire raged through the city, destroying almost 200 French-built buildings, most of them private homes, in less than three hours. Yet once again the Vieux Carré was rebuilt, and if its well-planned streets were sometimes filled with rotting sewage, slops, and garbage, the graciously appointed interiors of many of its homes belied this reality. Some of these, such as the Hermann-Grima Historic House, the Gallier House, and the Beauregard Keyes-Le Carpentier House and Garden, are still standing and are described later in this chapter as "Museum Houses" (see pages 98-101).

■ JACKSON SQUARE

The heart of the French Quarter remains its central plaza, **Jackson Square**, originally constructed in 1721 as a drill field and called the Place d'Armes. The square was renamed in 1848 to honor Andrew Jackson, the hero of the 1815 Battle of New Orleans. In 1851, the Baroness Pontalba installed the fences and gardens landscaped in the sun pattern made popular in France during the reign of Louis XIV, the Sun King.

The early Place D'Armes, the center of the Vieux Carré, which later became Jackson Square. This drawing is of the second of three cathedrals on this site. (Historic New Orleans Collection)

The pigeon-covered statue of Jackson ("Old Hickory") atop a rearing steed was fashioned by sculptor Clark Mills. It was the world's first equestrian statue in which the horse has more than one foot off the base. The statue now bears the inscription, "The Union must and shall be preserved," which was added in the 1860s by the occupying Union army during the War Between the States.

Jackson Square is dominated by St. Louis Cathedral, the oldest continually active cathedral in the United States, and the third church to be built on this site. (The first, constructed in 1722, was lost to fire, as was the second.) The present cathedral dates in part from 1794, but was largely remodeled in 1845-1851 by J. N. B. de Pouilly. Its interior contains magnificent stained glass, murals, frescoes, and the graves of many early New Orleans dignitaries. The cathedral's rectory serves as the repository for church registers that date back to 1731. Nearby St. Anthony's Garden and Père Antoine's Alley are named for the late-eighteenth-century priest, Père Antonio de Sedella. There is a monument in St. Anthony's Garden to those caregivers who were stricken in the yellow fever epidemic of 1853, which killed over 11,000 people.

The cathedral is flanked by original late-eighteenth-century Spanish Colonial government buildings, the Cabildo (to the left of the cathedral) and the Presbytère, which has the Confederate submarine in front. The Presbytère at 713 Chartres Street stands on the site of an early French monastery. A wealthy Spaniard, Don Almonester, financed this new building as a home for the priests of the Cathedral. While being built a fire destroyed much of the building in 1794, and it sat abandoned until the Americans rebuilt it in 1813 for use as a courthouse.

The Cabildo was once a Spanish government building, the *Casa Capitular* where the "Very Illustrious Cabildo," or city council, met. Destroyed in the 1788 fire, it was rebuilt with an ornate wrought-iron balcony rail attributed to Marcelino Hernandez. The Louisiana Purchase was turned over to the United States in the left-side room on the second floor of the Cabildo on December 20, 1803. From its chambers French, Spanish, Confederates, and Americans have ruled the city. In 1847, mansard roofs were added to both these Colonial-style buildings in an effort to modernize them. In 1988, yet another fire greatly damaged the upper floors. Today both buildings are part of the Louisiana State Museum system.

Flanking Jackson Square on either side of the park are the Pontalba Apartments, which some call the first urban renewal project in the New World, and

St. Louis Cathedral in Jackson Square was built between 1849 and 1852. It is interesting to compare it to the drawing of the earlier cathedral on page 89.

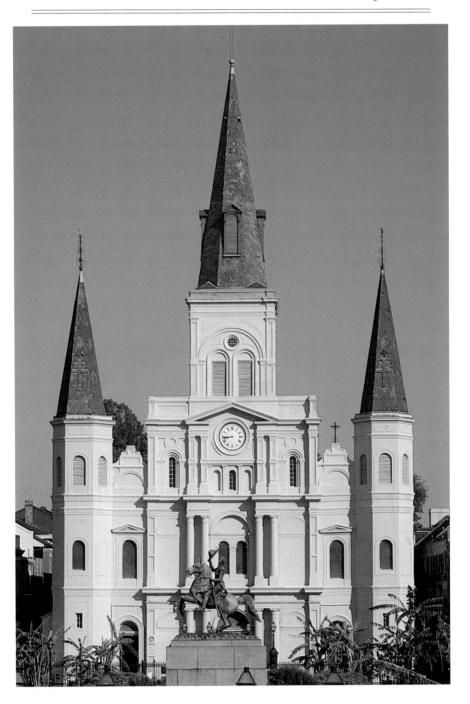

begun in 1849 by the Baroness Micaela Pontalba, the daughter of Don Almonester y Rojas. The infamous Baroness married her French cousin, the Baron Celestin de Pontalba; had a near fatal altercation with her father-in-law; and fled to Louisiana cloaked in scandal. The Pontalba buildings originally included commercial space on the ground floor, and palatial living quarters and slave quarters above. The first stage of the development includes the 16 elegant row houses along St. Peter Street. The complementary row, facing St. Ann Street, on the opposite side of the square, was completed in 1852. The rows of ground-floor offices and shops with residences above were conceived as a means of attracting up-and-coming Creoles to reinforce the commercial and social life of the Vieux Carré at the time that Americans were establishing their own commercial district across Canal Street. It was the baroness who introduced the use of cast iron for balconies and galleries instead of the hand-wrought iron previously used in the French Quarter. The design of her balconies and galleries intertwines the initials "A" and "P," her maiden and married initials.

Today the St. Peter Street Pontalba building is maintained by the city, while the one on St. Ann Street is owned by the state. The apartments are quite sought after, and one must be well connected to secure a lease. At Christmas when there is candlelight caroling in the square, local people consider themselves to be fortunate if they are invited to one of the parties hosted by Pontalba inhabitants. At 525 St. Ann Street, in the middle of the state's building, is the **1850 House,** a three-story period restoration. The square itself remains an active plaza. The Old World-style Cathedral, the Pontalba buildings, the Presbytère, and the Cabildo serve as a backdrop for street musicians, tarot card readers, Lucky Dog and ice cream vendors, mimes, and artists—slightly more upbeat replacements for the public executions that once took place there.

■ COLONIAL PERIOD

The earliest Ursuline Convent and the country's first Charity Hospital were located at 301 Chartres Street, in a townhouse leased to the Sisters of St. Ursula from 1727 until 1734. Here they founded the first convent and the first girls' school—the Ursuline Academy—in the United States. The sisters then moved to the **Old Ursuline Convent** at 1114 Chartres Street when it was completed around 1752.

Having survived the fire of 1788, it has stood longer than any brick-and-post building of the French Colonial style in the Mississippi Valley. There the Sisters continued to serve the community, and later started the first black and Native American school in the United States. Adjacent to the old convent is the Chapel of the Archbishops erected in 1845. Today it is called **St. Mary's**, and it serves as the St. Lazarus National Shrine.

Another structure evocative of the Colonial Period is **Lafitte's Blacksmith Shop** at 941 Bourbon Street. The building dates back to 1772 and was built with the timber and soft-brick construction used by the first colonists. Jean Lafitte and his fellow pirates are said to have sold their booty out of the back door of a blacksmith shop at this address, and it was here that illegally imported slaves were traded after the importation of slaves was outlawed in 1807. Some claim that the name comes from legend rather than fact, and that no one really knows where Lafitte's shop was located. No matter, the building now houses one of the city's most colorful bars.

Madame John's Legacy at 632 Dumaine Street is a rare remnant of the West Indian/Colonial-style architecture of the early French Quarter. Built in 1726, the house was partially destroyed by the Good Friday fire of 1788, rebuilt a few years later, and survived the fire of 1794. Some argue that it is one of the oldest buildings in the Mississippi Valley, predating the Ursuline Convent. The name "Madame John" comes from the short story written by George Washington Cable about fictional owner Captain Jean Pascal, who was killed by the Natchez Indians, and the free woman of color who was his mistress and the inheritor of his home.

The **Languille House** at 800 Royal Street was the tallest building in the city for many years after its completion in 1801. It soon earned the reputation as the hang-out for French Royalists, many of whom met at the Cafe des Exiles on the building's ground floor. But locals were truly horrified 10 years later when an honest-to-God skyscraper—the four-story **Lemonnier**—was built two blocks away at 640 Royal Street. For several generations neighbors predicted that it would collapse and kill pedestrians. (It is also known as the setting of the story by George Washington Cable, "'Sieur George.")

One of the loveliest homes of the early free people of color is the **Camponel House** at 717 St. Peter Street. This New Orleans home of the wealthy Parisian Bartholome Camponel was built in 1811. Another home, the **Magdelaine Bizot Cottage** at 719 Toulouse Street was given to a free woman of color by Joseph Bizot, who had it built in 1799. In the 1930s and '40s it was the home of writer

Roark Bradford, and it was here that Bradford and his wife entertained William Faulkner and Ernest Hemingway.

Spanish settlers favored private, shaded, interior courtyards and patios. One courtyard that is particularly lovely is at 615 Royal Street at the **Court of Two Sisters** restaurant, named for two sisters who ran a dry goods store here from 1886 to 1906. Originally, the site was occupied by the house inhabited by two Spanish governors, but that building was destroyed in the 1788 fire. Later, the president of the Banque d'Orleans built his house here with one of the largest slave quarters in the city, as he is said to have had over 35 household servants.

The **Historic New Orleans Collection,** 533 Royal Street, is housed in seven historic French Quarter buildings. The earliest was built in 1792 by a merchant and is one of the few existing buildings spared by the fire of 1794. This well-endowed private research facility mounts exceptional exhibitions related to the history of New Orleans; their wonderful gift shop specializes in fine historical reproductions.

The **Louisiana State Supreme Court Building,** covering the entire 400 block of Royal Street, sports an edifice that was added to the Spanish-style structure in

(above) The Ursuline Convent was founded by nuns from France and housed the first girl's school in the United States. (opposite) Jean Lafitte's Blacksmith Shop is one of the oldest extant buildings in New Orleans, having been constructed in 1772. His fellow pirates reputedly sold their booty out of the shop's back door.

1912. The building at 334 Royal Street was completed in 1826 as the Bank of Louisiana and now serves as the French Quarter Police Station.

■ LA BELLE EPOQUE

The U.S. Mint, one of the oldest mints still standing, is at the back of the Quarter at 1300 Decatur Street at Esplanade Avenue near the French Market. On the site of one of the city's original five forts, Fort San Carlos, it was designed by William Strickland and begun in 1837. While in service it minted $298,660,707.60 in United States coins. The State of Louisiana took possession of the mint when the Civil War broke out in 1861, and it became the mint for the Confederacy. When the city fell to Union hands, it became a prison for captured Confederate soldiers. After the war, it functioned as a federal mint again until 1909. Today, the building is part of the Louisiana State Museum system and houses an extensive collection on New Orleans jazz and Mardi Gras.

The **Lalaurie House** at 1140 Royal Street (at the corner of Governor Nicholls, formerly Hospital, Street), known as The Haunted House, was sacked by an angry mob in 1834. Louis McCarty built the house and presented it to his daughter, Marie Delphine McCarty Lalaurie, in 1831. Unfortunately, Madame Lalaurie found pleasure in torturing her slaves and enough of them "committed suicide" that the neighbors started to talk. When her neighbor called the volunteer fire brigade to her house to put out a fire on April 10, 1834, they discovered seven shackled, starving slaves. The lady of the house fled before the mob, determined to kill her, got there. Shrieks of the slaves are still said to fill the night air in that block of the Quarter. Mrs. Lalaurie later died in Europe, and her body was brought home to New Orleans to be buried in secrecy in St. Louis No. 2.

In 1814, the then-19-year-old master of local architecture, Henry Latrobe, built the house at 721 Governor Nicholls Street—probably the first example of Greek Revival architecture in the city. Latrobe is credited with inspiring New Orleans's love for the architectural style.

The **Quadroon Ballroom** and the Negro Sisters of the Holy Family's orphanage chapel were both once located at 717 Orleans Street. Originally built on this site were the Orleans Theatre and the Orleans Ballroom, which were destroyed by fire in 1816. The following year John Davis rebuilt the Orleans Ballroom at this address. (Davis also brought the French Opera to America, but his empire of theaters and dining rooms was lost in the aftermath of the defeat of the Confederacy, which he backed.) It was here that the famous quadroon balls were held, and here that magnificent mulatto daughters were presented by their mothers as potential mistresses to masked white Creole men. Wealthy Creole men sometimes supported quadroon mistresses and families in addition to their own "legitimate" white families. These balls lasted from 1838 until the early 1860s. In 1874, a free man of color, Thomy Lafon, bought the ballroom for an order of black nuns, the Negro Sisters of the Holy Family, founded in New Orleans in 1842 by the daughter of a quadroon mistress. The Quadroon Ballroom is now a restored meeting room within the Bourbon Orleans Hotel.

At 716 Dauphine Street at the corner of Orleans Street stands the **Gardette-Le Pretre** residence that dates from 1836. In June 1861, victorious Confederate General Beauregard sent part of the captured flagstaff from Fort Sumter to this house, where it was given to the Orleans Guards. Formerly occupying this site was the home of Cousrouf, brother to Sultan Selim III of Turkey, where both he and his five child-wives were murdered in 1792. In her 1922 account of the story, Helen Pitkin Schertz warned, "Highstrung, imaginative folk cannot abide in such ghostly quarters. . . . Holy water has proved ineffective in laying the little veiled figures which evanesce through corridors and up stairways, moaning in flight."

Another house of historical importance is the **President Zachary Taylor House** at 621 Royal Street. "Old Rough and Ready," the Mexican War hero, often stayed with his daughter and her husband in the 1840s at this address. In 1847 the city gave him a monumental celebration and in 1848 he was elected President of the United States, later dying mysteriously while in office.

■ IRONWORK

The French Quarter's lacy iron balconies and grilles were introduced by the Spanish governors between 1762 and 1800 and are a translation of North African metal-working traditions that date back over 2,000 years. Some of the nicest examples of cast ironwork can be seen in the 900 block of Royal Street in the three attached brick houses, the **Miltenberger Houses,** which date from 1838. It was here that Alice Heine, the first American princess of Monaco, was born in 1910. Miss Heine married the Duc de Richelieu, and later married Prince Louis of Monaco.

Don't miss the **Cornstalk Fence** across the street at 915 Royal Street, with its 1850s cast-iron motif of ears of corn and morning glories. The story goes that a doctor commissioned the fence from Philadelphia as a present for his wife, who missed the cornfields of her native Midwest. Another fine example of ironwork is offered by the oak boughs-and-acorns motif of the **La Branche House** at 700 Royal Street at the corner of St. Peter Street. The house was completed in 1840, and the ironwork was added in the 1850s.

■ MUSEUM HOUSES

The **Hermann-Grima Historic House** at 818-820 St. Louis Street was one of the earliest Georgian-style residences in the French Quarter. With the only functioning 1830s kitchen in the city, the house is the scene of fascinating open-hearth cooking demonstrations each Thursday from May until October. Throughout the year many homemade delights are available in the gift shop, including potpourris, pralines, and unusual jellies and vinegars.

An authentic 1830s kitchen at the Hermann-Grima Historic House.

(opposite) The ironwork typical of the French Quarter seems to define New Orleans architecture in the popular imagination.

Roughly from mid-October until All Saints Day, the museum house is transformed into a scene of "Sacred to the Memory," depicting the Creole funerary and burial customs of the 1830s. Black drapes cover the pictures, and a casket occupies the parlor. In addition to its other charms, the house is said to be haunted by a friendly spirit who smells of lavender and lights the fireplaces on chilly mornings.

Between the first of December and New Year's, the house is decorated Creole-style for the Christmas holidays. Decorations and furnishings are authentic down to the mop bucket filled with water that stands beside the candle-lit Christmas tree, just in case it should catch fire. An added enticement are the cooking demonstrations; call 525-5661 for details.

In 1857, 30-year-old Anglo-Irish Protestant architect James Gallier, Jr. began work on an elegant townhouse for himself, his Creole wife Aglae Villavaso, and their four young daughters. Today the **Gallier House** at 1118-1132 Royal Street, located three blocks from the Mississippi River in what was formerly the orchard of the Ursuline Convent, is a National Historic Landmark. James Gallier, Jr. (son of the architect, James Gallier, Sr.) was the noted architect of the famed French Opera House that stood on the corner of Bourbon and Toulouse streets from 1858 until it was destroyed by fire in 1919. Gallier's Bank of America Building (1866), designed in the Northern Italian Renaissance Style, can still be seen at 111 Exchange Place. It is thought to be the first building in New Orleans to have a structural cast-iron front.

Gallier House reflected the latest architectural innovations of its time, including an operable etched-glass skylight above the upstairs landing, ventilators in the master bedroom, and a flush toilet. Departing from custom, Gallier attached the kitchen directly to the house. An English cast-iron, coal-burning range minimized the cooking odors and fire hazards that had for so long made detached kitchens a necessity. Two 3,500-gallon cisterns provided water directly into the indoor faucets. Hot water circulated from a copper boiler through the range and then upstairs to the copper bathtub.

The home remained in the hands of the Gallier's three unclaimed treasures, his spinster daughters, until 1917, when they sold the house and moved Uptown. One of these daughters, Clemence, worked at the New Orleans Public Library from 1898 until her death in 1941. The Gallier House Museum was opened to the public in 1971 and painstakingly restored along the lines of the 1868 inventory of Gallier's estate. Of special interest are the portions of the house that are couched in "summer dress," the stylistic tricks employed to combat the brutal heat and humidity of Louisiana summers. Straw matting replaces the wool carpets. Mirrors, chandeliers, and all gilded objects are covered with netting to protect them from the permanent black-spotting damage of "flyspecks." Throughout the house in summer, upholstered furniture is covered in white cotton slipcovers that are cooler to the skin than velvet or brocade.

The **Beauregard Keyes-Le Carpentier House and Garden** at 1113 Chartres Street (at the corner of Ursuline Street, across from the convent) possesses one of the most captivating gardens and courtyards in the French Quarter. The house was constructed in 1820-1827 in the late Federal/Greek Revival raised cottage style (see essay "Architecture," pages 112-119). The original home was owned by the grandfather of chess champion Paul Morphy, who spent a portion of his early years here. Confederate General P. G. T. Beauregard rented a room here from 1866 to 1867. Later, the prolific writer Frances Parkinson Keyes (rhymes with "eyes") took up residence here, and moved her doll collection into the house. Ms. Keyes also took inspiration for her work from the prior inhabitants of her home, writing books about both a chess player and the general.

Ms. Keyes' doll collection and huge Victorian dollhouse remain special treats for guests. Each Christmas the museum house hosts the Doll's Tea Party on the second Saturday of December. Children of all ages are invited to bring their dolls along to have tea with the dolls in the collection. The children themselves enjoy Christmas caroling and cups of punch from the silver punch bowl.

While the house is decorated in a style appropriate to the turn of the century, its beautiful garden is authentic to 1830s New Orleans. The interior courtyard is dominated by a magnificent live oak tree which serves as a gigantic umbrella, keeping the garden 10 degrees cooler than the rest of the French Quarter. About the tree bloom pink ruffle azaleas, a profusion of ferns, Purple Dawn, and Louisiana Peppermint camellias. Like the garden in Jackson Square, the side garden is a "parterre" (a garden with ornamented plots separated by paths) which is laid out in a sunburst pattern. The Garden Study of New Orleans (Garden Clubs of America) maintains a formal, white, French garden that blooms year-round with white magnolia, petunias, azaleas, the parterre, and an herb garden. If a tour of the house isn't possible, peek through the gate at the garden.

■ ANTIQUES AND CABINETMAKERS

Both Royal and Chartres streets are lined with a plethora of antique shops specializing in fine French and English antiques. **French Antiques** at 225 Royal Street is noted all over the country for its selection of chandeliers; **Whisnant** at 222 Chartres Street specializes in the eclectic and unusual; and **Lucullus** at 610 Chartres Street is often featured in national design magazines for its collection of exceptional culinary antiques. Both areas have many shops specializing in antique jewelry and porcelains. (See "PRACTICAL INFORMATION" for more, pages 274-276.)

Two of the most famous nineteenth-century furniture-makers created their masterpieces in the Quarter. One is the Frenchman Prudent Mallard, who came to the city in the 1830s and opened his shop in the French Quarter. Mallard's Magasin was located at 301 Royal Street. The other is another Frenchman, **Francois Seignouret**, who fought at the Battle of New Orleans and was a wine merchant as well as a furniture-maker. In 1816, he built a house and wine importing business at 520 Royal Street, **Maison Seignouret**. His furniture (which is represented at the White House in Washington) always bears the initial "S" somewhere in the design. One example of this can still be seen on the left-hand side of the balcony on the third floor of his former home, which now houses Channel 6, WDSU.

■ ARTISTS IN THE QUARTER

The muses visited many while they resided in the French Quarter. While the French Opera House thrived at 541 Bourbon Street from 1859 until 1919 (when it burned), many chorus members stayed at the **Conrad Mansion** at 722 St. Louis Street. The more famous performers stayed at the Rouzan Mansion, 522 Bourbon Street, which would become the French Opera Hotel in 1884. The Tabary Theatre, the first Spanish theater in the United States, was built in 1791 at 718 St. Peter Street by a Spanish military officer; it now stands as the bar **Pat O'Brien's.**

The grandfather of French Impressionism, Edgar Degas, built the home at 417 **Royal Street** in 1801. Later it became the Banque of Louisiane, hence the "BL" in the balcony rail. After that it once more became a home, and in 1828 Andrew Jackson was entertained there. Much later, chess champion Paul Morphy lived there as an adult; it is now Brennan's Restaurant. The **Audubon Cottage**, 505

The French Quarter is well known for its fine antique stores such as Lucullus on Chartres Street.

AUDUBON

$\mathcal{J}$ohn James Audubon, ornithologist, naturalist, and artist, was born in Haiti in 1785, the natural son of a French slave trader and a Creole woman. After Audubon's mother was killed in a slave insurrection in Haiti, John James was raised in France by his father's wife. As a young man of 18, Audubon fled from conscription into Napolean armies, smuggled himself out of France, and came to the United States.

He tried and failed at a series of money-making schemes before he turned to painting. Once he did, his dogged pursuit of feathered subjects led him on hunting parties with the Osage Indians, whose language he spoke; and even into the company of Daniel Boone.

Audubon's spare and stylized paintings—accomplished by first killing and stuffing the birds he so admired—served as a foil to his chaotic life. The subjects' highly mannered poses bespeak the painter's romantic sensibility, and his pictures tell almost human stories of flirtation, pride, and anger.

"Wanderlegs" is how Audubon described the affliction that kept him adrift in the forests and swamps of nineteenth-century America. He once wrote to his anxious wife, in a letter written in New Orleans and dated May 3, 1821: "Thou art not, it seems, as daring as I am about leaving one place to go to another, without the means . . . without one cent." Audubon did hold for a time in 1821 at a cottage at 505 Dauphine in the French Quarter, working on his *Birds of America* series in his studio at 706 Barracks Street. Audubon never lost his French accent, and even permitted rumors to spread that he was the lost Dauphin of France. But when he returned to France on a few occasions to visit, Audubon posed as the wild outdoorsman of the frontier —a noble French savage in buckskin and leggings.

New Orleans has since honored the painter in its naming of Audubon Park and Audubon Zoo.

—Dan Duane

John J. Audubon. (Historic New Orleans Collection)

Dauphine Street, is where the artist John James Audubon lived from 1821 to 1822 while at work on his *Birds Of America* series.

The nearly destitute writer Lafcadio Hearn rented a room at **516 Bourbon Street** during his stay in the city from 1877 to 1887. The 1949 Nobel Prize-winning author William Faulkner lived in a humble garret at **624 Pirate's Alley** in 1925 while writing his first novel, *Soldier's Pay.* Tennessee Williams once rented rooms at **720 Toulouse Street**, where he wrote and set his play *Vieux Carré.*

■ HOUSES OF DRINKING AND ILL REPUTE

The Quarter has played host to other forms of inspiration as well. The cocktail is thought to have been invented in the 1800s at **Antoine Peychaud's Pharmacy**, 437 Royal Street. Peychaud created the first bitters, which he felt improved his bourbon's flavor when stirred into the liquor. The word "cocktail" itself derives from the egg cups, or *coquetiers,* in which Peychaud originally served his concoction, a drink known today as a Sazerac. Today, at 718 St. Peter Street, **Pat O'Brien's** sells more mixed drinks than anywhere else in the world. Built in 1791, the house found new life in 1933 as the home of the legendary pink drink, the "Hurricane." **The Napoleon House** at 500 Chartres Street, built in 1814, is a quiet place to stop in for a Pimm's Cup and a game of chess while enjoying the Mediterranean feel of crumbling plaster and the smell of antiquity. The French Colonial building is topped by the original tile roof and an octagonal cupola. The original owner, Mayor Girod, was said to have offered his home as a residence for Napoleon should he be able to escape.

The French Quarter has also played host to more than a few houses of ill repute. **The House of the Rising Sun**, 826 St. Louis Street, is politely known as "The Dancing Master's House" by those who claim this has always been the home of only the most prominent citizens. Its more common name is of uncertain derivation. The home was sold by the city's most famous dancing master in 1847 to widow Elizabeth Levant; *levant* in French means "rising," perhaps explaining the other name. Buggy drivers also like to pass along the rumor that **Villa Convento** at 616 Ursuline Street was once a famous bordello.

■ BOURBON STREET

Although most people do not visit Bourbon Street to savor the architecture, there are several structures that are worth strolling by. At 238 Bourbon Street is the Creole-style building that houses **The Old Absinthe House,** thought to be the oldest bar still in operation in the state. A block away, at 327 Bourbon Street, is **The Benjamin House,** the 1835 townhouse that was the home of Confederate Secretary of State Judah P. Benjamin.

■ ST. ROCH'S CHAPEL

St. Roch's Chapel was dedicated on August 16, 1876, in thanksgiving to St. Roch for sparing the congregation of the Holy Trinity Catholic Church from the yellow fever epidemic in 1868. The church looks as though it were a scale model of a Gothic cathedral or as some locals have described it, a Victorian parlor clock. The belief is that for every miracle St. Roch grants, he takes something away. The tiny shrine only has a few pews and an altar with a statue of St. Roch with his faithful dog.

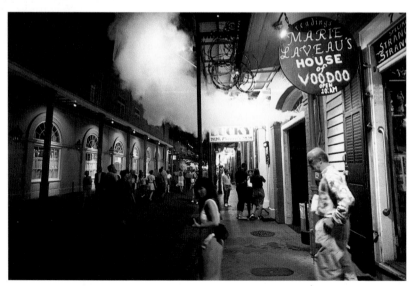

Bourbon Street is responsible for much of New Orleans's mystique.

Inside St. Roch's Chapel.

It is not unusual to see Catholic school girls in their white blouses and pleated skirts coming straight from school to one of the city's shrines, praying that St. Ann might take away their broken hearts and grant them the perfect boyfriend. They chant, "St. Ann, St. Ann, Send me a man."

A word of caution: The French Quarter has become quite dangerous. Even during the daytime, do not venture into the back of the Quarter or into the streets near Rampart unless you are with a group. At night take a cab if you venture out of the well-traveled areas of Royal and Bourbon streets. According to French Quarter tour guide Inez Douglas, "Don't do anything you wouldn't do in your home town."

MIDNIGHT ON THE WATERFRONT

*I*t was midnight when they drew near the waterfront and the roaring cabarets stood open along the banquette, the crowds dense around the long bars, air thick with smoke. Pianos tinkled in the din, and the shades of the flickering oil lamps were black with soot. White men and black men stood jostling on the stoops, gesturing, shouting or gathered on the damp bricks in the leaking light of the doorways, squatted on their haunches over games of dice or coins flipped in the air. An impromptu cockfight was in progress a pace from the markets, and suddenly the knot of men there let out a roar.

"I want a drink," Christophe said at once. He had made the same remark on leaving the cemetery and had not spoken again until now. Marcel's eyes were wide. He had seen these streets often enough by day when they were just as heavily thronged, but the night gave them a savage aspect which he instantly and absolutely loved.

—Anne Rice, *The Feast of All Saints,* 1979

RELIGIOUS TIMELINE

1700 First Catholic church in Louisiana territory established by Jesuit Father du Ru at Houma Indian settlement in West Feliciana Parish.

1724 Construction completed on original St. Louis Cathedral—first cathedral in the United States.

1727 Ursuline nuns arrive in New Orleans to open first school in Louisiana—a convent school for girls.

1748-1752 Erection of Ursuline Convent, designed by Ignace Broutin, the King's engineer. The oldest building still extant in the Mississippi Valley.

1763 Jesuits expelled temporarily from Louisiana.

1790 Capuchin Father Antonio de Sedella attempts to establish the Inquisition in Louisiana.

1794 Church of St. Louis rebuilt after being destroyed in fire of 1788.

1805 First Protestant Episcopal services established by Rev. Leander Chase.

1818 First Presbyterian Church established.

1826 Mortuary Chapel of St. Anthony (at Rampart and Conti), the oldest church in continuous operation in the city, is opened after funerals prohibited at St. Louis Cathedral due to fear of yellow fever.

1853 Trinity Episcopal Church built at 1329 Jackson Avenue. At onset of Civil War, Bishop Leonidas Polk, resigns to become brigadier general in Confederate Army.

1858 Hotel Dieu, oldest private hospital in the city in continuous service, is established on Perdido Street by Daughters of Charity of St. Vincent de Paul. It is now the state-run University Hospital.

1892 Mother Frances Xavier Cabrini arrives in New Orleans and begins to assist Italian immigrants. She eventually establishes 67 institutions and is the first American citizen canonized by the Catholic Church.

1899 Main portion of the Sacred Heart Academy, a girls' school, is erected on St. Charles Avenue.

1911 Jesuits establish Loyola University.

1962 Archbishop Joseph Rummel orders desegregation of Catholic schools.

1966 H. R. Perry, first black U.S. Catholic bishop since 1875, is consecrated in New Orleans.

1987 Pope John Paul II holds prayer service for clergy at St. Louis Cathedral. In honor of the event the pedestrian mall in front is renamed Place Jean Paul Deux.

(following pages) Modern New Orleans skyline as seen from across the river.

ARCHITECTURE

In much of America the purpose of architecture is to create isolated monuments. In New Orleans, to be considered successful, a structure must live in harmony with those buildings which have come before. The New Orleans style of architecture is a tantalizing repertoire of motifs and periods whose style is caught between romanticism and the first rumblings of functionalism.

In its early days, the city gave rise to a variety of styles from brick-and-post cottages to West Indian planters' houses; from columned antebellum mansions to Italianate townhouses; from Spanish-inspired stucco shops with living quarters above and hidden courtyards below to working-class shotgun houses with decorative scroll work. Many houses can boast of having been made of the barge boards from the keelboats that the hillbilly "Kaintock" traders broke up and sold to the Louisiana colonists in the early nineteenth century. Following is a brief description of classic New Orleans architectural styles.

CREOLE COTTAGE

The first French settlers framed their houses with cross-braced cypress and heart pine beams, then bound them together with mud, Spanish moss, and animal hair. These early one-room cottages were topped with palmetto-leaf roofs, which seemed to resist the swarms of termites, the torrents of rain, and the rot so common in a damp climate. Sometimes local bricks were used as infill, with clay or mud holding the structure together. This style can be seen at Lafitte's Blacksmith Shop, 941 Bourbon Street, which was constructed in 1772. Bricks were often covered in plaster, sometimes scored to resemble stone, as water tended to seep through those bricks left uncovered. Buildings were built on brick piers to avoid floodwaters, a construction which also increased ventilation.

(top) Audubon's former residence is a good example of a Creole cottage.
(above) Greek Revival style on an American mansion in the Garden District.

The Creole cottage soon adapted to a more urban context, often being built two-stories high and containing four rooms and no interior hallways. The Creole cottage was most often built flush to the sidewalk, with whatever small patch of garden space located in the rear. The exterior was finished in either woodlap siding or stuccoed brick and frequently painted in light-reflecting colors. The most common style of roof is side-gabled with chimneys breaking through the roof pitch at the center-line of the house, which is sometimes flanked by arched dormer windows.

Many homes of the urban Creole cottage style can be seen in the Faubourg Marigny Historic District (bounded by Esplanade Avenue, St. Claude Avenue, Press Street, and the Mississippi River). The area was the first "suburb" of the original city and the original plan dates from 1806. One of the finest examples of the Creole cottage can be seen at 1809 Dauphine, which dates from the 1830s.

Another area with some fine examples of this architecture is the city's largest local historic district, encompassing some 250 city blocks, the Esplanade Ridge Historic District (roughly the area from Bayou St. John to North Rampart and Philip Street and down Orleans Avenue to North Villere Street). Its earliest section, Faubourg Treme, contains several lovely Creole cottages dating from the 1830s. These include the residences at 1020-1022 Treme and 1308 St. Claude.

SPANISH COLONIAL

The great fires of the late eighteenth century destroyed most of New Orleans's earliest buildings. To limit the disastrous spread of fires in the future, Governor Carondelet instituted building codes requiring tile roofs and adobe or brick walls for all structures two stories or taller. The grandest and most baroque of these post-fire, Mediterranean-style buildings was the Renaissance-inspired Cabildo, the seat of the Spanish government. The present building was built in 1795 and was followed by its sister, the Presbytère, on the other side of the cathedral.

CREOLE TOWNHOUSES

The general plan of these houses consisted of a ground floor including the service rooms, which opened into a courtyard. Stairs were mounted outside the galleries in the courtyard. At the back was a two-story *garçonniere* (also known as a "carriage house") for older sons, male relatives, and guests; the kitchen was on the ground floor. The entertaining area was located in the main house on the second floor above the stench, noise, and mud of the street. The family bedrooms were on the third floor and the servants were quartered in the oppressively hot attics. **The Pharmacy Museum**, built in 1837 at 514 Chartres, is an excellent example of this architecture.

RAISED PLANTATION STYLE

As the city filled in its late colonial years, houses reminiscent of West Indian plantation houses were constructed on the outskirts of the town. The main living floor was built over a brick above-ground "basement," which served as protection from floods. West Indies-style double-pitched roofs extending over the galleries (galleries are balconies supported by columns or colonettes instead of brackets) created shady areas and allowed windows to be left open when it rained. As in the Creole cottage, there were no hallways; rooms were built parallel to each other, each opening onto the gallery through French doors.

The **Mayor Pitot House-Ducayet House** at 1440 Moss in Bayou St. John, the oldest of the city's museum houses, is constructed in this style with stucco-over-brick construction and wide galleries. The house, built about 1780 by the Ducayet family, was bought in 1810 by James Pitot, the city's mayor from 1804 to 1805, as the country home for his family. The house sits atop the 1708 site of the first French settlement in the New Orleans area.

AMERICAN STYLE

There are a few districts in New Orleans, developed after the city became American in 1803, that recall, heaven forbid, the Yankee architecture of Boston or Philadelphia. In them one finds asymmetrical three-story brick townhouses organized around a side hall which served as the main entrance. Creoles scoffed that these American houses were "lop-sided." A few American-style townhouses began to appear in the French Quarter prior to the 1820s, but the largest blocks of them were constructed in the years between 1830 and the War Between the States. The finest concentration of these buildings can be seen in the Lafayette Square Historic District (bounded by Baronne, Magazine, Lafayette, and St. Joseph streets), while the earliest homes still remaining were built in 1832 and stand at 535-545 and 602-646 (called Julia Row) on Julia Street.

GREEK REVIVAL

It was the Americans who were to add the classical stamp of the new republic to the city. Local architects such as James Gallier, Sr. (the St. Charles Hotel, the Boston Club), James Gallier, Jr. (the French Opera House), and Henry Howard were but a few who were able to influence the style of the burgeoning metropolis in the first half of the nineteenth century. The style's trademarks include galleries supported by columns, window architraves, and fanlight transoms.

Pitot House, with its open first floor, is representative of raised plantation architecture.

Bracketed "shotgun" houses.

The publication of Stuart and Rivett's *Antiquities of Athens* gave every architect and draftsman free access to a wide assortment of motifs for moldings and door frames which could be easily copied in wood. In addition, prefabricated wrought-iron detailing also became available in 1855, replacing the more expensive cast-iron versions. These innovations allowed other decorative styles to flourish as well, particularly the Italianate, Gothic, and Romanesque.

AMERICAN MANSIONS

Some of New Orleans's newly rich Anglo-Americans built free-standing villas with columns and wide porches, creating a style that took advantage of the rectangular lots and allowed for fresh air and landscaping. The houses were set back from the street, and often faced onto side gardens. They were embellished liberally with Greek Revival motifs, and later with Romanesque, Italianate, and other styles as well.

Many of the nicest examples of this grander style are located in the Lower Garden District, on streets named after Greek gods and muses. The house at 1531 Camp is thought to have been built in the 1850s. Other examples include 2000, 2018, 2026, and 2113-15 Prytania.

New Orleanians also built free-standing, sprawling homes which utilized larger lots and landscaping, recalling the houses some Americans were then building outside the city. The style refered to as "center hall villa" is characterized by a floor plan consisting of a center hall stretching from the front of the house all the way to the back, with rooms on either side. First appearing in the city in the 1840s, most of the homes were wood-framed, with wide, columned verandas. The proportions of the homes were lavish: 12- to 16-foot (4-7-meter) ceilings were designed to trap hot air in the warm months; wide galleries allowed interior furniture to be used outside in the hot evenings. Louvered shutters controlled the blistering rays of the sun and let in filtered breezes.

The Lower Garden District Historic District (roughly from Prytania to Chippewa and Erato to Jackson) contains many examples of this style of house which date from the period 1850 to 1880. The home at 1226 Camp is thought to date from the 1870s. On Jackson Avenue there is a center hall villa at 1007 and another at 1435; other fine examples stand at 1431 Josephine, 1805 Coliseum Street, and 2127 Prytania.

SHOTGUN HOUSES

Between 1840 and 1910, thousands of these railroad-car-shaped wooden houses covered in wood siding were built in each of the up-and-coming suburbs of the day, because they were an economical and cooler way to utilize narrow lots. The shotgun usually has no hallway and has from three to six rooms going straight back, with room opening into room. The American shotgun has a side corridor, allowing more privacy. And occasionally, a smaller wing has been added to one side, creating an L-shaped shotgun. Some shotguns have two stories, but more common is a second story only in the back, referred to as a "camelback" shotgun.

Shotgun houses were decorated elaborately and eclectically with details borrowed from Baroque, Greek Revival, Italianate, and even Moorish and Oriental styles. Galleries, overhangs, railings, columns, and bays were common design elements added to the basic shoebox homes. Prefabricated cast-iron decorations could be ordered from catalogs or purchased in New Orleans shops.

The shotgun, the side hall, and the camelback can be seen in abundance in Faubourg Marigny, Esplanade Ridge, Mid-City, Algiers Point, and the Irish Channel.

GARDEN DISTRICT
ST. CHARLES AVENUE STREETCAR

JUST A 10-MINUTE DRIVE away from the French Quarter is the Garden District, a residential area whose architecture bespeaks the exuberance of the Southern Belle Epoque of the early nineteenth century. After the Louisiana Purchase in 1803, New Orleans officially became an American city, a thriving port just a stone's throw from the rural sensibilities of the rest of the South. By 1810, it had 17,000 residents, making it the fourth largest city in its new country. Within 10 years, the population had more than doubled to 41,000, which caused something of a problem as the French Quarter was already jammed with Creole citizens, and the surrounding dry land was controlled by powerful Creole planters.

If the Creoles were the old-line aristocrats of New Orleans, the Americans were growing very rich indeed on cotton, sugar, and lumber. Just the same, the Creoles excluded them from their neighborhoods, and the Americans found themselves

Edgar Degas's painting of his uncle's New Orleans cotton office in 1873, now hanging at the Musée des Beaux Arts, Pau, France. (photo by Erich Lassing, Art Resource/NY)

Spring meet at the Metairie Jockey Club. (Historic New Orleans Collection)

corralled in a wedge of land between Canal Street, the end of the French Quarter, and Jackson Avenue, bordering the vast plantation of the powerful Jacques Francois Esnould Dugue de Livaudais. Livaudais, noted for building the first racetrack in New Orleans, had land holdings extending along the river to the beginning of what is now the Uptown area.

Livaudais greatly expanded his holdings when he married Celeste de Marigny, daughter of Philippe de Marigny de Mandeville, who owned a large plantation called "Fontainbleu" on the banks of Lake Pontchartrain. Mandeville's city residence was thought to have been in the Elysian Fields/Esplanade area, and an avenue of trees connected his white-pillared mansion to the banks of the Mississippi. The historian Grace King reports that in 1798 he entertained the Duc d'Orleans (who was later to become the king of France) and his two brothers the Duc de Montpensier and the Comte de Beaujolais. The area of the city where they lived is still known as the Faubourg Marigny.

After marrying Celeste, Monsieur Livaudais, possibly seeking to outshine his father-in-law, began construction on what many at the time considered to be the most palatial plantation house in all of Louisiana. Before the fabulous house could be finished, his land was visited by one of the worst spring floods of the decade.

His sugar crop was destroyed and his new house severely damaged. In 1825, Celeste up and left her husband and moved to Paris. After her divorce, she ended up with the plantation, which, as a result of the flood, had been left with rich alluvial sediment that made it the most fertile soil around. In 1832, she sold the Livaudais land for half a million dollars to a group of real estate developers who carved it up to make a new neighborhood for the emerging American gentry and nouveau riche. The area was to become a 14-block square bounded by St. Charles Avenue and Magazine Street, and by Jackson and Louisiana avenues.

One of the first things that the developers did was to hire a good engineer. Due to turmoil in France, one was available: Benjamin Buisson, fresh from his service to Napoleon. He divided the plantation into the pattern of streets that exists today. The oldest home in the area is thought to be **Toby's Corner,** built in 1838 (2340 Prytania Street) in the Greek Revival raised cottage style. The owner, a Philadelphia native, helped to finance his friend Sam Houston's revolt in Texas. The house was eventually sold in a sheriff's sale for $5,000 after the Union occupation.

The French and Spanish continued to exclude the Americans from their own neighborhoods and society. Nineteenth-century Creole writer Kate Chopin in her story "A Matter of Prejudice" describes the cold shoulder that a Creole mother gives her son when he marries an American girl from the Garden District. Creole society remained rooted in urbanity, exclusiveness, and the Latin traditions of Catholicism, while the leaders of the Americans personified the nineteenth-century ideals of exuberant decorative arts and straight-laced Protestant Victorian manners. Since the Creoles had a stranglehold on the politics of the area, they withheld city services from the ostentatious American sector of the city, and the American millionaires had to step from their palatial homes into the muddy streets. In an effort to control their own property, the Americans incorporated the section of the Garden District into the city of Lafayette. It remained as a separate city until 1852, when the Americans felt that they had attained enough clout in New Orleans to rejoin the city.

The grand era of Garden District development lasted only a few decades, but it was one of unbridled architectural innovation. The Greek Revival style was incorporated with great enthusiasm, with houses painted in Mediterranean colors complemented by wrought iron, louvered shutters, white columns, and elaborate gardens. By the 1830s, builders borrowed eclectically from Italianate, Moorish, Asian, and other design elements to suit the client's fancy.

■ GARDEN DISTRICT TODAY

In historic times Canal Street was the dividing line between the Creoles and the Americans; today it marks the division between the Central Business District and the French Quarter. At 171 feet (52 m) wide, Canal Street is one of the widest main thoroughfares in the United States. Both its name and width come from the fact that it was intended to be a canal. Though it didn't actually become a street until 1806 during Claiborne's governorship, all the addresses on the streets that cross Canal Street begin at 100 there, and move out to the north and south. All the streets to the north of Canal Street are prefixed "North," e.g. North Broad Street, and those to the South are prefixed with "South."

WHAT'S IN A NAME?

*M*errill Shackleford happened to be a poor man, but he knew New Orleans society. Actually, he *was* New Orleans society, a certain segment of it. Merrill's segment lived uptown in the hundred-year-old houses that were in states of legendary disrepair, where faulty wiring caused the crystal chandeliers to dim whenever the wind blew; where the parlor windows were hung with hemmed white bed sheets; where worn-out colored mothers worked for sixty cents an hour, serving Vienna sausages on heirloom silver trays to the ladies of the house.

❧   ❧   ❧

Because he knew the caprices of his native city's ruling class, Merrill did not make the mistake of instantly assuming that a New Orleans girl named Aimée Desirée was a whore, working Esplanade Avenue to the river. Hadn't he danced at the Comus ball with a frozen-lipped debutante called Lola, a name for a hot-blooded barmaid? Didn't he share a box each season at the symphony with a pedigreed divorcée christened Royal like a jockey out at the Fairgrounds? Once he'd gone to a funeral luncheon with a highborn, gilded widow called Evangeline, as if she were a Cajun housemaid.

In New Orleans, the chances were excellent than an "Aimée Desirée" was the darling of some madcap French aristocrat's frail heart and his robust last will and testament.

"What's her last name?" said Merrill.

. . . "That's Dreuil Vairin's only child," he said, rising. "She's richer than God. . . ."

—Sheila Bosworth, *Slow Poison,* 1992

The other navigational points of the American city are the river and the lake. Locals will say that their house is on the lake side or the river side of St. Charles Avenue, the uptown or the downtown corner. Up at the end of St. Charles Avenue is the University Section, where the St. Charles Avenue streetcar veers off to the right and rambles onto the neutral ground of Carrollton Avenue. The streetcar stops at Claiborne Avenue, but Carrollton Avenue continues under the expressway right through Mid-City, and Mid-City butts up on City Park. Past that the lakefront neighborhoods come into view.

Architectural styles were freely borrowed and added to (see essay on architecture). Many Italian "villas" were garnished with wrought iron and Greek Revival features. The Italianate and Greek Revival **Colonel Short's Villa** at 1448 Fourth Street was built in 1859, and stands behind an elaborate wrought-iron fence of intertwined cornstalks and morning glories. (The fence is remarkably similar to one in the French Quarter.) The **Musson House** at 1331 Third Street also exhibits magnificent lacy iron work. It was built in 1850 by Michael Musson, the president of the cotton exchange and the uncle of Edgar Degas. **The Bervard House,** 1239

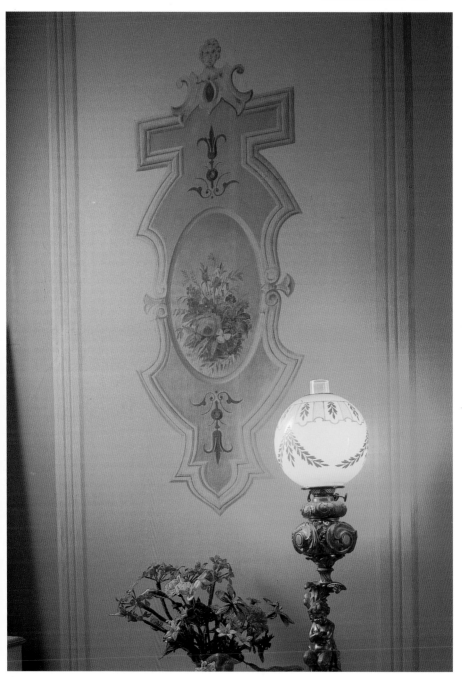

Belle Epoque interior of a Garden District mansion.

First Street, is embellished with lovely cast-iron grilles festooned in a rose motif. The home thought to have had the first indoor plumbing in the state is the **Robinson House** at 1415 Third Street. Built in 1865 with Italianate and Greek Revival features, this mansion is one of the largest private residences still in use in the city.

One of the loveliest streets to use as a starting point for explorations is Prytania Street. The street's name goes back to Bartheleme La Fon's original plan for part of the subdivision owned by Pierre Robin Delonge. La Fon had left a large plot of land for a school, and the owner offered the land to anyone who wanted to construct the "Prytaneum." One lavish architectural treasure is the **Louise S. McGehee School** for girls which stands at 2343 Prytania Street. It was constructed during the carpet-bagger era in 1872 by Bradish Johnson for $100,000 and transformed into a girls' school in 1929. Several other homes of special note include **2504 Prytania Street** built in 1859 in a marriage of Italianate and Greek Revival styles and capped with an octagonal turret. It now serves as the headquarters of the **Women's Opera Guild** and is open for group tours. Across the street is the **Brennan Mansion,** at 2507 Prytania Street, once the palatial home of some of the members of the Brennan restaurant dynasty (owners of Commander's Palace, Brennan's). Built in 1852, the Greek Revival home contains Ionic- and Corinthian-columned galleries and a magnificent gold ballroom. The Redemptorist Fathers now own the mansion at 2521 Prytania Street, **Our Mother of Perpetual Help Chapel,** built in 1856 as a private residence resplendent with cast-iron galleries and a marble entrance hall. One of the few surviving Gothic Revival-style homes is at 2605 Prytania Street, the **Briggs-Staub House,** built in 1849.

Coliseum Street was named after a large public facility that never materialized. Other homes of interests include the row of cottages in the 2300 block of Coliseum Street, known as the **Seven Sisters.** The **Payne Home** at 1134 First Street, built in 1849-50, is not only a mansion of magnificent proportions, but was also the residence where the former U.S. Senator and the only president of the Confederacy, Jefferson Davis, died on December 6, 1889, while a guest of owner Judge Jacob U. Payne.

The area abounds with gorgeous foliage. Many of the live oaks belong to the **Live Oak Society** (membership dues are 45 acorns a year). During most of the year, the fragrance of sweet olive, jasmine, and gardenia mask the odors of the city. They were first planted in the nineteenth century to shield the inhabitants from the stench of the neighboring slaughterhouse. In the late summer many of the streets are lined with white, lavender, and pink crape myrtles, magenta bougainvillea, and white or purplish oleander. The winter brings camellias, and in the spring most of the gardens are bathed in the stunning colors of azaleas.

■ ST. CHARLES AVENUE STREETCAR

To get a true feel for the city, it's worth your while to take a streetcar ride from Canal Street uptown along the oak-lined St. Charles Avenue—which runs along the edge of the Garden District. (Another famous New Orleans streetcar once ran along Desire Street, and inspired the title of Tennessee Williams's *A Streetcar Named Desire.*)

The St. Charles Avenue Historic District runs along the streetcar tracks from Jackson Avenue to Jena Street. The 13-mile (84-km) route (which goes outside the historic district) takes about an hour and a half, round trip. As it is the city's only commuter train and each of the cars can only accommodate 52 people, it is best to avoid rush hours and the end of the school day, about 3 P.M. The streetcar runs continuously 24 hours a day, roughly every quarter of an hour between 7 A.M. and 8 P.M. After 8 P.M. it runs every half hour until midnight, then every hour until 7 A.M. (It is never a mistake to know where a nearby bus line is or to have cab fare ready, as there is occasionally trouble on the line.) After 9 P.M. opt for the cab, as it is unsafe to wait on streetcorners at night, even on St. Charles. Along the route, the car will stop about every two blocks if passengers want to enter or exit.

The St. Charles Avenue streetcar line is the oldest operating street railway system in the country, dating back to 1835 when the New Orleans and Carrollton railroad connected the city of Carrollton to New Orleans. The 35 olive green cars in use today are Perley Thomas Arch Roof 900 Series cars built in High Point, North Carolina in the 1920s.

One of the city's old lines has recently been resurrected along the waterfront. Called "The Ladies in Red," these six vintage red and gold cars travel Canal Street to the French Market.

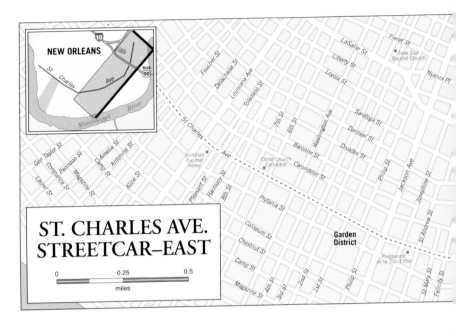

ST. CHARLES AVE. STREETCAR–EAST

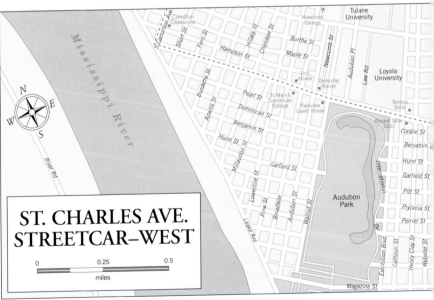

ST. CHARLES AVE. STREETCAR–WEST

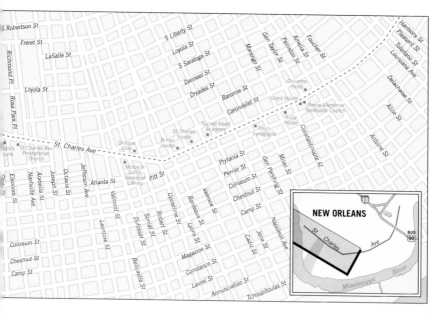

■ ST. CHARLES AVENUE STREETCAR TOUR

The following tour begins at the **St. Charles Avenue/Common Street** carstop off Canal Street. (In the French Quarter, Royal Street becomes St. Charles Avenue when it crosses Canal Street.)

Lafayette Square, 500 block of St. Charles Avenue. This was the central park of the early American sector. The statue on the white pedestal is of John Mc-Donough, benefactor of many of the public schools in New Orleans.

Gallier Hall, 545 St. Charles Avenue. Designed by James Gallier, Sr., this magnificent Greek Revival structure was the city hall from 1852 to 1957, also serving as the seat of the Reconstruction government. It's now used to hold receptions.

Julia Row, between Camp Street and St. Charles Avenue. To the left there are 13 American-style townhouses where prominent Americans lived in the 1840s.

Robert E. Lee Monument, Lee Circle at the intersection of St. Charles Avenue and Howard Street. Since 1884, a 7,000-pound bronze statue of General Robert E. Lee by sculptor Alexander Doyle has stood facing north atop a 60-foot (18-m) white marble column.

Howard Memorial Library, 601 Howard Street (on Lee Circle). This nineteenth-century landmark has been restored as the corporate offices of an oil company.

Confederate Memorial Hall, 929 Camp Street. The 1891 Gothic structure one block to the left houses the Confederate Museum, the oldest museum in the state.

St. Patrick's Church, 724 Camp Street. Patterned after Yorkminster Cathedral in England, it was opened in 1838 for an English-speaking congregation.

K&B Plaza, 1055 St. Charles Avenue. The sculpture garden in front of this modern office building includes works by Henry Moore and Naguchi.

Jerusalem Temple, 1137 St. Charles Avenue. The 1916 building features a beautiful tile mosaic. The Shriners use this as their headquarters; it is also used for balls and receptions.

Restaurant de la Tour Eiffel, 2040 St. Charles Avenue. This structure houses the painstakingly shipped and re-assembled interior of a restaurant that once operated in the Eiffel Tower. It found new life for a brief time in 1986 as a trendy bistro, and was later acquired by the Pontchartrain Hotel.

New Zion Baptist Church, 2319 Third Street. The site where Dr. Martin Luther King, Jr.'s Southern Christian Leadership Conference gained a foothold in Louisiana.

Christ Church Cathedral, 2919 St. Charles Avenue. Completed in 1887 at the height of the Victorian Era, the cathedral is the diocesan headquarters of the Episcopal Church.

Bultman Funeral Home, 3338 St. Charles Avenue at Louisiana Avenue. This amalgam of three wood-framed houses dating from 1852 was cut and pasted together in the 1930s to create the city's most opulent funeral home. The business was sold by the Bultman family in 1991.

Columns Hotel, 3811 St. Charles Avenue. This columned private home was built in 1884 and later turned into a hotel. Louis Malle used the interior in his film *Pretty Baby.*

Rayne Memorial Methodist Church, 3900 St. Charles Avenue. This Gothic style church was completed in 1875.

Grant House, 3932 St. Charles Avenue. Architect Thomas Sully built this home in 1887 in the Queen Anne Style.

Sully House, 4010 St. Charles Avenue. Architect Sully's private gingerbread palace.

Touro Synagogue, 4238 St. Charles Avenue. Named for the philanthropist Judah Touro when it was built in 1908, its new wing contains a rose window by sculptress Ida Kohlmayer.

Sacred Heart Academy, 4521 St. Charles Avenue. An elite Catholic girls' school opened by the Sisters of the Sacred Heart in 1899.

4621 St. Charles House. Once a country house, 4621 dates from the 1850s and is probably the oldest house on the avenue.

Brown House, 4717 St. Charles Avenue. No, it wasn't named for its color, and yes, this really is a single-family dwelling. Even back in 1902, this Romanesque Revival landmark cost $250,000.

Orleans Club, 5005 St. Charles Avenue. The Orleans (pronounced "Or-lee-*yawn*") was built as a private home in 1868, but was transformed into a ladies' club in 1925.

Latter Memorial Library, 5120 St. Charles Avenue. This Beaux Arts style mansion was built in 1907. In the 1920s, screen star Marguerite Clark lived here, and in 1947 the owners donated it to the city; it is now an elegant library.

St. Charles Avenue Presbyterian Church, St. Charles Avenue at State Street. Built in 1930, the Gothic structure hosts a group descended from the second Protestant congregation established in New Orleans.

Castle's House, 6000 St. Charles Avenue. The interior of this Georgian Revival House, completed in 1896, is often featured in design magazines. Architect Thomas Sully took his inspiration from Longfellow House, built in 1759 in Cambridge, Massachusetts.

Temple Sinai, 6227 St. Charles Avenue. Built in 1928, the temple hosted the first Reformed congregation in the city.

Round Table Club, 6330 St. Charles Avenue (near Audubon Park). A men's club that uses a King Arthur's court theme for its annual Carnival ball.

Loyola University, 6363 St. Charles Avenue. The Jesuit order established the college of the Immaculate Conception in the downtown area in 1840. The college merged with Loyola College, which existed on the present site in 1904. The Tudor- and Gothic-style university complex houses the largest Catholic university in the South.

Tulane University, 6400 St. Charles Avenue. Founded in 1834 as a medical college, Tulane was moved to its present Romanesque buildings in 1884. Its school of business is the oldest college of commerce in the United States.

Newcomb College, 1229 Broadway Street. At the back of the Tulane campus, and not seen from the streetcar, is the female wing of the university, Sophie Newcomb College.

Audubon Park, across from the two universities. This 400-acre park was named for naturalist John James Audubon, and was designed by noted landscape architect Frederick Law Olmsted. It contains lagoons, a golf course, picnic areas, and the zoo. It was developed after the close of the 1884 World's Industrial and Cotton Centennial Exposition which had occupied the site.

Zemurray House, 2 Audubon Place. This white-columned mansion was built in 1907 as the home of Sam Zemurray, president of United Fruit Company. The house now serves as the official residence of the President of Tulane University.

Parkview Guest House, 7004 St. Charles Avenue. This hotel was opened in 1884 to accommodate the visitors to the Cotton Centennial.

The Doll House, 7209 St. Charles Avenue. The small Tudor dollhouse in front of the home it duplicates actually has its own postal address.

St. Mary's Dominican College, 7214 St. Charles Avenue. The Dominican Sisters started a school for girls here at the end of the Civil War; later it became a college for women. The Sisters sold much of the campus to Loyola University in 1985, though their residence is still maintained on the site.

Carrollton Court House, 719 South Carrollton Avenue. Built in 1855, this columned structure once served as the townhall for the city of Carrollton, which became part of New Orleans in 1874. It is now the Lusher Extension, the junior high school portion of a public magnet school.

The American-style townhouses of Julia Row near the route of the St. Charles Avenue streetcar.

CITIES OF THE DEAD

The term "Cities of the Dead" came from both St. Louis No. 1 and No. 2 cemeteries, as their oven-like tombs, called *"fours"* by the Creoles, give the cemeteries the appearance of rows upon rows of windowless brick-and-stone dollhouses. Spaces in these cemeteries were completely sold out by 1820, though the original families may still reuse their family tombs, and do. Many of the more elaborate tombs were designed by J. N. B. de Pouilly, who designed St. Louis Cathedral and the St. Louis Exchange Hotel.

Thanks to the efforts of a local organization called "Save Our Cemeteries," many of the fine old tombs that were no longer being cared for have been restored and preserved. Until recently, unkempt tombs would bear notices such as, "Important: Anyone interested in the remains of persons interred in this vault, call the cemetery office." There are still many that have their slabs broken and ferns growing from empty crumbling tombs. Many are embellished with magnificent wrought-iron fences, balconies, crosses, and other objects.

St. Louis No. 1, the famous cemetery filmed in *Easy Rider,* stands just outside of the French Quarter, near the Iberville housing project (that stands atop most of what used to be Storyville). It is a maze of randomly spaced tombs, jammed into each other in no particular order. While it is fascinating, the cemetery is also a very dangerous place and should not be visited unless you go with an organized group. Contact Save Our Cemeteries at 588-9357 for tour information.

Here Étienne de Boré, the man noted for perfecting the sugar-refining process, spends eternity in the company of Paul Morphy, the famous chess champion; Homer Plessy of the 1892 Supreme Court case Plessy vs. Ferguson, which allowed Jim Crow laws in the South; Bernard de Marigny; and voodoo queen Marie Laveau I.

St. Louis No. 2 Cemetery was opened in 1822, four blocks away on Claiborne Avenue between Canal and St. Louis. It is here that Marie Laveau II, the daughter of the original voodoo queen, is supposedly buried, as are nineteenth-century mayors Pitot and Girod, and pirate captain Dominique You.

St. Louis No. 3 Cemetery, known as the Bayou cemetery, was founded in 1833 on the site of the city's early leper colony. It is at the end of Esplanade Avenue near Bayou St. John. Here James Gallier, Jr. designed his family cenotaph.

By the nineteenth century, due to the influx of large immigrant populations and the severity of the yellow fever epidemics, it became necessary for professional, ethnic, religious, trade, and social groups to band together to create benevolent societies for the purpose of providing medical assistance, burial services, and whenever possible actual tombs. The first black "perseverance, benevolent, and mutual aid society" was formed in 1783; about 200 more would soon be formed.

By the mid-nineteenth century New Orleans had become an amalgam of ethnic neighborhoods, each with its own cemetery. Along Washington Avenue, in the American sector, were Lafayette Cemetery No. 1, opened in the Garden District in 1833 as a final resting place for yellow fever victims; St. Joseph's opened in the 1850s, and Lafayette No. 2 in 1853.

St. Roch came into existence in 1868 to serve the new wave of French Quarter Italian immigrant residents. Down at the far end of Canal Street near Metairie, land was plentiful and cheap, and it was accessible by the transit system. Thus, a whole other group of "specialty" burial grounds grew up. The most interesting of these is the Egyptian-style Cypress Grove. Cypress Grove and Greenwood Cemeteries were started by the Fireman's Charitable and Benevolent Association in the 1840s for the volunteer firemen and their families.

Another oft-repeated local legend is about how Metairie Cemetery, the 155-acre former grand racecourse, got its start. Charles T. Howard, who created the state's first lottery in the 1870s, was also responsible for this cemetery. The story goes that Howard was blackballed from joining the Metairie Jockey Club in 1871. Instead of fighting a duel over it, he got even. In 1872, he bought the racecourse and turned it into an elegant cemetery where all of society would have to "die for admittance." Now Mr. Howard lies permanently where the track used to be. His neighbors once included Josie Arlington, the Storyville madam. However, Ms. Arlington's niece recently sold the tomb to the Morales family, had the famed madam's name chiseled off the face, and had the remains reburied in a humble, unmarked grave. But local legend has it that the $17,000 tomb still glows red on certain nights.

There's the miniature version of the Temple of Nike on the Acropolis where William Hellis lies encased in a ton of imported Greek soil. The largest tomb is that of the Moriarty family, part of the group of Irish immigrants shunned by "polite" society. When Mary Moriarty died, her husband, a bar owner and grocer, vowed to give her the grandest monument in the city. The massive granite monument is flanked by four female figures: Faith, Hope, Charity, and Mary Moriarty.

The favorite landmark of many a child is the tomb decorated with a dog that has a marble tear falling from his eye. It lies at the head of the tomb of Francis Masich.

continues

Evidently when his master died, the dog followed the funeral and remained at the cemetery to mourn. It isn't unusual to find notes, flowers, or bows left for the "Good Doggy."

Another tomb noted for its architecture is that of David C. Hennessy, the slain Irish police chief. This 26-foot memorial erection is worth the trip to the cemetery. The broken shaft is covered by a pall, over which is draped a police belt and nightstick. Its designer won a contest and received $3,300 for the finished masterpiece.

Self-guided walking tours can be obtained free of charge, seven days a week from the offices of the adjacent Lake Lawn Metairie Funeral Home Office. The information was gathered by Henri Gandolfo, who worked for the company for 72 years, and compiled a history entitled *Metairie Cemetery: Tales of Statesmen, Soldiers, and Great Families*. Call 588-9357 for times and days of cemetery tours conducted by Save Our Cemeteries.

St. Louis No. 1 Cemetery (above) contains the tomb of voodoo queen Marie Laveau I (right).

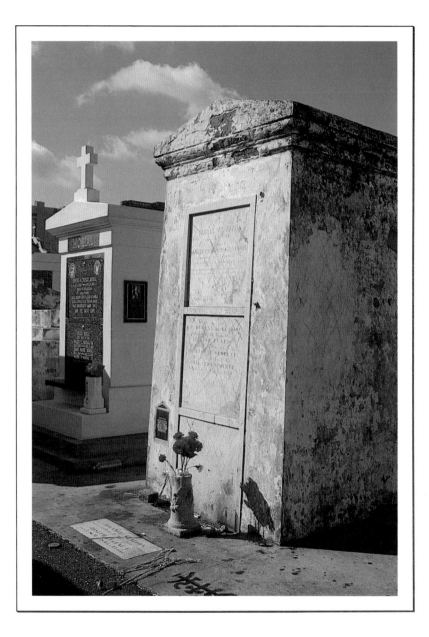

CULTURE BEHIND THE SCENES

NEW ORLEANS HAS LONG SERVED as a breeding ground for a rich assortment of plea-sures and vices. It is a city whose culture percolates from the ground up; where passions, intrigue, and funk intermingle on street corners to create cultural tradi-tions that move up the socio-cultural scale, rather than down it.

■ CREOLE WOMEN

As early as 1743, when the Marquis de Vaudreuil-Cavagnial, known as the "Grand Marquis," arrived as governor, New Orleans was taking a stab at having its own aristocracy. By all accounts the governor and his entourage of gold-braid-adorned officials led a life, amid the stench and cockroaches, as close to that of the Court of Versailles as they could muster. If the marquis' drop-dead elegance and stubborn courtliness provided inspiration to those who struggled daily against mud and fever, he was not similarly inspired by the colony, describing it as besotted with rum and "a chaos of iniquity and discord."

Nevertheless, the few "proper" families in town tried to avoid sinking into this chaos by maintaining strict control over their daughters. The Creole maiden was forbidden not only to wear velvet, but also to glance into the eyes of a young man, at least when her mother was watching. No young man was allowed to call on her at home after her first viewing; contact had to be made by relatives or friends and first approved by the girl's father or male head of the household. During the period between the Louisiana Purchase and the War Between the States, proper families showed off their daughters to society but once: at the opera, where ac-companied by her parents and grandmothers she would sit in the family box and receive callers. Parents had from their daughter's sixteenth birthday until her twenty-fourth to find an appropriate mate for her. Spinsterhood was a fate worse than death in a society that viewed marriage or the convent as the only two worthy vocations for women.

Once the proper husband or wife was found, the two families negotiated over the prospective bride's pedigree in order to determine dowry. A bonafide aristocrat in the family tree, even if he or she was somewhat impoverished, was worth more than a newly rich, salt-smuggling grandaddy.

Needless to say, the bride and groom were never allowed to be alone before their wedding. If they met at all, it was on a few carefully staged occasions and in the company of their families. Monday and Tuesday evenings were the proper days for Creole weddings. A detail of Swiss guards added pomp to weddings performed at St. Louis Cathedral (a practice that ended after 1803). Other than that, the Creole wedding was simple. After the service the bride's bouquet was sent to the convent where she had been educated.

On her wedding night, the young bride was dressed in a hand-embroidered peignoir and boudoir cap and left to lie in her own bed to await her first private moment with her new husband. The couple's "getting-to-know-you" phase lasted from three to seven days dur- ing which they were not even allowed to leave their room; all meals were brought to them. A newly married girl didn't show her face in public for several months after the marriage, and certainly never when she was with child.

Once married, Creole women had things a bit easier. For many, beauty and fine clothes were a passion. In letters written to her home in France, a young eighteenth-century Ursuline nun, Sister St. Stanislaus, observed, "Not withstanding the expense, the women (married) are dressed in velvets and damasks covered in ribbons, materials which regularly sold in the country for three times that in France."

"The Creole of New Orleans."
(Historic New Orleans Collection)

ELEGANT CREOLE LADIES

*I*cannot help to refute with great indignations, as a woman and as a French woman, the lines of Madame de G.: "The Creoles of the plantations talk mostly the Creole French . . . and their neglect in their clothes and their lack of education is such that it completely hides their pretty faces. Everything in them appears to be ugly and stupid."

I think that I can say with great certainty that Madame de G. during her very short visit in Louisiana has never been invited on a plantation. This is the reason she shows such bitterness against the Creoles living on plantations. But the ladies on the plantations have a right to be prudent and wanting to know to whom they give hospitality. They are so hospitable and so gracious to their guests, but they are very reticent in inviting strangers to participate in the life and customs of plantation life. Madame de G. mentions also that these Creole ladies in the plantations are a sort of savages who hide from strangers or laugh at them not knowing how to address them.

These ladies do not live isolated and alone as they would live in a desert. . . . These ladies have their city home. They usually spend the winter in New Orleans, they go to receptions, balls, theaters, operas. They have gone to hear the conference of Mrs. G. Finally they are part of society and form the very best society of Louisiana. Their mothers, sisters, friends are ladies living in this city. Their daughters are sent to the best boarding schools of the city and in the convents of the Ursulines, either one, for there is one on the levee outside the city limits and the other one on Rampart and St. Claude. The Ursulines have the reputation of giving a complete course of instruction giving excellent music lessons.

To give an idea of the hospitality of the Creoles I will relate a day spent on a plantation at the beautiful home of Mrs. X. . . . Received with the greatest of cordiality, I was given the best room in the house. It opened its wide windows in all directions and faced the wide river that rolled along the contours of cyprieres, the fir tree and the immense fields of sugar canes.

With the perfect service from the well trained servants, the exquisite politeness of the young master of the house, the simple manners of the young girls and the amiability of the ladies of the house, one could easily imagine oneself to live in one of the most elegant and refined French castles. But . . . there was a difference. A big fan was suspended above the dining room table sending us its refreshing breezes, near the dining room could be seen the orange trees covered with fruits, the young Negro butler and his assistants proved to us that we were not in France but in America. The breeze from the river brought to us the exquisite and elusive fragrance of jasmine.

. . . In the afternoon, we met in the big parlors to talk, embroider or sew, and read in instructive [literature] in a loud voice, some one taking the book, reading

The Musson sisters, relatives of Degas, quintessential Creole ladies.
(Historic New Orleans Collection)

while the rest occupied themselves with their needle. We did not read novels or newspaper clippings, but we read works of well known writers. For instance: *Tableaux de l'Eloquence chretienne au IV siecle* par M. Veillemain. La Bruyere, Pascal, beautiful plays from Racine. The young girls would then learn those verses by memory and recite them to friends and visitors. The touching story of "*La Servante*" of Lamartine, the charming *Novelles Genevoises* by Topffer, and many other renowned authors.

After dinner we took a walk on the river bank, sometimes we went in the carriage to visit other plantations, but we preferred to walk near the river admiring the splendid effects of the sunset reflecting itself in the great water of the Mississippi River, beautiful crimson and blue clouds losing [themselves] into an immense horizon bordered by the dark cypress forests, extending in the distance. This majestic effect of nature that I have seen only in America spoke to our heart in such a tender manner that it lifted our souls beyond this world, in the regions of the infinite.

—Helen d'Aquin Allain,
letter written in 1850s in Paris describing life in Louisiana

During this period, colonial families moving up the social ladder usually tried to send to France for a private chef. An invaluable status symbol, a chef also served as the facilitator for admittance into the whirl of the provincial "court." Nothing was more important than hosting a banquet in order to dazzle a newly arrived French aristocrat.

For over 175 years, proper Creole entertaining revolved around an event called the "soirée." In their purest form, these were supper dances for close family friends. They took place in the double parlor of a home, where a small band provided music for dancing and the dining table was laden with delicacies.

Creole society could be a joyous place for men, who were wont to ride about town, gamble, duel, and carouse with mistresses, but for unmarried upper-class women, the rules were as rigid as a whalebone corset.

■ DUELING

The Spanish both embraced and added to the culture of Louisiana when they arrived on the scene unexpectedly after a treaty between France and Spain. After they established themselves, the masculine tradition of brawling gave way to an entirely new, and more "orderly," means of settling disputes. The *duello* became the forum through which men of honor soothed their wounded pride, often killing one another in the process. The European-inspired etiquette governing these altercations was remarkably strict and demanded great proficiency with the rapier.

While both illegal and condemned by the church, duelling thrived in the Creole community until well into the nineteenth century. Aristocrat Bernard de Marigny is still remembered with admiration for the vast number of successful duels he fought.

Things didn't change much when the U.S. government took over the city: one of the combatants in the first duel fought in New Orleans under American rule (in 1803) was supposedly none other than the governor of the Louisiana territory, William Claiborne. The *Daily Picayune* of July 29, 1837 reported that "duels are as common these days as watermelons." *The Code of Honor* was published in 1866 by an expert duelist who settled in New Orleans from Cuba, and became a favorite text for those to whom loss of face was a fate worse than loss of life.

St. Vincent de Paul Cemetery located on Louisa Street was one of the business ventures of New Orleans' most famous duelist and proprietor of a *salle d'armes,* Señor Jose "Pepe" Llula. He operated the cemetery from 1857 until 1888 (when he died of old age) and was buried alongside some of his victims. The cemetery is now owned by Stewart Enterprises, the same corporation that owns Metairie Cemetery.

As Americans became gentrified they increased the use of their weapon of choice: the pistol. The "Dueling Oaks" off Bayou St. John, now in City Park, was an ideal spot to settle scores, for it allowed the duelists to stand exactly the right distance apart and yet stay out of earshot of the worried ladies in the Vieux Carré (French Quarter). (The site has also served as a location for pivotal scenes in literature, including Tennessee Williams's *Suddenly Last Summer.*) One of the last times a duel was mentioned in the press occurred in 1889, when the police arrested two duelists who had raised a ruckus after managing to miss each other with three rounds.

■ DEATH

European colonists brought with them their Old World funeral and mourning traditions. As in Catholic European countries, New Orleans Creole society required months of mourning following a relative's death. During the Victorian era, mourning periods became more codified and rigid: wives mourned husbands in carefully prescribed fashion for over a year. Even slaves were required to mourn the people who had enslaved them.

Traditional and often elaborate funerary rituals were also carefully observed. At the hour of a loved one's death, the lady of the house was responsible for stopping all clocks. Black crêpe was hung on the front door, and mirrors were draped in black; the wake and the funeral service were conducted at home, and funeral directors sometimes loaned fine furnishings to the home of the deceased so that the bereaved might make a better impression. Cabinetmakers built the caskets, and livery business owners arranged the transportation for funerals. Funeral coach drivers dressed in black top hats and tails. Their horses wore black plumes on their heads and were specially trained to march in funeral high step. The burial wagon would be followed by a procession of black coaches filled with black-clad mourners.

On one Sunday in 1849, ten duels were fought in the city. (Historic New Orleans Collection)

BITTER SORROWS

We must also say that the Americains, who are, for the most part, all protestants, follow with great zeal the rites and practices of their cult. How could it be otherwise in a city where death is constantly reaping its prey? Here in this city at each stop, one meets with a funeral. Why? Because we have not only the yellow fever epidemics but also cholera, pernicious fever, scarlatina with such violence that at times they exist and bring havoc together. We do not only have one disease . . . but several at the same time. These funerals that are seen at every corner, do they not talk of the short span of existence? of the rapid passing of time? and of the useless necessity of making plans for this world, terrestrial hopes should be abandoned. Each year every family counts several members who are victims to these epidemics. These bitter sorrows are so hard to bear. These sudden catastrophes are much more frequent here than anywhere else, and bring to the hardest sinner thoughts of a better world, religious and deep thoughts.

—Helen d'Aquin Allain,
memoir describing New Orleans c. 1830s.

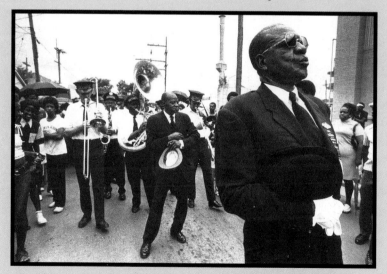

Frank Dorsey's funeral march on its way to the cemetery in 1973. (Michael P. Smith)

Despite their fancy dress, not all funeral coach drivers were entirely respectable. *Gumbo Ya-Ya: Folk Tales of Louisiana* includes the following story from the *New Orleans Bulletin*, of May 29, 1875: "Buried alive. Sickening tale of our hospital dead: A man in the charity wagon revives. He attempts to get out of his coffin. The driver smothers him." The story goes on to detail eyewitness accounts of how the driver, Jim Connors, struck the still-living man, a 19-year-old black smallpox victim named George Banks, with a brick. "You—," Connors shouted, "I have a doctor's certificate that you are dead, and I'm going to bury you." Witnesses reported that the driver took off the coach seat and smothered the man with it.

Graves that might receive the dearly departed represented a distinct problem for New Orleanians. Because much of the city is below sea level, coffins buried in the ground during the first days of the colony had the horrible habit of washing into the streets whenever floods hit. By the late eighteenth century, wealthy colonists solved the problem by laying the dead to rest in above-ground vaults. Of course, throughout the city's history, the poor had to be buried in the cheapest way possible, which meant planting the corpses in holes in the ground and hoping that they stayed put. Early accounts describe caskets being stomped into pools of viscous mire. During the yellow-fever epidemics, cast-iron coffins with glass faceplates, thought to protect the mourners from disease, became popular with those who could afford them. Then, as now, all New Orleanians showed respect for both their loved ones and their tropical climate by promptly entombing the dead.

Today Louisianians faithfully preserve the time-honored tradition of visiting family graves on All Saint's Day. In the rural areas of Cajun country, a nocturnal mass is performed in the graveyards on Halloween night. Families light candles and spend the night praying over their departed love ones. Burial sites all over New Orleans are whisk-broomed; tombs are scrubbed with brushes and often white-washed. Ladders are used to place chrysanthemums on top of the vaults. While these cemeteries may be visited, they are also dangerous—not because of the ghosts, but because of thieves who lurk around the tombs. It's best to see them by taking a tour: try contacting Save Our Cemeteries at 588-9357.

Although the use of funeral parlors did not become popular until this century, New Orleans today has many opulent funeral homes, some hosting more than funerals. The Bultman Funeral Home, at 3338 St. Charles Avenue, holds free public classical music concerts on several afternoons a year.

Former tomb of Josie Arlington in Metairie Cemetery. This cemetery was once the Metairie Jockey Club racetrack.

■ VOODOO

Voodoo, the ever-evolving practice akin to black magic and spirit worship, originated from the syncretic melding of the ancient practices of Africa's Fon (or Dahomey), Yoruba, and Kongo tribes. The practice of voodoo probably originated in Santo Domingo (modern-day Haiti) where slaves devoted rituals to the power of nature and the spirits of the dead. The term "voodoo" that the slaves adopted to describe their rituals probably derives from the name of the African Fon spirit, "vodu."

For many enslaved Africans such spiritual traditions and practices provided a vital means of mental and emotional resistance to bitter hardship. Indeed, although their beliefs and rituals may not have freed them, Africans do seem to have successfully frightened their captors: slavers so feared the powerful spirits of their human cargoes that by the mid-eighteenth century, they made certain to mix their load of Africans, breaking up tribes in order to prevent captives from banding together and taking over the ship.

Slaves who'd worked for a time in the Caribbean brought to New Orleans some of the rituals which were being practiced in Haiti. Once they got to New Orleans, slaves originally from different tribes were drawn together by what they did have in common—miserable living conditions, music, and spiritual practices. By 1782, the governor of Louisiana sought to outlaw the practice of voodoo out of the fear that its evil forces would serve as a rallying point for a slave uprising, especially as white colonists were greatly outnumbered by those they held in bondage.

Such fears came true in Haiti, where slaves ultimately used these African-born rituals to fuel their own rebellion. Between 1791 and 1804, a series of slave revolts inspired by spirit worship finally culminated in the expulsion of the French from the island. Many of the French who were able to escape fled to Louisiana, some accompanied by their French-speaking, occult-practicing slaves.

When these Haitian slaves arrived in New Orleans, voodoo began to emerge as a specific religious system that incorporated elements of the Catholic church's icons and rituals. At its core was the act of sacrifice as a means of establishing a direct link with the sacred. Forging that link were voodoo practitioners who through intuition, devotion, and practice, offered solace to their followers. Voodoo practices themselves evolved through each priest's or priestess's successful methods. If one priest or priestess succeeded in soliciting the aid of the spirit world—and thereby cured a straying lover, prevented illness, or harmed an enemy—then his or her practices would be emulated.

A doctrine for the practice of voodoo was first formulated by the witch queen of New Orleans, Marie Laveau, or "Madame L," an early nineteenth-century folk heroine whose reputation has been kept alive in songs, movies, and novels. Born in New Orleans, sometime during the 1820s she became the wife of a cabinet-maker named Glapion, whose descendants are now involved in the funeral business and local politics. Marie worked as a hairdresser in many prominent Creole homes, but on the side, this practicing Catholic was also a voodoo spiritual advisor to slaves and masters alike. She presided at the voodoo rites of St. John's Eve (June 23) and at many of the rites in Congo Square, and she was tireless in her efforts to care for the victims of the various fever epidemics. To this day, true believers in her power mark her tomb, located just a few steps from the Basin Street entrance of St. Louis No. 1, with red X's. The tomb of the "Widow of Paris," as she is called, is a white-washed, three-tiered structure bearing the inscription "Marie Philomen Glapion dece'de'e le 11 Juin 1897."

A drawing of a voodoo dance as it appeared in an issue of Harper's Weekly *in the 1880s. (Historic New Orleans Collection)*

QUEEN OF THE VAUDOUX

Now one word about the Vaudoux. In the center of a great plain, that is no doubt covered with houses today, there was formerly a wooden house, painted in grey and isolated completely from other houses. It was surrounded by a high grey wooden fence. I remember even today the feeling of terror when my young friends and myself would pass close to . . . that mysterious place. We would never walk close to these sad and lonely high fences. No trees, no flowers, no galleries, no traces of any one living there. . . . One day by the greatest of chance, I happened to meet face to face with the queen of the Vaudoux. . . .

We had hired to work in our garden of Bayou Street a small negro boy, intelligent but a liar and a hypocrite. When he had spent all his wages in playing scraps, or "caniques" (marbles) he would spend his nights away from home. He greatly feared that Vaudou Queen who happened to be his grandmother. One day, wanting to inquire about her grandson, she came to our home and I found myself face to face with this Vaudou Queen. I was not thirteen anymore and instead of being paralyzed with fear, as I would have been if it had happened in my childhood, I was calm and composed and rather took pleasure in finding myself in the presence of this beautiful woman. She was tall and elegant, well proportioned, slim waist line, and dressed with a good deal of taste. Her features were regular, piercing eyes, and intelligent expression, and a queenly bearing. Her walk was really imposing. She expressed herself not only in very correct grammar, but she had a melodious voice and a great deal of elegance in her speech. She talked of the many important people she had met, and if my memory is clear, she mentioned a trip to France. She did not seem to be bad, and had nothing to frighten any one. She was a queen without a throne and had all the imposing manners of a queen. However Baptiste did not seem to share my admiration for his grandmother. He entered in the room with his head low, trying to duck the blows that his grandmother was inflicting on his ears and his head.

—Helen d'Aquin Allain, memoir describing New Orleans c. 1830s

Marie Laveau I and II appear in this print looking as witchy as possible. In fact, both were said to be quite beautiful. (Historic New Orleans Collection)

It was Marie I's daughter, Marie II (born in 1827), who set nineteenth-century society afire with her elaborate rites. Legend has it that her advice was sought by politicians, well-born matrons, and even conventional religious leaders. Marie II may have been buried at the back of St. Louis No. 2 (in a tomb that can be distinguished by all of the tiny X's on the wall made with a scrap of soft brick), but almost every Catholic and Protestant cemetery in town claims Marie II's remains. Both Laveau women were protéges of the mid-nineteenth-century voodoo priest, Dr. John Creaux, a flamboyant slave-owning free person of color, who was purported to be descended from Senegalese royalty. (Dr. John the singer adopted his name.)

Voodoo continues to evolve today, and its ferocious appetite for new ideas and practices has kept it alive and vital. Like its symbolic snake, voodoo swallows and is nourished by other cultural practices, religions, and philosophies. New Orleans still has Spiritual churches, some of whose practices bear a resemblance to the original voodoo rituals. These small, tightly-knit Christian congregations are characterized by ritualistic dancing and exotic altars. (See essay, "Spiritual Churches," pages 218-219.)

Voodoo traditions also live on in other forms. Many folklorists claim that the reason why the Mardi Gras Indians parade on March 19, St. Joseph's Day, is that it is actually the date of *Legba,* the voodoo feast of spirit communication (see chapter "MARDI GRAS").

A visit to **F&F Botanica** at 801 North Broad, 482-9142, or any of the other neighborhood groceries that sell "potents" (voodoo charms) will attest to the fact that voodoo in various manifestations is still alive and well. The shop sells candles to ward off evil spirits, incense to promote potency, medicinal herbs to enhance longevity, and powders to sap the strength of an enemy. It is a commonly held belief that once a woman adds her menstrual blood to a man's food he will never be able to stray, and if she can possess some of his hair or fingernails she can make an effigy doll of him and control his every move from afar. Some men are so tormented by the potential threat of a voodoo-practicing damsel that they refuse to eat any food she may prepare and guard every strand of their own hair with their lives.

■ PROSTITUTION

The city's earliest female settlers were the first to establish the world's oldest profession on the North American continent. In 1744, a French officer commented that there were not 10 women of blameless character in the entire city. Whether this is a criticism or a compliment is unclear, but perhaps he appeared to be such a rake that no man wanted to take him home to meet his sister. But what kind of a port city would New Orleans have been if it didn't offer a bit of companionship to sailors after months at sea, or to those frontiersmen who had braved the voyage down the Mississippi River on flatboats?

After the more puritanical Americans took control in 1803, they attempted to clean up the rampant bawdy atmosphere of certain quarters of the city. As the practice of prostitution was prohibited on the ground floor of any building, the street level of such establishments became reserved for gambling and the serving of alcohol. By 1857 madams and their "girls" were required to obtain licenses, and their taxation was personally administered by the mayor.

If the solution did not mollify upstanding Protestant Americans, the soldiers of the occupying Union army seemed to be less scrupulous about their virtue. A clump of bordellos along the old basin canal became popular with the lonely Yankees, and in the early 1870s Josie Arlington, New Orleans's most famous madam, formally opened her "sporting house" in the neighborhood.

Forty years after licenses were first issued, Alderman Sidney Story proposed an ordinance to rid the better residential neighborhoods of the repugnant activity. Sporting houses were restricted to a single area on the far side of the French Quarter from "the north side of the Customhouse (Iberville) from Lower Basin Street to South Robertson streets, to the south side of St. Louis from South Robertson to Basin." Ironically, the area came to be called "Storyville" after the fastidious alderman. It was during this time that the photographer E. J. Bellocq (the subject of the Louis Malle film *Pretty Baby*) made his famous photographic portraits of prostitutes.

In Storyville, women such as the "Countess" Willie Piazza and Josie Arlington ran posh and decorous houses with "real" oil paintings and potted palms. Many of the houses were staffed by the madams' stunning quadroon and octoroon "nieces," usually girls whose families had fallen on hard times. The popularity of female Creoles of color among the patrons of bawdy houses caused many old-line Creoles of color to cloister their strictly raised daughters. Even today many Creoles of color will not let their daughters date until they make their debuts in the senior year of all-girl Catholic school.

For those who sought the services of the district's prostitutes, the *Blue Book* could be had for a mere 25 cents. Subtitled *Tenderloin 400,* this combination guidebook and *Who's Who* advertised the attributes of each establishment and listed over 700 ladies of trade in alphabetical order. Those who misplaced their copy of the *Blue Book* might consult a local newspaper called *The Mascot.* The paper ran a column called "On the Turf" that detailed the newsy goings-on from Storyville.

For many years, the central authority in the area was Tom Anderson, a member of the state legislature who owned three salons in the district. The official sanction Anderson represented, however, was soon a thing of the past. When World War I began, Josephus "Tea Totalling" Daniels, Secretary of the Navy, threatened to close down the New Orleans naval base if Storyville was not shut down. Thus, the district was officially closed by ordinance in 1917, and prostitution once more became a clandestine activity. Ladies of the evening relocated to the French Quarter, Julia Street, Tulane Avenue, and North Rampart Street. Most of the area of Storyville itself was demolished in the 1930s to make way for the Iberville Housing Project.

THIS place is one of the few gorgeously furnished places in the Storyville District, located so that the most particular person in the world can reach it without being seen by anyone.

This mansion is under the sole direction of Frances Morris, who is one of the handsomest landladies in the District and is a princess. Her ladies are of like type.

The success and reputation enjoyed by this establishment in the past is more than surpassed under the able management of Miss Morris, who has not overlooked anything that goes to make a place famous and select.

You make no mistake in visiting 1320. Everybody must be of some importance, otherwise he cannot gain admittance.

PHONE MAIN 2318

Advertisement for a house of ill repute in the "Blue Book." (Historic New Orleans Collection)

(following pages) This Enrique Alferez sculpture in City Park appears to symbolize the "good life" of New Orleans.

One Storyville operation that did escape notice until the 1950s was run out of the building at 1205 North Rampart, now occupied by the New Orleans Jazz & Heritage Foundation. When the Jazz Festival's music production staff began renovation of the building in the 1980s, the first thing they had to do was remove the wash basins from all of the rooms.

◼ GAMBLING

New Orleans, the unofficial American capital of stylish indulgence, not only boasted the first grand casino in the United States, opened in 1827, but is also credited as the American birthplace of the game of craps. It was the popular European game of hazard, imported through the port of New Orleans, which became the inspiration for craps. The name "hazard" comes from the Arabic word *az-zahr,* or dice. The game came to Louisiana with both the French and the Spanish in the eighteenth century. Bernard de Marigny, nicknamed "Johnny Craps," is given the credit for introducing the game to Creole society when he returned from being educated in Paris; "craps" probably derives from *crapaud,* or frog, for the frog-eating reputation of the French held by some American New Orleanians. From New Orleans the game was spread up and down the river by the hill-dwelling Kaintocks.

French soldiers who had fought under Napoleon in the Middle East are given credit for bringing a card game called *as nas* to Louisiana, incorporating elements of the game into a more interesting version of the French game of *poque.* Again the Kaintocks gave it a name that was easier on the American tongue: poker.

Blackjack, or twenty-one, is another of the gambling games that was born of the cultural assimilation of various nationalities in New Orleans. In the 1700s, faro, a guessing game played with cards (similar to blackjack) had taken the royal courts of Europe by storm. At the same time the French aristocracy were enjoying other card games called *vingt-et-un* and *chemin de fer* (or shimmy), while the Spanish had an Arabic-conceived game called one-and-thirty. By the time that New Orleans had her own grand casino, twenty-one was on the menu.

Legal gambling fell out of favor after the Civil War, but in 1868, during Reconstruction, the legislature chartered a state lottery to a group who agreed to pay $40,000 toward the operation of the Charity Hospital. (Lotteries were relatively common fund-raisers for schools and hospitals in nineteenth-century Louisiana.)

The lottery operators advertised a $600,000 prize, kept the proceeds minus the hospital donation, and maintained a slush fund of $15,000 to pay off state legislators. When the scam was in danger of failing in 1877, Confederate generals Jubal Early and P. G. T. Beauregard were hired to appear decked out in full dress uniform to conduct the weekly drawings. The federal government finally shut the lottery down in 1895, prosecuting all state officials implicated.

Up until 1887, gaming establishments were operating in the French Quarter, but pressure from American government officials led police to begin closing them down. Nevertheless, New Orleans's attraction to such decadence never waned, and in the 1930s populist demagogue Senator Huey Long is thought to have given the nod to mobster Frank Costello, allowing him to install slot machines in the city in return for a contribution to local widows and orphans. Whether or not the widows and orphans benefited is unclear at best, but there are still a few old-fashioned one-arm bandits dotted around town that have escaped detection.

In the 1950s, Mickey McDougall, the self-styled "greatest gambling detective in the world," stated to the local paper, "As Mayor Morrison so often points out, there is no wide-open gambling in New Orleans proper. But in Jefferson Parish the temples of luck seem to outnumber temples of God; in St. Bernard more paved roads apparently lead to gambling houses than to schools." Meanwhile, the Southport Club, an illegal gaming casino, advertised that it was just 10 minutes from downtown New Orleans. The Southport Club was owned by the local organized-crime kingpin, Carlos Marcello. (See "The Mob," below.)

The Beverly Country Club, a gilt-and-marble miniature Monte Carlo-style gambling villa, was the brainchild of Meyer Lansky, Frank Costello, and Carlos Marcello, who had a 12.5 percent stake in the operation. The club opened in 1945, a year before Bugsy Siegal opened the Flamingo in Las Vegas. This strictly illegal gambling palace had its own version of the Rockettes—the Beverlettes, who backed up headliners such as Danny Thomas and Rudy Vallee. Celebrities (among them, Rita Hayworth) were photographed against the dining room's tufted silk wall-covering. World War II American military officers lived it up at the lavish Beverly on summer nights, cooled by its 120-ton air conditioner. In the early 1950s, a Senate investigative committee led by Senator Estes Kefauver came to New Orleans to look into the Beverly's entertainments. The sheriff of Jefferson Parish swore that he'd see to it that the federal law against gambling would be upheld, and the Beverly was closed. (The Beverly reopened in 1972 as a dinner theater, but closed in 1983 when the building burned.)

After World War II a reform movement in Louisiana sought to wipe away the taint of gambling, and over 20 gambling operations were closed in Jefferson Parish, 12 in New Orleans, and an equal number in St. Bernard.

It wasn't until 1991 that legal gambling came back to the city with the passage of state legislation authorizing a lottery, riverboat gambling, and a single land-based casino. The move was prompted by the state's dire financial straits.

But flagrant gambling, and not unobtrusive, behind-the-scenes gaming, seems to bother the local community. A 1977 University of New Orleans study revealed that an estimated $144 million was spent on illegal gambling in the area, and no one said much about it. By 1987, local law enforcement officials argued that the figure was well over a quarter of a million a year. On weekends bookies are a common sight in many neighborhood bars or at streetcorner pay phones where they balance their bulging notebooks with fistfuls of quarters. Legal charity-based bingo games in the area bring in close to $30 million annually as well.

Harrah's new land-based casino, located at the end of Canal Street near the river, opens in 1996 with 6,000 slot machines and 200 gaming tables. While legally there is to be only one land-based casino, floating casinos seem to multiply like cockroaches. But don't expect the boat to do more than float. A technicality in the

Lucky Dog stand on Bourbon Street.

law lets the boats' captains determine when it is safe to take gamblers cruising. While the tour boats and ferries move up and down river, the boats hug the shore, allowing more patrons to come on board.

Some of the most popular boats include the Flamingo Casino boats, which feature Dixieland jazz, Lucky Dogs, groaning and inexpensive buffets, and nearly 80 gaming tables. The boomtown Belle Casino sits on the West Band at the Harvey Canal in Jefferson Parish and features a country-and-western saloon atmosphere, free baby-sitting, and many nationally known performers, as well as 850 slot machines and over 50 table games.

■ THE MOB

One of the most notorious crimes of nineteenth-century New Orleans involved the assassination in 1890 of David C. M. Hennessy, the first superintendant of the New Orleans Police Department. Nineteen members of a Sicilian gang were accused of the crime. When they were acquitted of the crime in 1891, an angry mob broke into Parish Prison and lynched 11 of the Italians. For years afterwards, the slur "Who killed the Chief?" could lead to a renewed outbreak of violence

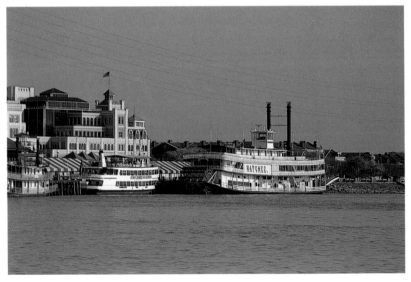

Paddle-boats such as this one are favorites for family outings.
Similar ones house riverboat casinos.

against Italians. (Today Hennessy's tomb remains a popular attraction in Metairie Cemetery.)

The upstanding Italian community has been dogged by the unsavory reputation of a handful of their kinsmen, in part because New Orleans, port of entry for most Sicilians into the United States, served as the cradle of America's first Mafia families. Most moved on to Chicago and New York.

The most notorious Mafia boss to stay in New Orleans was Carlos "Little Man" Marcello. Born Calogero Minacori in Tunisia in 1910, Marcello came to Louisiana as a baby. His family settled in Algiers, the community across the river from New Orleans, and as a young man Marcello launched his career by stealing autos, selling marijuana, and operating a bar in Gretna on Teche Street. He moved into the big time in the 1940s, when he went to work for New York mobster Frank Costello in the slot-machine business. In May of 1947, Carlos Marcello was made the head of the local Louisiana-based crime family at a ceremony held at the Black Diamond, a club that stood at the corner of Galvez and Conti.

At his federal bribery trial 34 years later, Marcello swore that he was nothing more than a humble tomato salesman employed by the Pelican Tomato Company. But he never denied owning a little bit of property, estimated to be worth $30-40 million. His eventual conviction kept him in prison for six years. In 1989 he returned to his suburban brick home in Jefferson Parish, where he resumed his life as a doting husband, father, and grandpop of 11.

When Carlos Marcello died in his sleep at the age of 83 in March of 1993, many touted the event as the end of the godfather era. To some he remains a folk hero, a modern-day Jean Lafitte. To others—if books such as *Contract on America* and *The Mafia Kingfish* are to be believed—the five-foot-three don was the power behind the Kennedy assassination.

CULTURAL TIMELINE

1764 Sieur Braud sets up the first printing press.

1792 Tabary Theater opens featuring raucous French political satire. Ultimately closed-down by a shocked Spanish government.

1794 Publication of first newspaper, *Le Moniteur de la Louisiana*.

1796 Staging of first opera in North America, André Grétry's *Sylvain*.

1803 The University of New Orleans is chartered.

1817 Betting on fights between bulls and dogs a popular pastime.

1821 Naturalist painter John James Audubon rents studio in the French Quarter.

1829 Composer Louis Moreau Gottschalk born in New Orleans.

1837 First issue of the *Picayune* is published. Chess player Paul Morphy is born.

1838 First Mardi Gras parade takes to the streets of New Orleans.

1847 New Orleans becomes leading horse racing center in the United States.

1857 Mystick Krewe of Comus presents its first Carnival procession.

1870 Writer Kate O'Flaherty Chopin comes to New Orleans.

1872 Rex presents its first parade—in honor of the visit of His Imperial Highness Alexis Romanoff, Grand Duke of Russia.

1885 Ferdinand "Jelly Roll" Morton born in New Orleans.

1890 Andy Bowen and Jack Burke fight the longest boxing match in history, lasting 100 rounds and ending in a draw.

1894 The Original Illinois Club, reputably the oldest black carnival and debutante presentation organization in the world, is founded.

1917 "Tarzan of the Apes" filmed amongst moss-draped oaks, pecan trees, and palmettos. Members of the New Orleans Athletic Club play apes.

1920s William Faulkner lives at 624 Pirate's Alley; Sherwood Anderson in the Pontalba Apartments.

1925 The *Louisiana Weekly*, a black newspaper, begins publication.

1935 Tulane defeats Temple, 20 to 14 in the first Sugar Bowl.

1941 Tennessee Williams makes his first extended visit to New Orleans, staying for three months at 1525 Louisiana Avenue.

1953 Duel is fought with automobiles at Tulane and South Broad.

1985 The New Orleans Saints are sold for approximately $71 million to Ted Benson.

1991 Oliver Stone's *JFK* is filmed in Louisiana.

C A R N I V A L
M A R D I   G R A S

IN CHRISTIAN COMMUNITIES around the world, the 40 days preceding Easter comprise Lent, a period of fasting and penitence. It begins with Ash Wednesday, the day many Catholics (and some Protestants) go to church to receive the sign of the cross marked in ash on their foreheads—its purpose being to remind them of their own mortality. For much of the country, the Tuesday before Lent is just that, a Tuesday, but in New Orleans this Tuesday is "Mardi Gras" (literally, "Fat Tuesday") and represents the last gasp of frivolity before a period of austerity. The date on which Mardi Gras Day falls is determined by the church calendar—always 41 days before Easter, and as early as February 3 or as late as March 9.

In New Orleans, the term "Carnival" refers to the season of balls and parades that begins on Twelfth Night, or January 6, and continues until Mardi Gras. On January 6, Christmas decorations come down, Carnival colors go up, and the six-to-eight-week season begins. Also on that day, one krewe (club)—the Twelfth Night Revelers—hosts the first ball of the season. (A "krewe" is a club that mounts a ball, a parade, or both.) The high point of Carnival is the parade-filled, four-day weekend that begins on the Saturday before Ash Wednesday and culminates in an all-out bash on Mardi Gras Day with the daytime parade of Rex, King of Carnival—the main event of Carnival.

MARDI GRAS DATES

1996 . . . . . . February 20

1997 . . . . . . February 11

1998 . . . . . . February 24

1999 . . . . . . February 16

2000 . . . . . March 7

2001 . . . . . . February 27

2002 . . . . . February 12

(opposite) The Rex float is adorned to look like a Thai royal barge during the main-event parade of Mardi Gras Day. (Syndey Byrd)

■ HISTORY

Mardi Gras was celebrated in the Christian countries of Europe long before the founding of the Crescent City. The day French-Canadian explorer Sieur d'Iberville and his men camped 60 miles (97 km) south of New Orleans in 1699 happened to be Mardi Gras, March 3, so he named the place Pointe du Mardi Gras. It didn't take long for the French to start celebrating this holiday in the New World. Historians say that Mardi Gras was observed by masked balls and bawdy street processions in New Orleans as early as the 1700s. A report issued in 1791 to the Louisiana colonial government warned that Mardi Gras provided dangerous opportunities: "People of color, both free and slaves, are taking advantage of carnival, going about disguised, mingling with the Carnival throngs in the streets, seeking entrance to the masquerade balls, and threatening public peace." By 1806, the festivities had gotten so rowdy that Mardi Gras celebrations were forbidden, but by all accounts, this law was summarily ignored. In 1817, masks were declared illegal. But by 1823, the celebration that had been going on all along became legal again, and by 1826 even masking was legalized. "Bals masque" (masked balls), also known as "tableau balls," were so fashionable in the nineteenth century that by law the season was limited to January 1 through Mardi Gras Day in order to keep the population from celebrating all year long. In 1827, it was reported that John Davis's *Theatre d'Orleans* was such a glorious event that it continued straight from Mardi Gras until St. Joseph's Day (on March 19). By 1837, the "season" was lengthened to last from November 1 to June 1. There is much debate as to whether the first formal parade was held in 1835 or 1838, but no matter, the parades that traversed the muddy streets are said to have been wicked and satirical. The first krewe to parade was the Mystick Krewe of Comus (see "Krewes").

Much of the pomp employed by the old krewes comes from the entertainments planned in 1872 when the Russian Grand Duke Alexis Romanoff came to New Orleans at Carnival time in hot pursuit of actress Lydia Thompson. Forty businessmen got together and founded the Krewe of Rex, mounting a daytime parade in the archduke's honor. The city's upper-crust folks, always socially ambitious, decided to adopt the Romanoff household colors—purple (signifying justice), green (faith), and gold (power)—as the official Carnival colors. The local gentry also learned that the Grand Duke Alexis's favorite song was a regrettable ditty called "If Ever I Cease To Love" from the New York musical *Bluebeard* that starred Ms. Thompson. All these years later, it remains the official song of Carnival. (The song is indeed so forgettable that many a jazz band gives up on the melody and plays a tune akin to "Little Brown Jug.")

■ PARADES

There is no question that Mardi Gras is about parades. About 60 Carnival parades fill the schedule between January 6 and Ash Wednesday, particularly during the two and a half weeks before Mardi Gras. But the four-day Carnival weekend is when parading reaches its crescendo. The pages of the *Times-Picayune* should be able to supply you with the three parade routes and the list of who parades on each. Among those held during the four-day weekend are two super-parades. The first is the Endymion parade on Saturday, which bills itself as the largest non-military parade in the world. Endymion first paraded in 1967 and continues to make good its motto, "Throw 'til it hurts!" The second is the Bacchus parade on Sunday. Taken together, these krewes have a combined membership of 2,300 men, and each year toss to bystanders more than 1.5 million cups, 2.5 million doubloons, and 200,000 gross of beads.

The crowds who attend these celebrity-studded parades tend to be denser, louder, and more aggressive than at other parades. Because these events fall on the weekend, people drive in from a 300-mile (483-km) radius just for a chance to see the likes of Henry Winkler or John Goodman dressed up in crown and blond wig, and to have their tax attorney or former professor throw them handfuls of 12-inch (30-cm) pearl strands.

Carnival Day (Tuesday) is more for families. Eager parade-goers wake up before dawn and stake out a spot along a parade route. By 7:00 A.M., St. Charles Avenue is blanketed with parade-watching equipment and essentials: special ladders, folding deck chairs, ice chests, generators; crockpots filled with red beans, barbecue pits, and buckets of Popeye's fried chicken; and video cameras and hand-held TVs. Out in Metairie, across the river, and in St. Bernard Parish, the scene is repeated for the suburban parades. By nine o'clock the streets are filled with paraders, dressed in costume and strutting their stuff. The parades begin snaking through the streets in earnest by 11:00 A.M. A lot of the local high school bands also

KREWES

Krewes are the masking and parading clubs for which New Orleans is both famous and infamous. Several of these are described below.

Babylon. Started by a New Orleans dentist, Frank Oser, in 1939, it remains one of the 10 oldest parading krewes in the city. Its membership is made up largely of physicians.

The "flambeaux" are a Babylon custom. These burning "torches"—really tubes filled with chemicals that produce a brilliant, sometimes colored, light—are traditionally carried by African Americans who march alongside the floats. The image of the torch was inspired by the slave ritual of Bois Caiman, performed on August 14, 1791, at the beginning of the Haitian War of Independence. After a fiery parade the slaves swore allegiance to their priest leaders. (When the war ended in 1804, Haiti emerged as the second country in the Western hemisphere to gain its independence, and the first free black nation.) Although some parade-goers find it demeaning to black men that they carry these torches, as blacks are rarely, if ever, allowed in this conservative krewe, flambeaux (the term applies to the torch carriers as well as the torches) still accompany the Knights of Babylon.

Barkus. In 1993, a new krewe was founded with membership limited to dogs and headquartered in the vicinity of the "Flea Market." Krewe of Barkus rules include this warning, "Cats, while welcome, will not be provided with security;" as well as, "No dogs may be 'in season' and owners are responsible for their own dog's scoop." This annual French Quarter event is open to the public and is a benefit for local animal shelters and national humane societies.

Comus. From the Greek *komos,* meaning revelers. They are the oldest parading krewe, having originally been called "The Mystick Krewe of Comus." In 1856 six men (all Protestant, white Americans) who had moved to New Orleans from Mobile, Alabama, met at Dr. Pope's drugstore to discuss introducing their brand of Carnival to the city (parades had begun in Mobile a few years earlier). They formed a secret society along with 13 New Orleanians and mounted a tableau ball for 3,000 at the Gaiety Theatre. Their first parade included two floats lighted by flambeaux.

In keeping with the early Masonic traditions of secrecy, the members of Comus never reveal the name of their king. Comus members are the most discriminatory of the old-liners, and up until a generation ago they wouldn't even admit Catholics to their ranks.

In protest to the city council's anti-discrimination ordinance, some members of Comus have replaced their Carnival night parade with a procession from Antoine's restaurant to their ball at the Municipal Auditorium. The revelers ring cowbells in honor of the group that inspired them, the Cowbellion de Rankin Society of Mobile, Alabama.

Iris. A ladies-only krewe formed in 1917, this group held its first parade in 1959, and today has over 500 members. They parade during the day on the Saturday before Mardi Gras.

Krewe du Vieux. Inside jokes and a no-holds-barred sensibility characterize the only parade allowed in the Quarter. This is probably the only krewe to capture the old spirit of Carnival, before high society and commercialization put the clamps on naughty expression and behavior.

Momus. Chartered soon after Rex in 1872, the group was named after the god of mockery. Their motto is "Dum vivimus, vivamus" ("While we live, let us live"). Members come from the ranks of the all-white Louisiana Club.

Okeanos. A krewe founded in 1949 by a group of Ninth Ward businessmen who wanted to bring Carnival to St. Claude Avenue, Carnival's original parade route.

Original Illinois Club. One of three old-line black krewes that presents debutantes, the Original Illinois Club was formed by several Creole-of-color community leaders in 1894. The "Chicago Glide" is the dance unique to this club. Though the club has less than 50 members, they mount an elaborate ball for over 700 guests.

continues

A Zulu coconut, a prize "throw" of the Mardi Gras parades.

Phunny Phorty Phellows. This group of costumed men and women celebrates the official opening of Carnival season by riding a decorated streetcar along St. Charles Avenue. The group eats king cake as they toss throws to the spectators and serenade them with a jazz band. The name comes from a nineteenth-century krewe.

Proteus. Taking its name from the ocean shepherd of Poseidon's seals, Proteus presented its first procession in 1882. One of the more stingy krewes in their parading days, they have now halted parading altogether due to MCS 14984, the ordinance that denies parade permits to discriminatory groups.

Rex. The main-event parade of Mardi Gras Day. The King of Rex is the King of Carnival. He is always a civic and business leader, and generally a member of the old-line Boston Club (an old, conservative, Christian club). The krewe itself has the most liberal admittance policy of all of the old-line groups, as they are a shade more interested in professional stature than in pedigree.

When Frank Howard became Rex's King of Carnival in 1895, he ended up married to his queen, Lydia Fairchild, and it got tongues to wagging. Nowadays kings are old enough to be the grandfathers of queens. A feature of Rex parades is the *boeuf gras,* the fatted beef, bull, or ox that symbolizes the last meat eaten before the beginning of Lent. Rex calls the Queen of the Carnival and the Maids of the Rex Court the "Carnival Court." No other organization is entitled to use this designation.

The charter name for the Rex organization is "The School of Design," the same group that presented the first daytime parade in the city in 1872. All Rex objects bear the motto, "Pro Bono Publico" ("For the Good of the Public").

Thoth. (Say "Toe-th"). This parading krewe was formed in 1947 to bring Mardi Gras to institutions for children and adults with disabilities.

Tucks. In 1969, two Loyola University students created a rag-tag parading krewe and named it for their favorite local hang-out, Friar Tuck's. Today the krewe maintains its *Animal House* reputation.

Zeus. The krewe that began the Metairie parade tradition in 1956.

Zulu. The Zulu Aid and Pleasure Club was founded in 1909, held its first parade in 1914, was incorporated in 1916, hosted its first celebrity monarch when Louis Armstrong became their king in 1949, and remains the most permeable of the old krewes. It has just under 400 members and several dozen are white. Zulu is the only krewe in which the king gets to choose his own queen. During parade time, any friend of a member can pay a fee and ride in the parade.

KING OF MARDI GRAS

*U*ncle Jules is as pleasant a fellow as I know anywhere. Above his long Creole horseface is a crop of thick gray hair cut short as a college boy's. His shirt encases his body in a way that pleases me. It fits him so well. My shirts always have something wrong with them; they are too tight in the collar or too loose around the waist. Uncle Jules's collar fits his dark neck like a tape; his cuffs, folded like a napkin, just peep out past his coatsleeve; and his shirt front: the impulse comes over me at times to bury my nose in that snowy expanse of soft finespun cotton. Uncle Jules is the only man I know whose victory in the world is total and unqualified. He has made a great deal of money, he has a great many friends, he was Rex of Mardi Gras, he gives freely of himself and his money. He is an exemplary Catholic, but it is hard to know why he takes the trouble. For the world he lives in, the City of Man, is so pleasant that the City of God must hold little in store for him. I see his world plainly through his eyes and I see why he loves it and would keep it as it is: a friendly easy-going place of old-world charm and new-world business methods where kind white folks and carefree darkies have the good sense to behave pleasantly toward each other.

—Walker Percy, *The Moviegoer,* 1960

march in parades. The good ones will march in many parades, and the money they earn goes a long way to support their schools.

Anything goes on Mardi Gras Day. *Everyone* dons flamboyant costumes or bizarre make-up. Locals and out-of-towners stroll the streets dressed as packs of Energizer Rabbits, condoms, tap-dancing bottles of Chanel, the Rolling Stones, Nubian royalty, Oscar Wilde, the Romantic Poets, French Revolutionaries leading Marie Antoinette to the guillotine, and troupes of topless clowns. Some people dress as nuns; some nuns dress as bag ladies. Transvestitism reaches the pinnacle of the art form, as the French Quarter hosts one of the most elaborate gay beauty-and-costume contests in the world. Usually, the costumes worn in the Quarter are a great deal more lascivious than those worn by the families in Metairie and along St. Charles Avenue.

Each year New Orleans festers with rumors concerning the goings-on at Carnival season. As the old-line krewes pride themselves on secrecy, getting the scoop on who is doing what becomes part of the fun. Good sources for the skinny on what's happenin' are limousine drivers who have been booked to tote the royalty around; the lunch crowd at Galatoire's on Friday; the noon street-corner crowd around Common and Carondelet; alteration staff at Town & Country on St. Charles Avenue; awning installers; and the maids who work on Palmer Avenue and shop at Langenstein's on Arabella Street. Perennial rumors include: one (or all) of the krewes are bankrupt; Schwegmann's Giant Supermarket has sold out of ice picks; a rider in Iris threw her three-carat diamond to the crowd by mistake; or the real queen of Comus got pregnant and the new one is a last-minute replacement.

To get some meatier info, try visiting the Mardi Gras Museum—a 10,000-square-foot exhibition of Carnival films, memorabilia, traditions, costumes, sounds, and photographs that can be viewed year round in the Rivertown section of South Kenner. Other collections of Carnival memorabilia include those of the Louisiana State Museum, and of the Germaine Wells Mardi Gras Museum, 813 Bienville Street on the second floor of Arnaud's Restaurant.

The biggest gossip in recent times has occurred in connection with the new non-discrimination rules implemented by the city and aimed at the krewes. It all started in December of 1991, when Councilwoman Dorothy Mae Taylor co-authored an

The Scene Highlighters, a marching club (above).
Carnival revelers crowd balconies in the French Quarters (right). (both photos, Syndey Byrd)

DESIRE

ordinance, MCS 14984, prohibiting race and sex discrimination by krewes. Those groups who had exclusive admissions policies were denied access to city services and parade permits. Of the 60 or so parading krewes, only three old-line krewes whose traditions stem from nineteenth-century elitist sensibilities viewed this as "cultural terrorism" and refused to comply: they were Mystick Krewe of Comus, the Knights of Momus, and the Krewe of Proteus. Also as a result of the ordinance, other krewes are changing their routes and schedules. It's best to consult the *Times-Picayune* for the most up-to-date parade information.

Krewe members aren't the only participants in the parades; marching or walking clubs feature prominently as well. The Jefferson City Buzzards is considered the oldest of marching clubs, as it was begun in 1890. They get going about 6:45 A.M. on Mardi Gras morning in the vicinity of Audubon Park and leisurely stroll toward the downtown madness. The Corner Club begins its day before 7:30 A.M. at the corner of Second and Annunciation streets. Pete Fountain's Half Fast Walking Club kicks off from Washington and Prytania streets about the same time.

Truck parades also feature prominently on Mardi Gras Day, when five of them follow the parade of Rex downtown (they follow Argus in another neighborhood). These are comprised of over 350 decorated flatbeds with nearly 15,000 costumed maskers. The trucks are decorated by families and friends who meet on the weekends and do all the decorating and costume-making themselves. In preparation for the parades the riders must get up before dawn, drive to the starting point of the parade, and wait for up to four hours to roll.

■ T H R O W S

Throughout the parade, masked riders stand atop two- and three-tiered papier-mache, tractor-towed constructions from which they throw plastic cups, panties, and beads, as well as metal doubloons inscribed with the logo of the krewe, to the eager crowd. The riders often spend over $1,000 on their individual stock of "throws" to give out during the parade.

In the early days of the festivities, merry-makers used to carry bags of flour that they would throw at each other. When a mischievous few mixed pepper with their flour, the practice had to be discontinued and safer things thrown. These days, the typical throws are beads, "doubloons" (fake coins), and, in recent years, Zapp potato chips, which come packaged in Carnival colors. Probably the most valued throws are the hand-painted coconuts tossed by the krewe of Zulu. Onlookers vie energetically—sometimes boldly—to catch the most "stuff." In recent years, it's become more commonplace for women to expose their breasts than to shout the conventional phrase, "Throw me sumtin' Mista!" in return for a long strand of faux pearls. *Be warned*—many an ordinarily gentle, little old sterling-headed grandmother will stomp your knuckles bloody for that aluminum doubloon, and that adorable tyke has no qualms about jerking your knees out from under you for a bamboo-and-rubber spear. Most importantly, never ever put your hand on the ground to pick up anything! If you want those beads or that doubloon, put your foot on it and don't lift your toe until you have it firmly in your hands.

Other tips for catching favors include taking a nun in habit with you, and standing under a street lamp: she'll be a favorite target for the good Catholics on the floats. Or make a posterboard sign that says "John" and hold it up at each float, figuring that there must be at least one guy named John on every float. Or cut a large bleach bottle in half and attach the spout to a broom handle so that you have a handy tool to hold up to the riders. Another version of this is to turn an umbrella inside out and hold it up to the floats. Some parade-goers with kids use a special 8- to 10-foot (2-m to 3-m) ladder fixed with a bench at the top for the little ones, while parents stand below balancing them. These pre-made parade ladders can be bought at many local hardware stores and cost about $60. Ladders should not be hooked together, placed at intersections or against barricades, or left unattended—or the police will confiscate them.

Those who live within walking distance from the parade routes sometimes joke that "Mardi Gras" must be an old Creole expression meaning, "May I use your bathroom?" Nowadays the city puts out a lot of Port-O-Lets, and restaurants and bars will let their patrons avail themselves of the facilities. Those groups who have large packs of newly toilet-trained kids or big drinkers in their party might consider renting a hotel room on the route.

The estimated size of the Mardi Gras crowd is based on the amount of trash generated. A good crowd is one that has produced 2,000 or more tons of refuse. Each parade is followed by the Sanitation Department with its street sweepers, water-and-brush trucks, and blowers. Watching them is almost as much fun as watching the parade.

■ MARDI GRAS BALLS

Nowadays, there are over 130 krewes who center their year's activities around the Carnival season. Of these, close to 60 mount an annual parade. But all of them host at least one affair: a ball, which is the popular term for a bal masque, masquerade, or tableau representation. The money to mount the tableaux and balls comes from the dues paid by krewe members. These can be as low as $100 or as high as several thousand dollars; the additional initiation fee for new members can be as much as $1,000. The older krewes take their balls very seriously, so these tend to be long on pomp and short on life. At the other end of the spectrum are the gay balls—a combination of Las Vegas and the Lido with just a dash of camp thrown in. They're presided over by a grand female-impersonating queen in a multi-thousand-dollar gown. All of the other krewes' balls fall somewhere in the middle. There are krewes for youngsters, oldsters, neighborhoods, the visually impaired, Italians, artists

An invitation to a Mardi Gras ball from the nineteenth century.

—you name it and there's probably a krewe and ball for it. Some balls are for members of the krewe only, some are for "PLU" (People Like Us), while other krewes are thrilled to have any visitors enjoy their spectacle. Endymion holds its ball/rock concert in the Superdome, and many revelers eagerly buy tickets to attend.

One tradition that krewes (and other partiers) continue is the "king cake" served at Mardi Gras parties. The authentic Carnival version of this confection is a brioche decorated with purple, green, and gold sugar and containing a tiny gold bean. Today the gold bean has been replaced by a plastic baby, a loose reference to the baby Jesus. The person who finds the token in their piece is responsible for hosting the next king cake party.

(Historic New Orleans Collection)

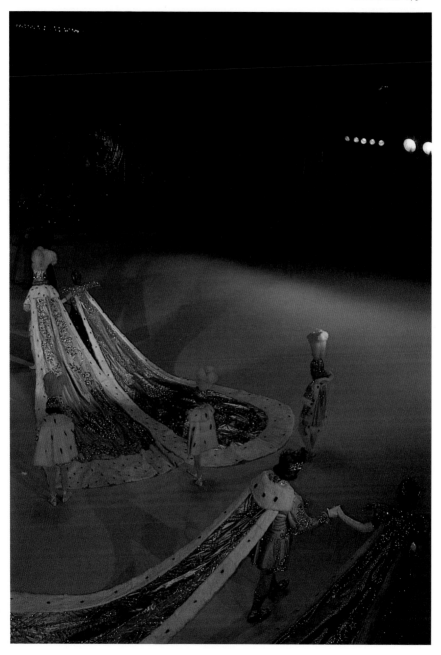

Elaborate costumes and ritual are the hallmarks of the Meeting of Courts of Comus and Rex. (Syndey Byrd)

■ SOCIETY BALLS

Among the many balls that krewes give during the Carnival season between January 6 and Ash Wednesday, only a few attract the city's society debutantes to their "courts." The stakes of Carnival are the highest for socially ambitious New Orleanians—a father belonging to one of the "right" krewes will begin a campaign at his daughter's birth to ensure that she will become queen of the ball when the time comes. Little girls who attend private girls' schools such as Sacred Heart and McGehee's learn early that an indiscretion at a childhood birthday party might permanently relegate them to a slot in the court of the queen, while others are tapped to become krewe royalty. Having a mother who was a queen certainly helps a girl's chances. Failing to achieve the status of queen can, within certain circles, lower a family's social status in a way that not even a good marriage can remedy.

Belonging to one of these "old-line" krewes today entails making social standing a priority. A family will make financial sacrifices so Dad can be in the right club, and Sis can make an impressive debut. For those not yet belonging to the right krewe, the willingness to make such sacrifices is not enough to guarantee membership. Regardless of an applicant's credentials, he may still be "blackballed," or rejected, by just one or two members; guests may also be blackballed from some invitation lists.

Few are invited to these "exclusive" balls, and as most krewes do not include an address on their invitation, it is difficult for those who are invited to reply; however, guests may return their admit cards to signify that he or she will not be in attendance. Those who do get invited are expected to wear *costume de rigueur,* or "full dress," consisting of white tie and tails for men, and a floor-length dress for women. Or the ball may be a bal masque, or masked ball, in which an elaborate costume is *de rigueur.* Once you get there, be sure not to take one of the "reserved seats," since space reserved on the floor and balcony is for specific, special guests.

When you get there, you'll notice the members of the court, including the king, queen, dukes, and maids. The king occupies the throne at the ball along with the queen. Attending him is a page, a little boy in costume. The queen is the lucky debutante (probably the daughter of a krewe member) sitting next to the king and wearing a grand, expensive ball gown. Though he may not appear with the other court members, the most powerful member of the krewe is the captain. This elected officer is placed in full charge of the pageantry, including any street parade or tableau ball. Kings may come and go, but it is the captain who decides the krewe's

A debutante is introduced at the Comus ball. (Syndey Byrd)

theme and court. When parading, the captain generally rides a horse, and his identity—particularly in the exclusive krewes —is rarely made public.

Before or after being presented, these royal folk may all be found in the "Captain's Room," or the "King's Room." This dressing room is reserved for the members of the court, the captain, and the aides. Here, champagne and other drinks are usually served by the king. Certain kings provide large quantities of wine and liquors as well as light refreshments. Admittance is restricted to members of the cast of the tableaux and committeemen.

After the king, queen, dukes, and maids are assembled on the throne, the king and queen perform the "Grand March" around the floor followed by their retinue, in the style of Old World royalty. Most European tradition dictates that ladies walk to the left of their escorts because knights of old used their right arms for weapons. But the custom of New Orleans Carnival is that the ladies should always be next to the audience so that they may appear to greater advantage: At most balls the king and queen turn to the right upon beginning the Grand March, and the queen is on the king's right; maids are likewise to the right of the dukes.

Depending on the type of ball, another significant event may be the "tableau," an enactment of the ball's "theme." Following this are the "call-outs," the first three or more dances allocated to members of the cast of the tableau. The term "call-out" may also refer to an invitation to participate in the maskers' dances, or to a person occupying a seat in the call-out section. When a masker calls out a partner, the partner is presented with a "favor," or souvenir. Some favors are obtained by the krewe for their members, while others are purchased by their wives. A few maskers bestow handsome gifts upon favorites: the cost of favors varies from a few cents to thousands of dollars. At the end of the ball, the court and their select guests will attend the Queen's Supper, a late-night party honoring the queen.

■ OTHER CELEBRATIONS

While the obvious focus of Mardi Gras for most is the many parades, New Orleanians and their visitors celebrate the holiday in other ways as well. One big celebration takes place in **Spanish Plaza on Lundi Gras**, the Monday before Mardi Gras. Free and open to the public, the event features the arrivals of the Kings of Zulu and Rex, as well as a free concert and fireworks. For folks with kids, there's also the Mardi Gras Mask-a-Thon, a family-oriented costume contest held on Mardi Gras afternoon in the 600 block of Canal Street.

For those who haven't brought kids along, there's an option that may cure you forever of any desire to party. The **six-block-long party** along Bourbon Street over Mardi Gras weekend somehow manages to be a combination of VE and VJ Day, New Year's Eve on Times Square, *Animal House,* the California Gold Rush, Spring Break in Daytona, and a Fellini movie. When the parades are over, many fun-seekers of the beer-gut and college set line the historic, lacy wrought-iron balconies to shimmy at passersby in return for beads. The aroma of beer, Hurricanes, and bodily fluids can be enjoyed as far away as Garden District. But at midnight on Mardi Gras the street is closed, and police with bullhorns announce, "Mardi Gras is officially over!" This kind of partying is enough to make anyone stumble to a pharmacy the next day for a bottle of XS, the locally produced hangover reliever.

One interesting incarnation of the holiday festivities is the **Courrir de Mardi Gras.** Taking place on the Cajun prairie northwest of Lafayette, this celebration of Carnival strikes a different note. Literally translated, this "Mardi Gras Run" resembles a celebration brought to Louisiana by the early Acadians. The Courrir is a rowdy, exuberant procession of locals going from farm to farm, collecting the ingredients for a pot of gumbo symbolically meant to feed the entire community.

Amid all the revelry, local Catholics do not forget their own heritage—or at least, don't neglect the devotion necessary to compensate for their wild behavior. Many devout Catholic families demand that their children go to confession on Mardi Gras morning *before* the parades to atone for sins, just in case they should over-party and meet their Maker before attending mass on Ash Wednesday. Once that first day of Lent does roll around, hard Mardi Gras partying can cause even pagans to embrace this day of atonement.

■ MARDI GRAS INDIANS

One of the most magnificent spectacles and most elite of all Mardi Gras celebrations is the elaborate tradition of the black neighborhood "tribes" who dress up to honor the Native Americans who first befriended them. Born of a completely original aesthetic tradition, the Mardi Gras Indians have contributed a costuming and parading style that has become integral to Carnival. The inspiration for the

Indians was an event in the 1790s, when several dozen slaves escaped and were hidden by the Chickasaws, who also tried to assist in a slave rebellion. Black oral history kept the contributions of the Louisiana natives alive, and by the time of Reconstruction a few groups from the secret black pleasure clubs (many of whose roots went back to Congo Square) formed their own Carnival clubs. They took to the streets during Carnival dressed in turkey feathers, fish-scale ornaments, and ceremonial regalia to honor the Louisiana Indians.

Tribes soon developed rivalries, and Mardi Gras (referred to as "That Day" in the Indian songs) also provided the perfect opportunity to settle grudges. Dressed as Indian warriors, rival "gangs" could fight outside the law's reach on a day when the rest of the city was celebrating in the streets. Indians then fought ritualistic duels set to music (see "MUSIC"). Challenges are still made these days, but on strictly aesthetic grounds.

The first official tribe was begun in the 1880s at 1313 St. Anthony Street by Becate Battiste. Hailing from the Seventh Ward, born of both African and American Indian stock, he named his gang the "Creole Wild West Tribe." Today the descendants of the tribe are the **Yellow Pocahontas**, previously led by Battiste's nephew,

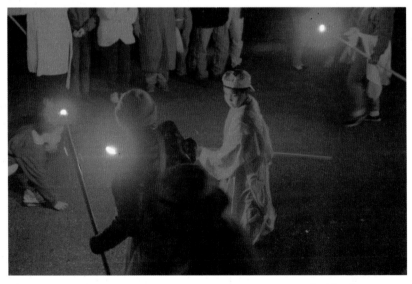

During Carnival, nighttime revelries follow fabulous parades (above).
Mardi Gras Indian tribes are noted for their elaborate plumage (right photo, Syndey Byrd).

Alfred Montana, Sr., and now by his son Allison "Tuddy" Montana. The original Yellow Pocahontas tribe was formed across town in the uptown Garden District in 1896 by a man who was part Louisiana native and part African American, and who married a pure-blooded Choctaw. It is thought that these tribes were in part inspired by the World Centennial Cotton Exposition of 1884, when New Orleans played host to Buffalo Bill's Wild West Show for four months. As part of the show, resplendent (authentic) Indians whooped and hollered, strutting their stuff to New Orleans' people of color. During the Mardi Gras celebration of 1885, American Indians who had performed in the show evidently took to the streets in celebration.

After World War II another wave of tribes was formed, including the Wild Magnolias and the Black Eagles. Tribes are founded by a chief, the man in the neighborhood able to gather the largest personal retinue. Today there are over 20 Indian tribes—among them the Wild Apaches, White Eagles, Wild Tchoupitoulas, and Golden Star Hunters—with between 10 and 40 members each. Most members come from inner-city, working-class black neighborhoods. (One tribe is integrated, however: a Finnish fellow who makes his own costumes has been the Second Chief of the Black Eagles for the past 20 years.) Fifteen of the 17 tribes have decided to "bury the hatchet" and joined together in 1987. The proceeds from their first official poster in 1993 went to benefit the preservation of their Indian culture.

When the tribes march on parade, those watching will see the First Spy Boy, then the First Flag Boy, and several series of Spies and Flags, the number depending on the size of the tribe. Near the end of the procession is the man who carries the Gang Flag, followed by the Wildman or Medicine Man, with the Second Chief and the Big Chief bringing up the rear. The Big Chief is followed by his secondline, his civilian bodyguards, who often carry weapons. Their trademark plumage, which can weigh up to 50 pounds (23 kg), is designed and crafted by the wearer, an effort that takes months and costs thousands of dollars. Nowadays, the ferocious tribal rivalry focuses on the costumes: the Big Chiefs all seek to be deemed the "prettiest" by other gang members and neighborhood followers. The Uptown tribes —among them Golden Star, Creole Wild West, Black Eagles, Golden Eagles, Wild Magnolia, Carrollton Hunters—are considered to be the fanciest dressers. The Downtown tribe noted for its plumage is the Monogram Hunters. Musician Charles Neville remembers that his mother used to mask as an Indian on

Mardi Gras Day with his uncle, Chief Jolly. She'd carry scissors to keep people around Jolly from stealing his feathers. You can also see the Mardi Gras Indians march a few weeks after Mardi Gras—on St. Joseph's Day, the holiday tradition begun by New Orleans' Italian Americans in the nineteenth century.

Mardi Gras Indian with a live bird in his feathery hat. (Michael P. Smith)

M   U   S   I   C

THE RHYTHMS OF NEW ORLEANS JAZZ were born of Africa and the West Indies, fed on the spicy food, tropical heat, and oppression of the Deep South, and intertwined with melodic structures brought along by European immigrants. Once its early structures were formed, jazz grew up on the collectively improvised back-of-town ragtime and an unbeatable *joie de vivre*, bite, and swagger.

If there is one place in the United States that can be credited with being the spiritual and mythological birthplace of jazz, it must be the *Place des Negres*, or Old Congo Square, in what is now Louis Armstrong Park. Here, enslaved Africans were allowed to meet and dance, speaking in their native African tongues and playing their traditional instruments. The square bustled with these activities from 1817 until 1867.

Following the Civil War, bands such as Kelly's Silver Cornet Band performed concerts there. These were times of transition when the melodies of the black minstrel shows, syncopated music, slave work chants, and the blues were mingling everywhere that people gathered. The style of music practiced in the early years of the twentieth century in New Orleans was a buoyant, simple music in 2/4 or 4/4 rhythm. This style of jazz is now often referred to as "traditional" (or "trad," the British term), and in New Orleans there are a good number of 80- and 90-year-old founding fathers still doing nightly gigs.

During these early years, white musicians began to hang out in the streets and clubs of the African-American community, trying to learn their style. Many black musicians were also listening to recordings of white musicians such as Larry Shields of the Original Dixieland Jazz Band. Shields was influential in creating the "trick bag" of jazz riffs common to all New Orleans jazz. The term "Dixieland" was used to connote the syncopated music played by white bands, a distinction made by 1930s jazz critics. The jazz music played by the Creoles of color and the blacks was more improvisational than Dixieland and was rooted in African and West Indian traditions. Added to the mix were Irish, Jewish (cornetist Johnny Wiggs), and Italian musicians who moved into the same urban neighborhoods and took to the American music form as quickly as the Acadians had taken to the swamps. Some of the early bands often improvised on handmade instruments such as banjos made of cheese boxes and percussion instruments of kitchen implements.

Charles Neville, one of the legendary Neville Brothers, performs at Jazz Fest.

DANCING THE CALENDA

*T*o dance the calenda, the Negroes have two drums made with hollow pieces of wood, all in one piece. One of the ends is left opened and the other end is covered with the skin of a goat or a sheep. The shortest of these drums is called the "bamboula" because most of the time the drum is made of a very large bambou tree. A Negro is seated on each drum upon which he beats the skin with his fingers and wrist. One Negro keeps the time slowly like a basso drum while the other keeps time rapidly with fingers and wrist. To this is added the sound of many gourds half filled with small stones or grains of corn. These are shaken by beating them with the hands by means of a handle that crosses them. When the orchestra is increased or completed the banza is added to these drums and the gourds. The banza is a coarse violin made with four cords that are pinched with the fingers. The Negresses standing in a row keep time with their hands, clapping them together, and they take the chorus from a song improvised by one or two Negresses who sing with a very loud and piercing voice. Negroes have great talent to improvise music and words adapted to the music.

The dances, always a pair, a man and a girl, dances in the middle of the circle that is formed on a level piece of ground and always out of doors. This dance consists of the following: The dancer turns around, spinning on himself around his partner. He keeps his arms close to his body, wrist tightly closed, then raises alternatively the arms one after the other. In the meanwhile, the Negresses forming the circle keep time with the beating of their hands. The dancer moves her feet forward alternatively, hitting the ground sometimes with the point of the toes and sometimes with the heel. Each one has a turn to dance in the middle of the circle, and the rhythm is always perfect. They are so fond of dancing that they would keep on dancing all night, and

when orders are given to stop the dancing it is always with regret that they leave their ball.

—Helen d'Aquin Allain, memoir describing
New Orleans, c. 1830s

Pieces of a journal kept by Benjamin (Henry) Latrobe illustrate the instruments he saw being played at Congo Square in 1819. (The Maryland Historical Society)

The word "jazz" was not applied to the new sound until a good 20 years after the music had already found its way to the ears and tapping feet of New Orleanians, who referred to it with slang terms such as "gutbucket," "ragtime," or "ratty music." Ironically, it is believed that a white band was first called a "jazz" band. In 1915, Tom Brown took his white Dixieland band to Chicago and audiences requested uptempo, or "jass" music. Meanwhile, the Chicago Musician's Union angrily used "jass" as a slur against the musicians for playing that dirty New Orleans "jass music." ("Jass" was an Elizabethan English word that meant roughly "to do with enthusiasm," and later came to refer to sexual fluids.) Back in New Orleans, on June 20, 1918, the good reporters at the *Times-Picayune* referred to jazz as a "musical vice."

The Chicago audiences knew a catchy word when they heard it and began calling the group "Brown's Dixieland Jass Band." By the time the next white band went north, the five-man ensemble led by Nick LaRocca was officially called the Original Dixieland Jazz Band. This group was to have a great impact on audiences in London, Chicago, and New York. In 1917 they became the first New Orleans jazz group to make successful records, some of which sold more than a million copies. The hits from their 20-year career, including "Tiger Rag," "Ostrich Walk," and "Clarinet Marmalade," continue to be mainstays for both black and white traditional bands.

Buddy Bolden (1878-1931) is the man credited with throwing all of the city's musical ingredients into a big pot and turning out a feast with a uniquely New Orleans flavor. With his fiery cornet, he and his band added pepper and spice to the "legitimate" music of the day. They played music that was raunchy and gut-bucket, born of poverty and passion. An example was Bolden's theme song, "Funky Butt Blues." No recordings exist of his music, but accounts from those who heard him play say that he was the greatest cornet player who ever lived. He was also thrown out of his own band on occasion when he drank away all of the band's profits. His career was cut short when he went wild at a Labor Day Parade in 1907, and was committed to the East Louisiana Mental Hospital, where he spent the last 24 years of his life, rotting away with venereal disease.

After Buddy Bolden left town, **Freddie Keppard** (bandleader of the Original Creole Orchestra) became the "king" of the New Orleans cornetists. Cornet virtuosos Keppard and his O.C.O. spread the sounds of New Orleans on vaudeville tours between 1914 and 1918. Asked to make a jazz recording, Keppard reportedly refused saying, "Why should I put my stuff down on a record for other people to steal?"

■ STORYVILLE SOUND

While legend has it that New Orleans jazz was born in the brothels of the infamous Storyville district, the truth is that the music was most often played in saloons nearby, or to accompany social activity. Buddy Bolden himself played in Lincoln Park and the streets of the city more often than in Storyville. Outdoor musical processions, a concept practiced by Bolden, Jelly Roll Morton, Freddie Keppard, King Oliver, and Louis Armstrong, created wide audiences for jazz. Nonetheless, the popular brothels of Storyville were a venue for this music, and steady gigs—usually for pianists—meant steady income and the opportunity to grab the attention of the upper-class patrons.

Meanwhile, ragtime was setting feet to tapping in low-life juke joints. Made popular by Missourian **Scott Joplin** and characterized by highly syncopated melodic lines played against a 2/4 bass, ragtime was to have great influence in the New Orleans jazz scene. In New Orleans, ragtime aquired a heavy dose of Latin rhythms.

Jazz pianist **Jelly Roll Morton** (Ferdinand Joseph La Mothe, 1885-1941) insisted that he, and only he, had created jazz. While that might not have been exactly accurate, most agree that at the very least, Jelly Roll was the first notable jazz composer and arranger. As a Creole of color, he tended to feel that he was superior socially and musically to black musicians. He was quite a dandy, and had a diamond embedded in his front tooth to add flash to his smile. He led a colorful life as well—he was a ladies' man, and an expert pool hustler. Possessed with a terrific fear of the power of voodoo, he was known to throw away a good suit of clothes and completely re-outfit himself if he thought someone had thrown voodoo powder on him. Morton's autobiography, *Mr. Jelly Roll,* based on Alan Lomax's 1938 interviews, was published in 1950. Jelly Roll died in 1941 in California.

The ragtime pianists, such as **Steve Lewis, Spencer Williams,** and **Manuel Manetta,** were known as the Storyville "professors." This mock title went to talented musicians who served as mentors to the younger ones.

While performing in bordellos such as Hilma Burt's Mirror Mansion and Lulu White's Mahogany Hall, Spencer Williams, the ward and a blood-relative of Lulu White, began playing music as a young child and went on to write such jazz standards as "Basin Street Blues," "I Ain't Gonna Give Nobody None O' My Jelly Roll," and the "Mahogany Hall Stomp." In 1925, he migrated to Paris where he wrote music for Josephine Baker.

Jelly Roll Morton playing piano in a Storyville bordello. (Hogan Jazz Archive, Tulane University Library)

During the same period "spasm bands" were filling the back alleys, train stations, and markets with their hot music. These bands began with street urchins playing on improvised instruments—comb and paper, cigar box guitars, barrel basses, bottles and jugs—for whatever coins passersby were willing to throw. These grew into more established ensembles, among them "Stalebread" Lacoume's Razzie Dazzie Spasm Band. The popularity of these hot dance bands bolstered the city's mania for dancing in Storyville, Treme, and Seventh Ward dance halls, at places such as the Economy and the San Jacinto. Dance halls sprang up in many neighborhoods, rich and poor, particularly in the years between the Spanish American War in 1898 and the Great Depression in 1929.

■ MAJOR PLAYERS

Several other great stars were to emerge in the early years of the twentieth century. **Edward "Kid" Ory** was a Creole of color who grew up upriver from New Orleans at San Francisco Plantation (a home owned by a white family also named Ory). Here, he and some of the other teenagers formed a spasm band, the Woodland Band. By the time that Ory found an audience in New Orleans, the group had become a woodwind, horn, and percussion ensemble in which Ory played the valve trombone. After this ensemble split up, he began leading bands at Economy Hall and the prestigious, whites-only New Orleans Country Club, as well as spots in Lincoln Park and Storyville.

In 1919, Ory left New Orleans for a Creole-of-color community in California. There he organized the Sunshine Band, which in 1921 became the first black New Orleans jazz band to record in Southern California. After stints playing with King Oliver, Louis Armstrong, and Jelly Roll Morton in New York and Chicago, he retired from music in the early 1930s. Ory later returned to perform for an even wider audience in the '40s as the grand old man of jazz, continuing to play professionally until his death in 1973.

Joe "King" Oliver, one of the immortal cornetists and bandleaders of the early years of jazz, took what he perfected in New Orleans and spread it around the world. After migrating from rural Louisiana, he began playing in New Orleans in 1904, with the Onward Brass Band. By 1910, Oliver had begun to perform in Storyville and with Kid Ory at Pete Lala's. After the closing of the Storyville district during World War I, Oliver left for Chicago, sending for Louis Armstrong as his second cornetist. It was here in 1919 that his nickname "Bad Eye" (an accident blinded him) was replaced with the moniker "King." During the 1920s King Oliver and his two bands, the Creole Jazz Band (1920-24) and the Dixie Syncopaters (1925-1930), enjoyed great popularity and recorded over 30 records. Those who knew him remember him as being "cocky, cute, and meaner than a nine-balled tomcat." By the 1930s, Oliver was losing his teeth and finding himself increasingly unable to play the cornet. More and more frequently he asked Armstrong to replace him. When Oliver died in Savannah in 1938, he was destitute, and the world of jazz had passed him by.

Another star of these years was **Sidney Bechet** (1897-1959), a master of the clarinet and soprano sax, known for his particular "bending" of notes. Bechet began playing clarinet at age six, and by 1914 he had already worked with many of the city's greats. After working with Clarence Williams and King Oliver, he moved to Chicago, and later to New York. Bechet ended up in Paris and continued to play the New Orleans style of jazz, ultimately becoming something of a legendary figure in Paris. His autobiography, *Treat It Gentle,* was published in 1960.

King Oliver's Creole Jazz Band, from left: Honore Dutrey on trombone; Baby Dodds on drums; Louis Armstrong on slide trumpet; and behind Armstrong, King Oliver on cornet. Armstrong's wife, Lil Hardin, is on piano; Bill Johnson plays banjo; and Johnny Dodds on clarinet. (William Ranson, Hogan Jazz Archive, Tulane University Library)

The name **Louis Armstrong** is virtually synonymous with New Orleans jazz. Born on August 4, 1901 (he claimed July 4, 1900), Armstrong got his earliest musical training when he was on the streets and a ward of the Jones Colored Waifs' Home. He began playing professionally with Kid Ory in Lincoln Park and later with King Oliver. By 1918, Armstrong was playing on river boats, and in 1922 he left New Orleans to join King Oliver's band in Chicago. He spent the next 40 years performing around the globe, but rarely in the city that was his home. The sponsorship of the State Department enabled Armstrong and his All Stars to tour the world as a "goodwill ambassador" from the 1940s to the '60s. He died in 1971.

■ MARCHING BANDS AND SOCIAL CLUBS

The tradition of brass band street parades goes back well over a century to the first jazz funerals, held by jazz musicians when one of their brethren died. In the jazz funeral parade, the band follows the coffin, behind which is the "second-line"

Opening night in August of 1923 of the Pythian Temple Roof Garden, an elite Creole-of-color nightclub. (Hogan Jazz Archive, Tulane University Library)

made up of family, friends, and mourners. On the way to the grave the mood is somber, the bands often playing "Flee as a Bird," a slow dirge with muffled drum. On the walk home, jubilation and rejoicing overtake the crowd as they celebrate the departed's joyful entry into heaven, often to the tune of the up-tempo jazz "Oh, Didn't He Ramble." Today, these marching jazz bands are made up primarily of brass, reeds, and percussion. While they can be hired to play at both funerals and parades, they still often donate their services for fellow musicians. Contemporary practitioners include Duke Dejan's Olympia, The Onward, The Original Tuxedo, and The Dirty Dozen.

The early brass-band parading tradition expanded after the founding of the African-American benevolent societies known as "social aid and pleasure clubs" or "SA&PCs." In the 1880s, these clubs began hiring brass bands to play at their social functions. By the turn of the century, some of the clubs decided to hold an annual second-line parade strictly for the fun of incorporating a brass jazz band into the day street celebrations. Their names bespeak their spirit of pleasure, such as The Money Wasters and the Calliope High Steppers. In the uptown area, clubs include The Fun Lovers (a women's club), Kool & Gang, and The Avenue Steppers. The Young Men's Olympia Social Aid & Pleasure Club was founded in 1884

The Young Olympian Soul Rebels play at Jazz Fest.

and is the oldest SA&PC in New Orleans. It is a non-profit organization whose purpose is two-fold: performing civic work, including acting as a funeral society within the African-American community; and mounting an annual parade. Their annual parade, advertised by word of mouth, is generally held on the fourth Sunday in September, though club members also parade at the Jazz Fest.

The Scene Boosters, another of the uptown groups, were chartered in the summer of 1973 as a combination of SA&PC and marching club. Their annual parade is the first Sunday in November; they're also regulars at the Jazz Fest. The most prestigious of the downtown clubs is the Jolly Bunch, organized in 1941. Members alternate their annual parade between uptown and downtown routes. They can be seen in the Zulu parade at Carnival, and each January the club celebrates its anniversary with the Majestic Brass Band or the Pin Stripe, parading from church to church. Another of the downtown groups is The Louis Armstrong Golden Trumpets, which was founded in the Seventh Ward in 1974 by Freida Germaine, a member of the Ladies Auxiliary of the Jolly Bunch. Their parade is distinguished

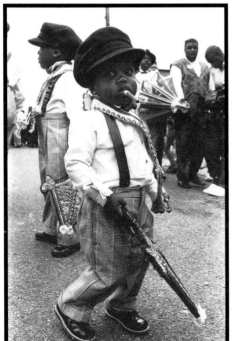

by the use of the basket, the fan, and the umbrella to signify the first division, second division, and preppy division, respectively.

The social clubs assume all the expense of the parade, including hiring the bands. Bands can cost well over $1,000, and the police escorts and parade permits cost over $1,500. The total expense for a parade can be $5,000; obviously, this is difficult for those groups who have but several handfuls of members and want to continue to mount parades annually for the thousands of second-liners that participate.

At the Sudan Club parade.
(Michael P. Smith)

■ OTHER JAZZ SPOTS

Beyond Congo Square and Storyville were many other venues for New Orleans's jazz musicians. Musicians sometimes congregated in the clubs and cottages in the Treme area, including Perseverance Hall, still standing at 1644 North Villere as the Holy Aid Comfort Spiritual Church. Another early jazz site was located in Faubourg Marigny, the Francis Amis Hall, an exclusive Creole-of-color Social Aid and Pleasure Club. These halls became popular with the freed slaves who had migrated into New Orleans during and after Reconstruction. In the early years of the twentieth century, Buddy Bolden, Kid Ory, and King Oliver entertained local residents in Lincoln and Oakland parks. The racially mixed Oakland Park was later sold at auction and redeveloped as the New Orleans Country Club, an elite whites-only club. (It's sad to note that while whites could "hang out" with black musicians and learn from them in their clubs, the reverse was not true.)

The old gym (now the ROTC building on Freret Street) at Tulane University introduced jazz to the Uptown/Garden District students of both Tulane and its sister school, Sophie Newcomb, as early as 1917 at their "script" dances. Here the kids could boogie to the music of King Oliver, Johnny Wiggs, Papa Celestin, and Kid Ory. Many parents were horrified at this revolutionary form of wild dancing, preferring their children listen to Guy Lombardo or other orchestras at hotels. But by the '30s, jazz was embedded in popular culture and constantly played on the radio.

New Orleanians also went to nightclubs in the Milneburg area, a series of "camps" constructed in the late nineteenth century on pilings over the waters of Lake Ponchartrain. Here New Orleanians could go to nightclubs and listen to Dixieland, "Sweet" Emma Barrett, and A. J. Piron's Society Orchestra. Piron is remembered for promoting jazz as a socially acceptable form of music with the polite society of both races. He even played at debutante balls.

Later on, it was the gambling circuit that supported some New Orleans musicians—among them Louis Armstrong, who visited New Orleans to entertain the patrons of the Suburban Gardens casino in 1931. If Armstrong played to packed houses, they were white only, causing a great deal of resentment within his own black community. In July of 1935, he returned to New Orleans again, this time playing for black audiences at the Golden Dragon.

In the city, the era of ragtime-inspired jazz lasted until the end of World War I, when it evolved into the uninhibited dance crazes of the Roaring Twenties and the Swing Era of the '30s. With the advent of the swing bands in the rest of the country, the national popularity of the classical jazz of New Orleans began to fade. In the 1940s jazz shaded into be-bop and mixed with the funk and blues of urban blacks to become rhythm and blues.

New Orleans enters the last decade of the twentieth century, having played host to the soul of jazz for over a hundred years. New Orleans now nurtures music as a living, breathing link with the past. For many native sons, this musical heritage is a foundation on which to build new styles. Artists who emerged during the 1980s tip their hats to traditional styles of composition and performance. The fame of such musicians as Terence Blanchard, Donald Harrison, and the Marsalis family —Ellis, Wynton, and Branford—fostered a resurgence of interest in New Orleans jazz and, as a result, in venues where traditional jazz and Dixieland can still be heard. The great living museum for the city's early jazz is **Preservation Hall** at 726 St. Peter, and another superb venue is the **Palm Court Cafe** at 1204 Decatur Street.

(above) Frank Frederico's Dixieland band (Syndey Byrd). Preservation Hall is New Orleans' most famous venue for old-time New Orleans jazz (right).

BECHET ON JAZZ

*P*eople come up to me and they ask me, "Are you going to play Tin Roof Blues?" They ask me, "What's be-bop?" or what do I think of some record Louis Armstrong put out. But if I was to answer that, I'd have to go back a long way. That's why I have to tell a lot more than people would expect.

They come to tell me they like this record or that, and they ask me what I'm trying to do by my music. They ask me what's going to happen to Jazz? Where's it going? One night a man came to see me when I was playing in Paris; I'd known his son in New York. He came in with this party, and after the band had finished playing I got to talking with him. He started to tell me it meant a lot to him to hear me play; he'd had an experience he'd never had before. I told him I played like I always played. That's really all I can say.

But he was in a kind of feeling he wanted to talk. . . . "This music is your music," he said.

But, you know, no music is my music. It's everybody's who can feel it. You're here . . . well, if there's music, you feel it—then it's yours too. You got to be in the sun to feel the sun. It's that way with music too.

—Sidney Bechet, *Treat It Gentle*, 1960

Music in the sun: the Kid Thomas Band opens a gas station in 1961.
(Hogan Jazz Archive, Tulane University Library)

■ BOURBON STREET

There is no other seven-block stretch in America more evocative of excess, the erotic and exotic, and traditional jazz and R&B than Bourbon Street. One might guess the street was named for the Kentucky whiskey rather than an eighteenth-century royal family. Between the world wars a rather sedate residential street in the French Quarter turned into a raucous strip designed to titillate tourists and tempt them into parting with their money. Although the architectural treasures are upstaged by the neon and fluorescent lights, and there's a scent of old oyster shells and beer in the air, Bourbon Street's bustle and flamboyance are quintessential New Orleans.

The musicians who hold down the regular gigs on the strip are all remarkable professionals and masters of their art form. They have played each song a thousand times but can still pump it out with enthusiasm. Even after one club closes down for the morning, the musicians will drift down the street to jam with a band at another club.

Somehow going to hear traditional jazz on Bourbon Street in the afternoon is a more down-to-earth experience than going after dark. Many Quarterites like to begin their music evenings at Donna's, across from Congo Square and Armstrong Park at 800 North Rampart, for terrific brass band music. From there they move over to Fritzel's at 733 Bourbon for another infusion of jazz.

■ MARDI GRAS INDIAN TRIBE MUSIC

If there is a black roux at the base of the gumbo of New Orleans jazz and R&B, it is the warrior chants of the Mardi Gras Indians. Beginning in the 1880s, these semi-organized "gangs" melded the old call-and-response chants of their African heritage with diverse percussion instruments—cowbells, whistles, conga drums—thus beginning the traditional music of the Indian tribes. The chants also included voodoo terms from the Caribbean and even some North American Indian words and intonations. Handmade percussion instruments are still beaten in rapid backbeat time to arouse dancers to a fever pitch of excitement.

Tribes speak to each other through rhythms, chants, and dance. Traditionally, rival tribes greet each other with a war dance. In earlier days, if a warrior couldn't dance a rival to the ground, he would knock him down, and the rest of the elaborately clad tribe would join in. The waving of handkerchiefs and the chant

Birthday party for Norman Bell, second chief of the Wild Tchoupitoulas. (Michael P. Smith)

"Hecky Pocky Way" (the modern version of a nineteenth-century Mardi Gras Indian phrase) were originally just a smidgen more inflammatory than giving a rude hand gesture. Today, when tribes move through the streets, their meetings consist of dancing, formal costume display, tribal gestures, and shared "Indian" pride. (See "CARNIVAL" for further information.) Their influence can be heard in the music of everyone from Jelly Roll Morton to Sugarboy Crawford, Professor Longhair to Dr. John. The Indians' music directly touched the Neville Brothers, as it was their uncle, George Landry, Big Chief Jolly, the founder of the Wild Tchoupitoulas, who first called the family together to make an album.

The raucous sound of the Mardi Gras Indians seems to voice the untamed, emotional charge of New Orleans itself. The closer to Carnival, the wilder the music. Musician Charles Neville explains, "You just sing the bad spirits of the week on their way before you have to go back to work Monday. The Big Chief could hit that tambourine so loud it sounded like a pistol shot." Today's tribes are becoming more organized, with official posters and a museum under development near Armstrong Park.

(opposite) Dancers and musicians at Jazz Fest.

■ RHYTHM AND BLUES

During the '40s, music played on the now ubiquitous radio drew a wider and wider audience and brought the taste for big-city, Harlem-generated be-bop to New Orleans. The term "rhythm and blues" is said to have been coined in *Variety* as a category for its hit charts. Of course, in the back streets of New Orleans, the local musicians put a slightly different spin on what they heard. They added soul and jazz, and began to hammer out rhythm and blues. The Dew Drop Inn (at South La Salle and Washington Avenue) was noted as the club where this fusion took place. Originally opened in 1938 as a lunch stand and barber shop, it featured blues players Gatemouth Brown and Big Joe Turner, the jazz orchestras of Lionel Hampton and Duke Ellington, and local entertainers such as Irma Thomas, Allen Toussaint, Charles Neville, and Guitar Slim. (Although the Dew Drop no longer exists, each year the Jazz & Heritage Festival produces a "Dew Drop Inn Revisited" concert to showcase many of the musicians who performed there.)

In 1949, a former tap dancer and blues pianist named Henry Roeland Byrd took the professional name of **Professor Longhair,** "Fess," and created a musical

Professor Longhair (above) plays his birthday cake in 1977 (right), three years before his death. (Michael P. Smith)

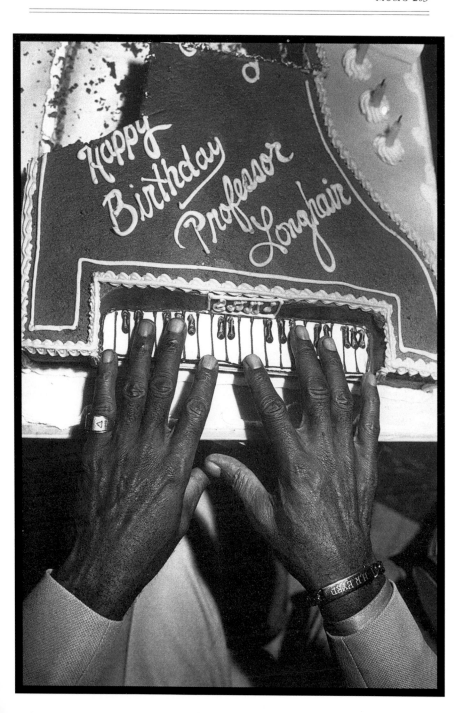

tornado with his unique blend of mambo, rhumba, calypso, jazz, Mardi Gras Indian music, and the blues. Until his death in 1980, the Professor's style had a profound influence on most of the younger R&B performers that were recording. Fats Domino hit the national scene in 1950 with a rocking and rolling piano style for such chart toppers as "Blueberry Hill" and "Walkin' to New Orleans." One of the musicians most influenced by Fess was a white pianist named Mac Rebenneck. In 1968 Rebenneck hit it big as "Dr. John," a name taken from the famous voodoo priest of the nineteenth century.

In the 1960s, Allen Toussaint, a Creole of color from a musical family, had the foresight to gather and nurture the talents of many popular local talents: Aaron Neville ("Tell It Like It Is"), Ernie K-Doe ("Mother in Law"), the Dixie Cups ("Chapel of Love"), Lee Dorsey ("Working in a Coal Mine"), and Irma Thomas ("It's Rainin'"). By 1966, when the ground-breaking Meters hit the stage with their fusion of indigenous funk and jazz, the New Orleans audience responded enthusiastically.

In the 1970s, the Warehouse, a psychedelic brick dungeon that sat wharfside on Tchoupitoulas Street, served as a venue for white rock from England and the West

The Dixie Cups take their audience to the "Chapel of Love" in 1977 (above) while Aaron Neville tells it like it is at an early Jazz Fest event. (Michael P. Smith)

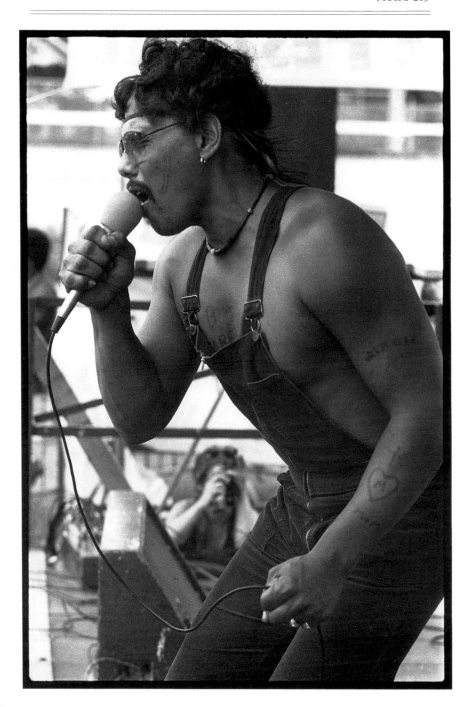

Coast, while local music often seemed to be relegated to a few clubs and fraternity parties. Then in 1977, Aaron Neville joined his brothers to form the legendary Neville Brothers and began performing at the Nitecap on Louisiana Avenue.

The 1980s saw a renaissance of New Orleans music. Two former students from the New Orleans Center for the Creative Arts, inspired by the early sound of jazz, managed to win Grammy Awards while they were still in their twenties. These were Wynton Marsalis, son of a noted jazz pianist and educator, and Harry Connick, Jr., whose father is a local district attorney *and* a cabaret singer.

Today **Tipitina's** (the name comes from the title of a Professor Longhair song) at 501 Napoleon Avenue is the forerunning venue for the classic R&B of the 1950s through the '70s, as well as the R&B and alternative rock of today.

■ CAJUN AND ZYDECO

The motifs and themes of Cajun, swamp pop, and zydeco share the same ingredients—Acadian folk, the accordion, homespun percussion instruments, and the French language. Acadian folk stems from the eighteenth-century French ballads

(above) Dr. John, named after one of voodoo's most famous nineteenth-century priests, plays at Tipitina's. (opposite) Ambrose Thibodeaux, Cajun music master, at the first Jazz Festival in 1970. (Michael P. Smith)

that the first Acadian settlers brought with them when they were ousted by the British from Nova Scotia and eastern Canada. A generation later, German farmers, encouraged by the French to come grow wheat in Louisiana, brought the accordion. The Acadian dance party, *"Fais Do-Do,"* literally means "Make Sleep," though it is really a joyful social event. Unlike jazz, with its sometimes mournful feeling, Cajun music is usually upbeat.

The Cajun music of the white Acadians is still characterized by the fiddle and hand-held triangle. Its danceable tempo favors the timing of a waltz or two-step. The typifying "chanka-chanka" sound is a blend of European and African rhythms synthesized in the 1920s and '30s by Amadée Ardoin. In the late '20s, Ardoin was the first black accordion player to be recorded. Stylistically, Cajun music holds hands with American country and bluegrass music. In the 1970s, a new generation of Acadian musicians began to rejuvenate the old music, among them Michael Doucet and his band Beausoleil, who've continued to build on the traditional Cajun sound. Other such groups include: Bruce Daigreport, Eddie LeJeune & The Morse Playboys, and D. L. Menard. The legendary Cajun fiddler Dewey Balfa led his family band at the Newport Festival.

Zydeco combines African blues and R&B components with traditional Cajun dance music. Its name is an elision of the old dance tune "Les Haricots N'est Pas Sale," which loosely translated means "The Snap Beans Aren't Salty." In Cajun French, *les haricots* sounds like "lay-zy-de-co." Saxophones, "piano" accordions, and the rub-board—a corrugated metal vest that is played against the chest—are paired with electric guitars and pulsating rhythm to give the music its irresistibly danceable style.

The king of zydeco was the late Clifton Chenier of Opelousas, who won the Grammy in 1983 for Best Ethnic/Folk Recording. Some of those artists who continue the tradition are his son C. J. Chenier, Buckwheat Zydeco, Grammy-winning Queen Ida Guillory and her Bon Temps Band, and Willis Prudhomme & Zydeco Express.

"Swamp boogie" or "swamp pop" is rock and roll with a Cajun/country accent. The style goes back to the post-World War II era when songs written by Cajun white boys hit the charts. These chart-toppers included Bobby Charles's "See Ya Later Alligator" and Phil Phillips' "Sea of Love." Today, Zachary Richard, "The Zack Attack," is one of the hottest performers. He and young, hot zydeco musicians can often be heard at local clubs such as Jimmy's, Margaritaville Cafe, Tipitina's, and Mid-City Lanes Rock 'n' Bowl.

Jimmy Buffett at Jazz Fest.

■ NEW ORLEANS JAZZ & HERITAGE FESTIVAL

The last weekend in April and the first one in May showcase over 4,000 musicians, cooks, and craftsmen in a 10-day event, held in the infield of a racetrack. Performers include internationally known jazz artists, gospel choirs, Cajun and zydeco bands, R&B bands, and many others in between. The food offerings are impressive and tasty, and the crowd can be as entertaining as the musicians. Those who regularly attend have worked out a handful of money- and time-saving tips. Book tickets in advance in mid-February by calling Ticketmaster at (800) 488-5252, or write P. O. Box 53407, New Orleans, LA, 70153.

Once in the city for the "Jazz Fest," you'll find parking to be a nightmare; it's best to stay in a guest house in the back of the French Quarter or on Esplanade, then rent a bike or take a taxi to the fairgrounds. Having the proper equipment is also a must. Don't leave home without a pair of good rubber boots that won't come off even in squishy mud, a rain poncho, plenty of sunscreen, a hat, a long-sleeve cotton shirt for sun protection, and comfortable running shoes. Nighttime concerts, held in air-conditioned venues throughout the city, require much less equipment. Tickets for these evening events sell quickly, so order ahead.

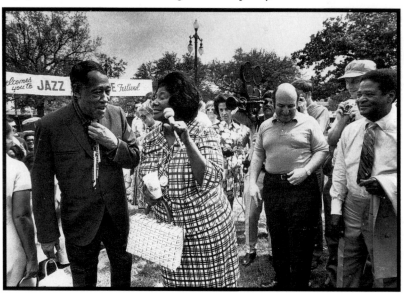

(above) Duke Ellington and Mahalia Jackson at Jazz Fest in 1970.
(opposite) Howlin' Wolf, the legendary blues performer, plays at a New Orleans club in 1973.
(both photos, Michael P. Smith)

There is something for every musical taste at Jazz Fest. (top photo by Michael P. Smith)

■ MUSIC CLUBS

Following is a listing of New Orleans clubs featuring live music. Call ahead for hours, since in New Orleans there are no official closing times. Get up-to-the-minute information from the monthly music newspaper *Off Beat*. For current listings, use e-mail: offbeat@neworleans.neosoft.com. Other good sources are the Friday "Lagniappe" section of the *Times Picayune*, the weekly paper *Gambit*, or listening to WWOZ at 90.7 FM. A favorite way to hear jazz in New Orleans is to catch "jazz brunch" at a local restaurant; see page 255 for listings.

*(S) Safer area, although caution is always advised.

Traditional New Orleans Jazz

Donna's Bar & Grill. 800 N. Rampart; 596-6914. Smack dab across the street from the new casino. Brass bands play every night from 8:00 P.M.

Famous Door. 411 Bourbon St.; 522-7623.

French Market Weekend Jazz Concerts. St. Philip St. at Dutch Alley; 522-2621.

Fritzel's European Jazz Club. 733 Bourbon St.; 561-0432. Popular with French Quarterite jazz aficionados.

Kemp's. 2720 La Salle between Washington & Fourth; 891-2738. A funky neighborhood, but terrific brass bands.

Little People's Place. 3334 Washington St. (no phone). Kermit Ruffins is a regular in this irregular, petit, early evening Treme jazz joint.

Louis Armstrong Jazz Club. Hotel Meridien, 614 Canal St.; 525-6500. *(S)

Maxwell's Toulouse Cabaret. 615 Toulouse St.; 523-4207. *(S) Good Dixieland.

Palm Court Jazz Cafe. 1204 Decatur St.; 525-0200. Best place in town to hear traditional jazz in comfort.

Pete Fountain's. Hilton Hotel, 2 Poydras; 523-4374. *(S) The club's namesake performs on selected nights.

Preservation Hall. 726 St. Peter St.; 522-2841. No food or drink, no A.C., but a museum for the "real thing."

Snug Harbor. 626 Frenchmen St.; 949-0696. Intimate setting for sitting back and listening to top contemporary jazz performers.

Treme Music Hall. 1601 Ursulines; 596-6942. Up-and-coming brass bands outside the range of most tourists.

Trombone Shorty's. 1533 St. Philip St.; 523-1481. Brass band music for locals in a tough part of town.

Vaughan's Lounge. 800 Lesseps; 947-5562. Take a cab to this rockin' Ninth Ward hotspot.

Vic's Kangaroo Cafe. 636 Tchoupitoulas St.; 524-4329.

Cabaret/Light Jazz

Bayou Bar. Pontchartrain Hotel, 2031 St. Charles Ave.; 524-0581.

Blue Room. Fairmont Hotel, 123 Baronne; 529-4744.

Bombay Club. 830 Conti St.; 586-0972.

Cabaret Lautrec. 1001 Toulouse St.; 586-8000.

Chris Owen's Club. 502 Bourbon St.; 523-6400.

Columns Hotel. 3811 St. Charles Ave.; 899-9308.

Joe's Cozy Corner. 1532 Ursulines St.; 561-9216.

Maxwell's Toulouse Cabaret. 615 Toulouse St.; 523-4207.

Pat O'Brien's. 718 St. Peter St.; 525-4823.

Pete's Pub. Hotel InterContinental, 444 St. Charles Ave.; 525-5566.

Rock/Blues/R&B

Café Brasil. Frenchmen at Chartres St.; 947-9386. Cutting edge bands.

Café Istanbul. 532 Frenchmen St.; 944-4180. Tightly packed crowds, great tunes with a salsa beat.

Carrollton Station. 8140 Willow; 965-9190. Jumpin' boogie bands in a small club.

Hog's Breath Saloon. 339 Chartres St.; 522-1736. Uninhibited crowd, lots of T&A.

House of Blues. 225 Decatur St.; 529-BLUE. Great music, but locally known as "House of Rules" for its heavy-duty security, and "House of Snooze" for the long wait to get in.

Howlin' Wolf. 828 S. Peters; 523-2551. Near the convention center, and catering to a student crowd with alternative rock tastes.

Jimmy's. 8200 Willow; 861-8200. Funk, hip hop, and blues in close quarters.

Lion's Den. 2665 Gravier; 822-3745. Irma Thomas usually performs on weekends to a standing room crowd.

Margaritaville Cafe. 1104 Decatur St.; 592-2565. Jimmy Buffett's local club.

Mid-City Lanes Rock 'n' Bowl. 4133 S. Carrollton Ave.; 482-3133. There's often a line around the block to get in and bowl to the beat.

Muddy Waters. 8301 Oak St. at Dante; 866-7174. Memphis blues to Austin sound.

Old Absinthe House, 400 Bourbon St.; 525-8108. A gut-bucket blues venue.

Pasquallie's. 938 Valence St.; 897-9711. Down-home, cheap, and rockin'.

Rendon Inn. 4501 Eve St.; 822-9858. College and 20-something crowd.

Rhythms. 227 Bourbon St.; 523-3800. Tourists and local band followers.

Rivershack. 3449 River Rd.; 835-6933. Hardcore partyers and tacky ashtrays; blues on the weekends.

Second Line. 216 Bourbon St.; 523-2020. Tourist spot with a good line-up of bands.

Tipitina's. 501 Napoleon Ave.; 895-8477/897-3943. An R&B institution.

Cajun/Zydeco

Michaul's. 840 St. Charles Ave.; 522-5517.*(S)

Mulate's. 201 Julia St.; 522-1492.*(S)

Country

Mudbugs Saloon. 2024 Belle Chasse Hwy.; 392-0202. Top national acts.*(S)

Wild Bar. 441 Bourbon St.; 566-1507. Local honky-tonk patina.

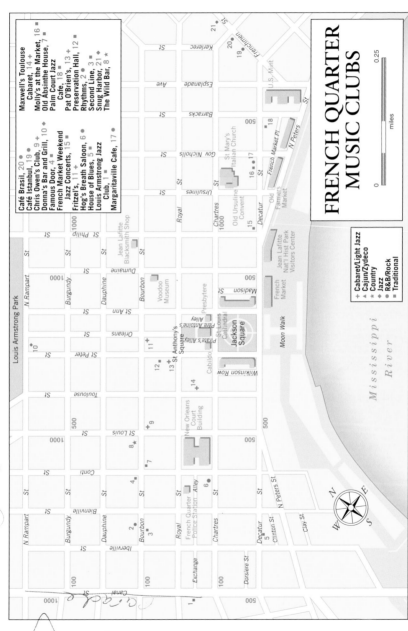

FRENCH QUARTER MUSIC CLUBS

Café Brasil, 20 ●
Café Istanbul, 19 ●
Chris Owen's Club, 9 +
Donna's Bar and Grill, 10 ■
Famous Door, 4 ●
French Market Weekend
  Jazz Concerts, 15 ■
Fritzel's, 11 +
Hog's Breath Saloon, 6 ●
House of Blues, 5 ■
Louis Armstrong Jazz
  Club, 1 ■
Margaritaville Cafe, 17 ◆

Maxwell's Toulouse
  Cabaret, 14 +
Molly's at the Market, 16 ■
Old Absinthe House, 7 ■
Palm Court Jazz
  Cafe, 18 ■
Pat O'Brien's, 13 +
Preservation Hall, 12 ■
Rhythms, 2 ●
Second Line, 3 ■
Snug Harbor, 21 +
The Wild Bar, 8 ★

Legend:
+ Cabaret/Light Jazz
▲ Cajun/Zydeco
● Country
◆ Jazz
★ R&B/Rock
■ Traditional

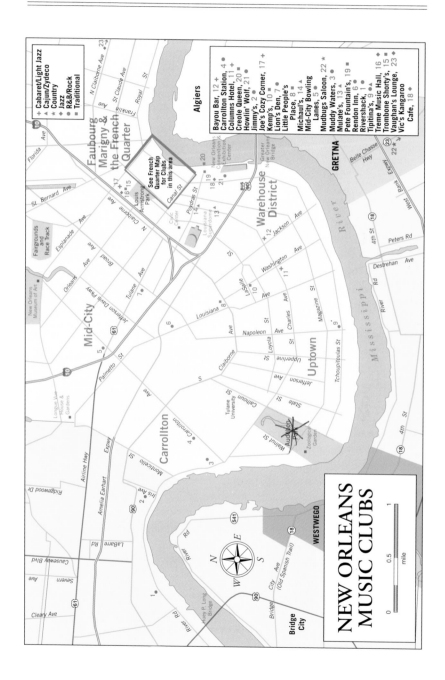

NEW ORLEANS MUSIC CLUBS

Faubourg Marigny & the French Quarter

See French Quarter Map for Clubs in this area

Cabaret/Light Jazz +
Cajun/Zydeco ▲
Country ◆
Jazz •
R&B/Rock ■
Traditional ■

Algiers

Bayou Bar, 12 +
Carrollton Station, 4 •
Columns Hotel, 11 +
Creole Queen, 20 ■
Howlin' Wolf, 21 ■
Jimmy's, 2 •
Joe's Cozy Corner, 17 +
Kemp's, 10 ■
Lion's Den, 7 •
Little People's Place, 8 ■
Michaul's, 14 ▲
Mid-City Bowling Lanes, 5 •
Mudbugs Saloon, 22 *
Muddy Waters, 3 ■
Mulate's, 13 ▲
Pete Fountain's, 19 •
Rendon Inn, 6 ■
Rivershack, 1 •
Tipitina's, 9 ■
Treme Music Hall, 16 +
Trombone Shorty's, 15 ■
Vaughan's Lounge, 23 ◆
Vic's Kangaroo Cafe, 18 +

SPIRITUAL CHURCHES

The Spiritual churches of New Orleans comprise a singular African-American religion which combines elaborate rituals, eclectic beliefs, and highly emotional services. Like other New World religions such as Santería, the Spiritual churches are syncretic, containing elements of Catholicism, Pentecostalism, and voodoo. Although members practice Christian rituals such as Holy Communion and baptism, they also observe unique rites including the "helping hand service" and the "candle drill." Worshippers honor Catholic saints with fervor, but also seek guidance from the American Indian warriors Blackhawk and Sitting Bull. The beliefs, practices, and structures of the church's individual congregations can vary widely. What distinguishes them are prophecy and healing, the two "gifts of the spirits" when worshippers may be filled with the Holy Spirit, as in Pentecostal churches, or "entertain" spirits, as in voodoo and other forms of spiritualism.

The beginnings of New Orleans' Spiritual churches remain something of a mystery. Today's Spiritual practitioners often credit Chicago Spiritual church organizer Mother Leafy Chase with bringing her faith to New Orleans on a 1920 visit, yet the church's beliefs—rooted in popular Catholicism, voodoo, and, to a certain degree, in 1850s American Spiritualism—well predate this woman's arrival. The churches more likely represent a religious movement that developed from the intersection of various belief systems during the latter nineteenth century, and became organized in the 1920s. Earliest records show that women filled the church leadership during the 1920s, suggesting that the Spiritual church was first organized as a women's movement. In the mid-1930s, in an effort to legitimize the religion, men assumed the most important leadership positions. Because membership then as now consisted largely of working-class women, this produced a certain unresolved male-female tension between hierarchy and church members which continues to this day. Nonetheless, members and leaders alike interact informally and familiarly, and many important church leaders are women.

Perhaps because of its diverse origins, the church fosters spiritual individuality, encouraging its members to have a personal relationship with the sacred. As Archbishop Lydia Gilford of the Infant Jesus of Prague Spiritual Church of Christ comments, ". . . So that's what I've been doing: trying to help the small individual, doing what God is telling me to do, and giving the individuals belief in themselves

... He says, 'Where you find two or three assembled, there will be God in the midst.' That means you don't have to have a big crowd to serve God. You've got three: God, you, and me in every church. You see, we feel the presence. That's what I like about it ..."

—Julia Dillon

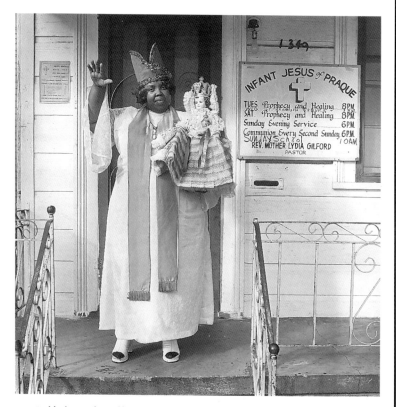

Archbishop Lydia Gilford of the Infant Jesus of Prague Church. (Michael P. Smith)

TASTE OF NEW ORLEANS

NEW ORLEANS CULINARY STYLE, which has been tickling palates for 200 years, was created with a secret recipe that is five parts tradition and one part instinct, marinated in generations of cultural isolation from the rest of the United States, and seasoned with the innate Latin desire to eat well. As the saying goes: "There are two times of day in Louisiana—mealtime and in between."

■ CAST-IRON MELTING POT

The local culinary traditions of Creole cooking, the sophisticated urban cuisine containing such jewels as trout meunière, and Cajun cooking, its country cousin known for its stew-like etouffées, did not evolve directly from French cooking. As internationally known chef Kevin Graham explains it, "The confusing part is that the Creoles felt no qualms about appropriating French names and techniques and then running off with them in another direction. The first time I ordered shallots I got green onions! And the local court bouillon is really an Italian or Spanish fish stew in a red sauce."

Bernard Guste, a direct descendent of Antoine's original proprietor, sees Louisiana's food as being truly Creole; i.e., of Old World parentage in New World surroundings. "Our Oysters Rockefeller is the perfect example of a Creole dish. It was invented in the New World by my ancestor who was applying the classical techniques he learned in France. Cajun cuisine is more of a one-pot, eat-to-survive kind of food that gets a lot of its sizzle from German salt meats and sausages."

Creole and Cajun cuisines have constantly evolved. In each bowl of gumbo served in Louisiana today, there is French roux, African okra, American Indian filé, Spanish peppers, Cajun sausage, and oysters supplied by Yugoslav fishermen, served over Chinese-cultivated Louisiana rice.

Paul Prudhomme, arguably one of the twentieth century's most influential chefs, is fascinated with dishes *with some age on them*: "What I learned is that if a recipe survives from one generation to the next, it serves a need. Some dishes build a fire in your body, and they are the ones worth remembering."

Classic Louisiana food labels from the Sharon Dinkins Collection.

History shows that had it not been for the kindness of the Indians, New Orleans's earliest settlers would have starved to death long before they had an opportunity to invent a cuisine. The Indians introduced the French to a variety of breads and mushy cereals made from corn; various kinds of squash, including the chayote (or "mirliton") and cashaw, which are still popular in Louisiana today; and dried beans. The French sweet tooth was satisfied with syrups made from persimmons, and piqued with chokecherries which were used to flavor smoked meats. Stews were thickened with powdered sassafras, today called filé powder.

Despite the abundance of these Indian foods, the colonists were still Frenchmen to the core and yearned for the flavors they had known at home. In France during this period thousands of new recipes were created and volumes written on the subject of food, and it was fashionable for every nobleman to have not only his own accomplished chef, but also a sauce named for him. Of course, settlers who classified as noblemen were few and far between. The majority of settlers were peasants, convicts, and prostitutes unaccustomed to a particularly luscious diet. Before coming to Louisiana, they had been eating the same thing as their ancestors—boiled, grainy, weevil-laden flour mush mixed with animal blood, carrots, turnips, and even topsoil. Bread was literally the highlight of their diet, and in Louisiana, far from home, that was what was missing. Unfortunately the area around New Orleans was too wet to grow wheat.

It was the Ursuline Sisters, the daughters of French aristocratic and middle-class families, who brought to Louisiana the knowledge of the latest French culinary skills. One of their order, Sister Xavier Herbert, was the first woman pharmacist in the New World. A condition of the contract between the Company of the Indies (the French company which first financed settlement of Louisiana) and the Ursulines was that Sister Xavier would plant an herb garden. The Ursulines taught settlers the benefits of using bay leaf in stews and soups to prevent souring and in flour to prevent weevils; dill for soothing sleep; oregano to reduce swelling; parsley to remove the smell of garlic; shallots for strength; and sage "to put fever to flight."

The letter of the young nun Sister St. Stanislaus, written between 1727 and 1728 to her family in France, provides a glimpse of the diet of the average colonist. She says it consisted of rice cooked in milk, and *sagamite,* a mixture of ground Indian corn boiled in water with butter or bacon fat (the forerunner of grits, no doubt).

GUMBO FILÉ

A gumbo can be a gumbo fevé, filé, or calalou.

Gumbo filé: The filé is a greenish powder usually prepard by the Indians, the degenerated and poor descendants of those proud Chactas Indians praised by Chateaubriand. To make the filé gumbo it is necessary to make a good stew with chicken, ham and oysters. The stew is strongly seasoned with a good quantity of water, and before serving, that aromatic powder is poured in it like a thin rain, and instantly it begins to "filé" (get stringy). That soupe should be eaten like the two others with boiled rice and seasoned with strong pepper.

—Helen d'Aquin Allain, memoir of life in New Orleans, c. 1830s.

Indian woman selling sassafras leaves, from which filé powder is made, in a New Orleans market during the 1890s. (Historic New Orleans Collection)

A Creole of color wearing a tignon, a required head-covering during the slave era that evolved into a fashionable headdress. (Historic New Orleans Collection)

"We [the Sisters] live on wild beef, deer, swans, geese and wild turkeys, rabbits, chickens, ducks, teals, pheasants, partridges, quail and other fowl and game of different kinds. The rivers are teeming with enormous fish unknown in France."

While the Ursulines were teaching the rudiments of French cuisine, the African slaves were on the culinary frontlines, trying to create edible fare from what was available to them. Noted chef Leah Chase, whose restaurant Dooky Chase is the black counterpart of Antoine's, says, "There isn't one famous Creole dish that didn't pass through the hands of a black chef or cook before it came to be written down." These black cooks came from an ancient and sophisticated African culinary tradition. Documents indicate that their African ancestors had traded with the Arab spice merchants since the eleventh century. By the sixteenth century West African farmers were cultivating peanuts, eggplant, corn, yams, garlic, and onions, which they had assimilated into their traditional diet of rice, beans, leafy vegetables, and okra. They prepared their food with various slow cooking methods or roasting. The popular Lenten Creole soup, gumbo z'herbes, came from a West African dish. In some parts of Africa and in Louisiana's Creole society, tradition has it that a new friend will be made for each green used in the soup.

In New Orleans, as in France, having a good cook was crucial to one's social status, and also as in France, a Creole lady did not venture far from the kitchen while the meal was being prepared. Male and female slave cooks were taught to read and write in order to better adapt French recipes to the Louisiana kitchen. An Anglican bishop was once visiting in a proper Creole household in the 1850s. As he sat at the breakfast table, he became fascinated by the loud chants of the servants in the kitchen as they belted out everything from French cane-cutting tunes to Anglican hymns. He puzzled over why these French-speaking Catholics would know one of his hymns. The lady of the house explained that her cook timed her creations, from coffee to breakfast cake to boiled eggs, by the time it took to sing various songs.

Black cooks took the French peasant's thickener, the roux (from the French *roux beurre,* literally "reddish brown butter") and transformed it into a dark, redolent base for many local specialties such as etouffée, gumbo, Creole sauce, grillades, and turtle soup. (Famed French master chef Escoffier scoffed that this type of "peasant" roux was indigestible.) To the roux a cook would add tough pork or fowl too old to lay eggs, a few herbs, lots of onions and garlic, and cook it all day in a cast-iron pot into a tasty, rich stew. Even today a jar of roux made by a master cook is considered a nicer gift than a box of store-bought chocolates.

Creole cuisine might have remained a slightly countrified reproduction of eighteenth-century French cuisine had not the Spanish come to Louisiana. When the first Spanish arrived, they brought with them a bag of tricks they had learned from the Mayans, Aztecs, and Incas. In the fifteenth century, Columbus had brought yams, kidney beans, maize, red pepper, and allspice back to Europe, and later explorers brought back the tomato (known as the "wolf peach," the "apple of the moors," or the "love apple") from Mexico. (While the Italians, Spanish, and Africans adored the tomato, the French and English suspected it might be poison. The French didn't begin to use it until the 1850s, when the Empress Eugénie introduced it at Napoleon III's table.) The Spaniards then reintroduced the pepper and the tomato back to the New World in Louisiana, and began the practice of adding green pepper to sauces and meat dishes in part to slow spoiling. The tomato, when coupled with a roux, became an integral component in Shrimp Creole; the rich gravy for grillades; and the base for court bouillon (pronounced "coo-bo-yon"), a thick seafood stew similar to bouillabaisse. The Spanish paella, a rice and shellfish dish, became the Creole dish jambalaya when *jambon,* or ham, was added to it.

Political turmoil throughout the world brought refugees rich and poor to Louisiana, adding more flavor to Creole culinary style. Aristocrats fleeing the French Revolution brought the newest innovations of eighteenth-century haute cuisine. Planters and free people of color from the West Indies and Santo Domingo introduced fish dishes with Spanish flavors. Sicilians added their talent for rich red gravies and dishes utilizing garlic and bread crumbs, such as stuffed artichokes and eggplant, inspiring the Louisiana dish, stuffed Indian mirliton (also known as a "vegetable pear").

The dishes that evolved from these early experiments are enjoyed to this day. From breakfast, with its calas (rice cakes) or pain perdu (French toast) served with cane syrup, to the after-dinner treats of café brulot and pecan pralines, the inhabitants of New Orleans happily eat a diet uniquely their own. For generations, red beans and rice seasoned with Spanish chaurice or Cajun boudin sausage have been eaten on Monday—wash or market day. Meatless gumbo z'herbes is eaten for Lent; bread pudding with whiskey sauce or pain perdu utilizes every last crumb of French bread; and what would the Christmas turkey be without oyster dressing, or breakfast without chicory café au lait?

Creole cooking was spared from becoming another outgrowth of the aristocratic gastronomy of Europe as a result of the Civil War, which drastically changed the

Fresh produce at the French Market, where Creole cooks have been shopping since the early 1700s.

household economy of the Creoles. Suddenly, the French-speaking Creoles had to take a back seat to the Americans and the carpetbaggers who arrived in the city during Reconstruction. As the Creoles' economic position foundered, they still found pleasure in social dining. They became the "red-beans-and-rice-aristocracy" —well-educated gentry who were "too poor to paint and too proud to white-wash." No matter, the Creoles still loved to eat and entertain. When they couldn't afford the finest meats, they would make a fine gumbo from fresh vegetables and a little leftover chicken or seafood. When the price of ice exceeded their means, they would crush glass and sew it into cheesecloth bags which were floated in pitchers of water to give the tinkle of ice. No matter, guests never suspected their hosts of skimping, because everything was prepared with such care and love that it was always satisfying and delicious.

It is this tradition of hospitality and pride that has fostered and preserved Creole cuisine. Ironically, tourism, which rejuvenated the city's economy in the 1950s, '60s, and early '70s, came close to destroying the flavors that were innately Creole. During this period most Americans were still gastronomic *ingénues*. Local hotel restaurants and popular large eateries were forced to create an Americanized version of the "exotic" local cuisine. Chicory was taken out of the coffee; filé powder was rarely used; murky morsels of crab and oysters were banished from the gumbo; and freshly ground black pepper replaced cayenne pepper in every dish. Creole home cooking and household resourcefulness retreated, staying alive only in homes and in the city's family restaurants.

In the 1970s nouvelle cuisine came and went in local restaurants, without making so much as a ripple on the roux-based sauces of Creole and Cajun home-cooking. By the late 1980s, foodies were hungry for spunky flavors, and suddenly Creole and Cajun cuisines were yanked out of the culinary closet—New Orleans cooking was native American, fervent, ethnic, inexpensive, relatively easy, and far more vital than the sleek, elegant culinary style of the past decade. Finally, after more than 200 years, Creole food achieved culinary respectability—and the rest is just history.

There is a Creole proverb, *"Jardin loin, gombo gaté."* It means that when the garden is far, the gumbo is spoiled. Two of the four top agricultural money-makers in Louisiana are edible crops—rice and sugarcane. There are over a hundred alligator farms in southern Louisiana. Add to this the fact that Louisiana is the world's number one producer of crawfish, and that catfish ranks just behind crawfish as the state's top aquaculture product. Now note that the number one vegetable crop is sweet potatoes. Louisiana's Creole tomatoes and Ponchatoula strawberries are about the best varieties in the world. That will give you an idea of the bases for this cuisine's best dishes.

To eat a meal in New Orleans today is to dive head first into tradition, flavor, and cholesterol. It is a city where food is fried to perfection in lard, where French-fried potato po-boys still appear on some menus, and where sugar, liquor, and coffee —the region's three favorite stimulants—can be obtained in one glorious after dinner concoction: café brulot. About the only nod to healthy eating comes when a local cleanses his palate with iceberg lettuce swimming in rémoulade sauce, or runs a lap or two around Audubon Park between a double order of Café du Monde beignets and a slab of Camellia Grill pecan pie.

■ CLASSIC CREOLE RESTAURANT

Today, more than 150 years since its founding, Antoine's is America's oldest restaurant under single-family ownership. One of the main reasons for its longevity is the power of the New Orleans palate. In the rest of America, a dish may become famous for its flavor; in New Orleans it only achieves greatness when it has fervor. New Orleanians cherish those dishes that prod the subconscious, bringing back memories of savory feasts. Antoine's is a living culinary museum. Devoted third- and fourth-generation patrons not only eat at their great grandparents' favorite table, but also enjoy the same Creole dishes created centuries ago in New Orleans. Not long ago, the late Helen Hayes requested that Bernard Guste, the great grandson of the founder, reconstruct the dinner that his grandfather, Jules Alciatore, had created for the actress in 1918. A bit of research produced the recipe for the orange brûlot that brought tears of pleasure to Mrs. Hayes's eyes.

Cecil B. DeMille once exclaimed, "Many a chef has created a dish, but only God could have cooked that fish." Supposedly he was referring to Antoine's *Pompano en Papillote* which had been created to honor a visiting French balloonist: the chef prepared the fish in a paper bag that was fashioned to resemble the fellow's magnificent balloon.

Antoine's menu has changed little since the 1840s. It is still written in French, and the dishes still reflect the preferences of the mid-nineteenth-century palate for sweet sauces and heavier food. The staff still dims the lights in the restaurant when *Café Brulot Diabolique* and *Crêpes Suzettes* are served, so that patrons can see the

Bernard Guste (right), owner of Antoine's restaurant and great grandson of the founder, stands with Samuel le Blanc, who is retiring after 50 years of service. (Photo courtesy of Antoine's Restaurant)

azure flames of the ignited brandy. The private library at Antoine's contains over 400 cookbooks as well as books on wine and other related subjects; some of the volumes are over 250 years old, with one dating back to 1659.

In the back Dining Room Annex, five American Presidents—Hoover, Coolidge, Taft, and both Roosevelts (Carter, Nixon, Reagan, Ford and Clinton have also eaten at Antoine's, but not while they were in office)—and two British Princesses—Princess Margaret and Princess Anne—have dined, as well as numerous celebrities whose photos grace the walls. The mirrored front room of Antoine's is considered to be a social no-man's land by many locals, but since it is also the "No Smoking" area, some prefer enjoying its mirrors and gilt to sitting in the darker back room, rubbing elbows with the elite amid clouds of tobacco smoke.

ALLIGATOR RIPPLES

*D*o you know why that alligator kept on attacking the man who was working on the plumbing under his house in Metairie—that alligator who had that guy by the leg and wouldn't let go—? 'Cause the man was crouched down under that peer-and-beam house and he just couldn't stand up. Peer-and-beam houses in New Orleans—at least most of them—are just high enough off the ground for you to crawl under and play, or do some plumbing or electric work or something like that. I expect that when the gator sees you crouched low to the ground, stooping on a log, or all curled up in a ball, he can't see you've got two long legs and maybe are five to six feet tall. He's looking down on you—not straight up. He's lookin' at the silhouette of dinner and, for sure, if he's hungry, he's gonna check you out—like the one that had that man by the leg and wouldn't let go.

continues

PHOTO BY MICHAEL P. SMITH

One day my daughter Josephine (who was about seven when this happened) and I went for a walk to go fishing for brim and sacalait down the old road by Half Moon Lake. We walked about a mile with worms, poles, and buckets way in the back where nobody usually goes. There's a good bank to fish from there. We fished, moving around the bank and around the far corner of the lake for maybe an hour or so, and caught a few blue gills perch and kept them alive in a bucket of water. Josie liked watching them swim. During the spawn they get so colorful—blue, orange, and green . . . look like tropical fish.

After a while, Josie and I got tired of moving around and the fishing got slow, so I sat crouched down on the ground with my back against this fallen-down tree on the bank of the lake. I laid my pole on the ground next to me where I could reach it if I got a bite. Josie sat and rested on the top of the log on the side of me. She looked like a little fur ball with her long hair shining in the sun behind her.

All the while we were fishing we were watching other things—like a big blue heron, white egrets, mosquito hawks, and regular hawks (the bird kind), and some alligators in the lake far away. The alligators were treading water still as stumps— they were almost on the other side of the lake. After 10 minutes or so of sitting down we noticed at least four alligators now in the middle of the lake closer to us. (It seems like an alligator can move in any direction with very little effort and make absolutely no disturbance in its surroundings.) I've seen a 12-foot alligator—which must weigh 700 pounds—treading water with head and back almost fully exposed on the surface of the water—then completely submerge itself and disappear without making the slightest ripple in smooth-as-glass water.

Josie and I counted the gators again. There were now five and getting nearer. In a matter of minutes we were counting eight alligators and the closest one was 20 to 30 feet from us. Josie asked me, "Daddy, how close will they get?" At first I didn't want to frighten her, but I decided she'd better know that to those alligators the way we were crouched we looked like their favorite appetizer and main dish—dinner for eight.

They treaded water even closer and Josie suggested that we stand up and show them how tall we were. Right away the gators eased off and we decided it was time to go back to the camp and get a bite to eat.

—Story told by Bernard Guste, owner of Antoine's restaurant, 1993

■ CREOLE AND CAJUN CULINARY LEGACIES

Cajun specialties are indicated with a ↶

Andouille. ↶ ("Ahn-doo-we") A fat, sassy country sausage containing hog stomach, or "chitterlings." Often used in jambalaya and gumbo, and as an accompaniment to red beans and rice.

Beer. Local beer brands are another point of honor. Many people won't consider serving boiled crawfish without a Dixie longneck, while others swear by Turbo Dog, Voodoo, or Abita Beer.

Beignet. ("Been-yay") Diamond-shaped, raised doughnuts without the hole which are doused in powdered sugar.

Bisque. ↶ ("Bisk") A rich, spicy roux-based soup with crawfish, oysters, or shrimp.

Boudin. ↶ ("Boo-dan") A spicy Cajun sausage. *Boudin blanc* is the pork-and-rice-dressing sausage generally available in the cooler months; *boudin rouge* is the blood sausage made in Cajun country.

Bread Pudding. French bread soaked in a custard and baked.

Café au Lait. ("Caffy-oh-lay") Chicory coffee served with steaming milk. The average American drinks 1.5 cups of coffee a day; New Orleanians consume 3.2 cups a day. What sets New Orleans coffee apart from that of the rest is the addition of chicory, which produces a rich cup of coffee with the same consistency but only half the caffeine of full-bodied crude. Chicory is the easily grown relative of the dandelion whose young leaves are known as endive. The root resembles that of the dandelion and when dried, roasted, and ground, produces a deep brown, syrupy beverage with an almost peppery tang that doesn't taste at all like coffee. Café au lait (literally coffee with milk) is served as Creoles like it 24 hours a day, seven days a week at Café du Monde, between Jackson Square and the river.

Kaldi's Coffee Museum and Coffeehouse is an excellent place to learn about the evolution of coffee. Located at 914 Decatur Street in the French Quarter, the old bank building is dominated by a two-story mural of Kaldi, the legendary North African goatherd who first touted the rejuvenating effects of coffee.

Calas. Fried, sweet, rice cakes.

Court Bouillon. ("Coo-bo-yon") A fish stew in an authoritative red sauce.

Crawfish. (never "cray-fish") These little spicy toy lobsters are best eaten spread out on newspaper on a picnic table. Sometimes called "mudbugs."

Crème Caramel. A custard similar to flan.

Dirty Rice. No, this is not the *nom de plume* that local author Anne Rice uses when she publishes erotica. It is a rice dish made with liver and spices, and is similar to a rice dressing.

Eggs Sardou. Artichoke hearts, poached eggs, spinach, hollandaise sauce. (At Brennan's they sell 750,000 poached eggs a year due to the popularity of this and their other brunch egg dishes, such as Eggs Benedict.)

Old coffee label. (Sharon Dinkins Collection)

Crawfish are an important ingredient in many Cajun and Creole dishes.

Etouffée. ☞ ("Ay-too-fay") A thick tomato-based sauce usually containing either shrimp or crawfish.

French Bread. Many of the finest restaurants in town continue to be as persnickety about the staff of life as the early French settlers. Those crusty small loaves of hot French bread, called "gigitts," come from Angelo Gendusa's at 1801 North Rampart.

Filé. The mature green leaves of the sassafras tree, which contain a mucilaginous substance, are dried and powdered to produce this aromatic thickening agent. In the days when flour was more scarce than truffles, this substance became essential in turning a weak stock into a hearty soup. Filé must only be added to gumbo after the soup has been removed from the heat, and stirred in a few minutes before serving. If the soup should boil with filé, it becomes stringy and inedible.

Garlic. The Creole cook believes what Balzac said about garlic, "even the chef should be rubbed with it." Local folk wisdom has always known that garlic can prevent both heart and vampire attacks, as well as cure digestive disorders.

Grillades. ("gree-yodds") A roux-based beef-and-tomato gravy with thin slices of beef or veal.

Gumbo. A murky roux-based spicy soup that can contain a variety of shellfish, okra, poultry, and/or sausage, depending on the mood of the cook.

Hurricane. During such events as the Sugar Bowl, Mardi Gras, and the Super Bowl, the French Quarter takes on a particularly cloying, fruity smell generated by the thousands of these rose-colored rum punches. They are served in souvenir glasses that will later be filled with Mardi Gras beads, decorating dorm rooms from San Diego to New Rochelle. The beverage has all the punch of a blow on the head with a baseball bat, with a similar day-after result.

Hush Puppies. A seasoned, fried, cornmeal ball used to accompany fried seafood.

Jambalaya. ("Jam-bul-eye-a") A rice-based dish similar to paella, but heavier on the local sausage and poultry.

Mint Julep. The French totally ignored mint as an herb. The Spanish (who got the herb from the Arabs) are thought to have brought the passion for mint tea to the sultry South. The name of the plant comes from a Greek myth that would do a Tennessee Williams's julep-guzzlin' heroine proud. It seems that Pluto became enamored with a wood nymph named Menthe, which greatly perplexed his beloved Persephone, the Goddess of Spring. Persephone knew that murdering her rival would push Menthe right back into Pluto's arms in the underworld. Thus, she transformed Menthe into a lowly plant doomed to be trampled underfoot. And as fate would have it, the fragrance of Menthe's spirit rose to haunt each time the plant was trod upon.

Mirliton. ("mill-a-ton") A pear-shaped vegetable known also as chayote, similar in taste to zucchini. It is generally served stuffed with bread crumbs and seafood.

Muffuletta. A round stormdrain-sized Italian sandwich stuffed with Italian meats and cheeses and liberally doused with garlicky olive salad. Try Progress Grocery, Central Grocery, or The Napoleon House. Bayou Ridge makes a luscious muffuletta pizza.

Okra. Most New Orleanians aren't born liking okra. Next to the first raw oyster, eating that first slimy piece of okra is a sort of culinary rite of passage for Louisiana children. Okra is a mucilaginous pod that grows on a tall, ornamental tropical annual of the hibiscus family, a cousin of the cotton plant. Legend has it that okra was brought to the New World by slaves who hid the seeds in their hair and ears. During the warm months when okra is in season, it replaces Indian filé powder as the thickening agent in gumbo. Okra was originally known as "kingcombo;" hence, "gumbo."

DESERAN GUMBO

This recipe yields a hearty gumbo for 6.

½ cup flour
½ cup butter
1½ cup chopped celery
2 cup chopped onion
1½ cup chopped green pepper
2 tsp minced garlic
¼ cup chopped fresh parsley

3 cups fresh or frozen okra, thinly sliced
1½ cup chopped fresh tomato
6 cup cold water

2 tsp lemon juice
2½ tsp salt
¾ tsp black pepper
1 tsp dried thyme
1 bay leaf
2 tsp cayenne (hot!)

1 lb. peeled shrimp
1 pint lump crabmeat

Optional:
1 pint oysters
4 gumbo crabs

Before beginning the roux, chop all of the vegetables. Then, in a heavy pan, slowly melt the butter (or, if you prefer, heat vegetable oil). Gradually add the flour, stirring constantly. Cook over medium heat, always stirring to avoid burning, until a medium brown roux is formed (the color of hazelnuts or pecans). This will take approximately 20 minutes.

Once the roux is medium brown, add the celery, onion, green pepper, garlic, and parsley. Stir quickly, then lower the heat, cover, and cook about 10 minutes.

Meanwhile, in a smaller pan, sauté the sliced okra in 2 tsp. butter until lightly browned (to eliminate its stringiness). Add this to the other vegetables and cook, covered, 10 minutes more.

Slowly stir the water into this vegetable mixture. Add the tomatoes, half of the shrimp, the crab, and seasonings (for a cooler gumbo, decrease the amount of cayenne). Bring the mixture to a boil, lower heat, cover, and simmer for one hour. Add the remaining shrimp and oysters. Traditionally: Cook covered over low heat for 15 minutes more. A more modern version: cook 5 minutes. The gumbo should be thicker than soup, with dark, rich flavors.

Serve over rice in bowls.

Oysters. There are about 50 oyster bars in New Orleans. In the 1930s U.S. Senator Huey P. Long included in his anti-Roosevelt-sponsored-legislation filibuster the recipe for fried oysters. Long concluded, "There is no telling how many lives have been lost by not knowing how to fry oysters, but serving them as an undigestible food. Many times we hear of some man who was supposed to have had an acute attack of indigestion or cerebral hemorrhage or heart failure, and the chances are the only thing that was the matter was that he had swallowed some improperly cooked oysters." Of course, New Orleanians like cooked oyster dishes too, such as fried oysters and Oysters Rockefeller.

An oyster specialty and crab cakes as served in the Grill Room at the
Windsor Court Hotel. (Photo courtesy of the Windsor Court Hotel)

Pain Perdu. ("Pan pairdo") This Creole version of French toast is made with French bread.

Pepper. There is an old Creole proverb, "Misery makes the monkey eat red pepper," which perhaps holds a clue as to why the use of hot peppers gained such a foothold in this region of the country. The Cajuns were economically, culturally, and geographically cut off from the more cosmopolitan areas.

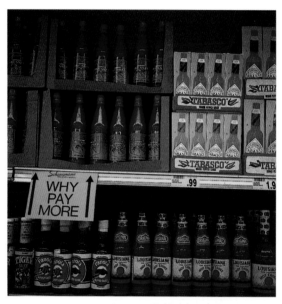

Hot sauces are the spice of life in New Orleans.

From the Spanish period onward, each household, no matter how poor, could easily grow one or two varieties of hot peppers. The flavors of food (be it anything from old raccoon meat to "mud bugs," or crawfish) were greatly enhanced by the addition of a little salt and a dose of red pepper. Pepper-eating (both pickled and raw varieties) remains a popular south Louisiana barroom sport.

If the Spanish influence on southern Louisiana cuisine was ever in danger of fading, the trend was reversed when hundreds of Louisiana boys went off to fight the war with Mexico in the mid-nineteenth century and returned home with a renewed passion for the pepper. One such man brought the McIlhenny family of Avery Island some special Mexican pepper seeds. The result was Tabasco sauce, which sells over 50 million bottles annually all over the world; other hot sauce brands include Cajun Chef, Crystal, Louisiana Red Hot Sauce, and Louisiana Gold—one of the hottest on the market.

Po-Boys. A sandwich served on French bread. To be served "dressed" means with mayo, lettuce, and tomato. Common fillings include ham, fried oysters, meatballs, or roast beef.

Pommes de Terre Soufflée. Puffed, twice-fried potatoes.

Pralines. ("Praw-leens") A sugar-and-pecan candy so sweet it will make your fillings itch.

Ramos Gin Fizz. Gin, orange water, lime juice, lemon juice, cream, egg white, powdered sugar, and ice. Huey Long's favorite cocktail.

Red Beans and Rice. The late Louis Armstrong used to sign all of his letters "red beans and ricely yours." The dish of beans and rice couldn't be simpler, but in the hands of a good cook they become a gloriously satisfying blend of the flavors of smoked pork, onions, garlic, and hot sauce.

Rémoulade Sauce. ("Rum-a-laad") A spicy, mustard-based, Creole cocktail sauce for seafood.

Roman Candy. One of the fixtures of the Uptown neighborhood is the Roman Candy Man. The mule-drawn white-and-red-painted wagon is now the base of operations for the founder's grandson, Sam Cortese to sell the toffee-like confection. Two places where he can be found are on St. Charles Avenue between Audubon Park and Tulane University, and near Spanish Plaza at the foot of Canal Street by the River, close to the Aquarium.

Root Beer. The Root Beer Institute of America reports that New Orleanians drink twice as much as other Americans. Until the last generation, there were 18 brands for sale in local stores and eateries. Nowadays Barq's is the brew of choice.

Sauce Piquante. ("Pee-cont") The local spicy version of an Italian red gravy.

Sazerac. Bourbon and bitters. Reputed to be the first cocktail.

Shrimp Creole. Shrimp mixed with a lusty red sauce with onions, garlic, and bell pepper.

Snow Ball. This ice and flavored syrup concoction makes the weather bearable. Some people like to buy one the size of a large bucket of popcorn, take it home, douse it with rum, and suck on it all day.

Tasso. A red-pepper-seasoned version of smoked ham.

Trout Meunière. A pan-fried filet of trout served under a rich butter sauce.

Turtle Soup. A New Orleans tradition, actually often made with alligator.

CULINARY TIMELINE

1699 Sieur de Bienville and Sieur d'Iberville eat their first meal in Louisiana. They are said to have dined on buffalo.

1751 First sugarcane is introduced by Jesuits from Santo Domingo.

1791 First recorded restaurant in New Orleans, Café des Emigrés, becomes a popular meeting place for exiles from uprisings in the Indies.

1800s Creole businessmen begin conducting much of their business in the local "exchanges" or coffeehouses.

1820 The owner-chef of the Tremoulet Hotel in the French Quarter invents meunière sauce.

1827 Antoine Alciatore brings the secret recipe for Pommes de Terre Soufflée to the Western Hemisphere.

1840 Antoine's restaurant opens at 50 St. Louis Street.

1868 McIlhenny Company begins production of Tabasco sauce.

1860s Café du Monde founded.

1880 Commander's Palace opens.

1881 La Louisiana restaurant is opened by a member of Antoine Alciatore's family.

1899 Jules Alciatore invents "Oysters à la Rockefeller." Since that day over 18 million Oysters Rockefeller have been served at Antoine's.

1907 Dixie beer makes its debut.

1908 Eggs Sardou, the city's first famous brunch dish, is created by Jules Alciatore at Antoine's, and named for his guest, the French playwright Victorien Sardou.

1918 Arnaud's Restaurant is founded by "Count" Arnaud Cazenave.

1920s Huey P. "Kingfish" Long's favorite drink, the Ramos Gin Fizz, is invented at the Stag Saloon on Gravier Street.

1937 Pat O'Brien's "Hurricane" is invented when the bar owner overbuys rum and a case of hurricane-shade-shaped glasses.

1941 Edgar and Emily Chase establish the famed eatery Dooky Chase.

1955 The Brennan family moves their Bourbon Street restaurant to its permanent location at 417 Royal.

■ RECOMMENDED NEW ORLEANS RESTAURANTS

Don't be fooled into thinking that any regular mortal can eat three meals a day in New Orleans and live to tell the tale. Take it from one who knows: plan one pull-out-all-the-stops meal a day, take one long walk, an even longer nap, and then buy a local cookbook so that you can create the dishes you missed in your own kitchen. **Note:** Because the restaurant business is ever-changing, please call the restaurants to check on days and hours before embarking on your food odyssey. **Attire:** In some of the nicer restaurants, shorts are not considered acceptable despite outrageous degrees of humidity. Call to see if coat and tie are required.

——— ⅋ ———

Prices (per person, not including drinks and tip):
$ = under $10; $$ = $10-20; $$$ = $20-30; $$$$ = over $30

——— ⅋ ———

The Cajun Restaurant Myth: The countrified, hearty cuisine of the Cajuns is a mainstay in most New Orleans homes and restaurants. A pure Cajun restaurant in the city, however, is viewed more as a hook for tourists than an ethnic dining experience. Antoine's, noted for its classic Creole recipes, offers one of the best Cajun-style crawfish bisques around. So when Cajun food is what you have a hankerin' for, go to a Creole restaurant and ask your waiter to recommend Cajun dishes on the menu.

Traditional Creole with Flair

Antoine's. 713 St. Louis St.; 581-4422
Owned by the same family for five generations, Antoine's offers over 130 dishes on its vintage turn of the century French menu. Some of the best dishes include the pommes de terre soufflée, and a combination of oyster dishes—Rockefeller, Foch, and Bienville—followed by a crème caramel make for one of the finest lunches or dinners in town. $$$$

Arnaud's. 813 Bienville St.; 523-5433
Jackets are required in this large (six public dining rooms, 12 private) French Quarter institution. Shrimp Arnaud in a tart remoulade sauce, trout meunièr, veal Wohl, crème brûlée, and cinnamony bread pudding are all delightful. (See "Jazz Brunch Hotspots," p. 255.) $$$$

Commander's Palace. 1427 Washington Ave.; 899-8221
Excellent food and service keep this restaurant's 12 dining rooms and cocktail courtyard full seven days a week with locals and tourists. Luncheon specials are always delicious and well-priced. Trout with pecans, fish Grieg and the crab and softshell crab dishes

shouldn't be missed. For dessert, crème brûlée, lemon crêpes, and bread pudding soufflé are tops. (See also "Breakfast," p. 251, and "Jazz Brunch Hotspots," p. 255.) **$$$-$$$$**

Dooky Chase. 2301 Orleans Ave.; 821-2294
Elegant black Creole food. The crabmeat Farci, the shrimp Clemenceau, the fried catfish, the sweet potatoes, and the bread pudding are all exceptional. **$$**

Galatoire's. 209 Bourbon St.; 525-2021
Oysters en brochette, the Godchaux salad (not on the 6-page menu), trout almandine or with crabmeat, and the crabmeat Yvonne are some of the finest seafood dishes to be found in the city. Best time to go is between 1:30 and 4:00 P.M. on a Saturday or Sunday. **$$$**

Neighborhood Soul

To experience New Orleans truly, it is essential to escape from uncomfortable shoes and snooty headwaiters, and git down with some real cholesterol-laced, carbohydrate-friendly food.

Cafe Atchafalaya. 901 Louisiana Ave.; 891-5271
On the fringe of the Irish Channel, a few feet from the Garden District, this is a "nothing-but-plain-food," bare formica top neighborhood restaurant. It is the brainchild of a feisty lady from the Mississippi Delta who is about as unpretentious as they come. Her daily specials are written on a board on the wall. The vegetable plate is great after a hard night (Not healthy, California-style veggies: southern greens cooked with pork, fried green tomatoes, black-eyed peas, lima beans, etc.). Other home cooking regulars include beef brisket and chicken and dumplings; also try a fruit cobbler and iced tea. **$**

Dunbar's. 4927 Freret St.; 899-0734
Five minutes away is another lady's personal statement of home cookin'. Guests who nestle into the red-tufted banquettes are in for a hard time, having to decide between some of the best fried chicken in the city, knock-your-socks-off mustard greens, fantastic red beans and rice, and bell peppers stuffed with shrimp and meat. **$-$$**

Jayde's Jazzy Soulfood Joint. 2523 Perdido St.; 822-6814
The new hotspot for all manner of greens and down-home seafood. Located in a former crack house. **$**

K-Paul's Louisiana Kitchen. 416 Chartres St.; 524-7394
K-Paul's chef, Paul Prudhomme, has made Cajun cuisine famous beyond its Louisiana borders. A recent New Orleans landmark known mainly for its blackened fish, it also serves creative gumbos, sweet potato-pecan pie, and jalapeño-laced martinis served in canning jars. Its national recognition has made K-Paul's extremely popular with tourists. Expect to wait in a long line due to the "no reservation" policy, and to be seated communally. **$$$**

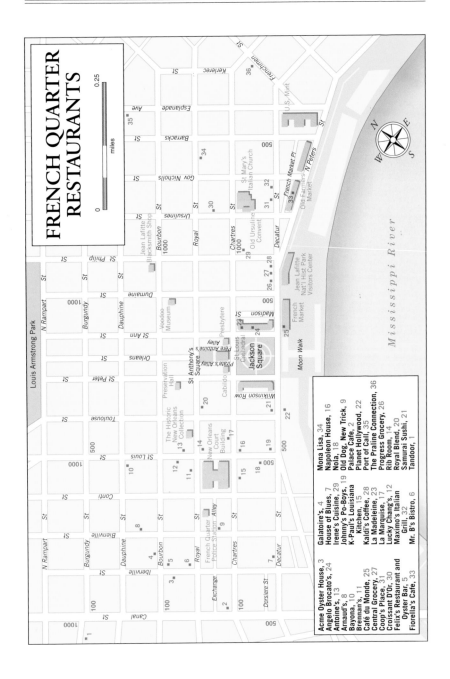

FRENCH QUARTER RESTAURANTS

Acme Oyster House, 3
Angelo Brocato's, 24
Antoine's, 13
Arnaud's, 8
Bayona, 10
Brennan's, 11
Café du Monde, 25
Central Grocery, 27
Coop's Place, 31
Croissant D'Or, 30
Felix's Restaurant and
Oyster Bar, 5
Fiorella's Cafe, 33

Galatoire's, 4
House of Blues, 7
Irene's Cuisine, 29
Johnny's Po-Boys, 19
K-Paul's Louisiana
Kitchen, 15
Kaldi's Coffee, 28
La Madeleine, 23
La Marquise, 17
Lucky Chang's, 12
Maximo's Italian
Grill, 32
Mr. B's Bistro, 6

Mona Lisa, 34
Napoleon House, 16
Nola, 18
Old Dog, New Trick, 9
Palace Cafe, 2
Planet Hollywood, 22
Port of Call, 35
The Praline Connection, 36
Progress Grocery, 26
Rib Room, 14
Royal Blend, 20
Samurai Sushi, 21
Tandoor, 1

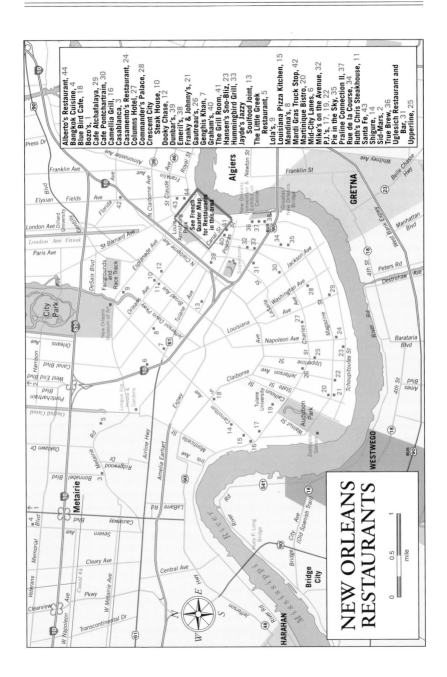

NEW ORLEANS RESTAURANTS

Alberto's Restaurant, 44
Bangkok Cuisine, 4
Blue Bird Cafe, 18
Bozo's, 1
Cafe Atchafalaya, 29
Cafe Pontchartrain, 30
Camellia Grill, 16
Casablanca, 3
Casamento's Restaurant, 24
Columns Hotel, 27
Commander's Palace, 28
Crescent City
  Steak House, 10
Dooky Chase, 12
Dunbar's, 39
Emeril's, 38
Franky & Johnny's, 21
Gautreau's, 26
Genghis Khan, 7
Graham's, 40
The Grill Room, 41
Hansen's Sno-Bliz, 23
Hummingbird Grill, 33
Jayde's Jazzy
  Soulfood Joint, 13
The Little Greek
  Restaurant, 5
Lola's, 9
Louisiana Pizza Kitchen, 15
Mandina's, 8
Mardi Gras Truck Stop, 42
Martinique Bistro, 20
Mid-City Lanes, 6
Mike's on the Avenue, 32
P.J.'s, 17, 19, 22
Pie in the Sky, 35
Praline Connection II, 37
Rue de la Course, 34
Ruth's Chris Steakhouse, 11
Santa Fe, 43
Shigure, 14
Sid-Mar's, 2
True Brew, 36
Uglesich Restaurant and
  Bar, 31
Uperline, 25

Mandina's. 3800 Canal St.; 482-9179
This Mid-City spot is famed for its stiff drinks, seafood, Italian food, and red beans. Waiters wear white coats; the patrons are generally more casual. **$$**

Praline Connection. 542 Frenchmen; 943-3934
Cool soul; white, lima, or red beans; stewed or fried chicken; and fantastic pralines. Outside the French Quarter is **Praline Connection II Gospel & Blues Hall** (901-907 S. Peters; 523-3973). Come here, lunch or dinner, for jambalaya, gumbo, and red beans and rice. Praline Connection II also hosts a jazz brunch. (See "Jazz Brunch Hotspots," p. 255.) **$-$$**

Shellfish—Crabs, Crawfish, Shrimp, and Oysters

Acme Oyster House. 724 Iberville St.; 522-5973
The oyster shuckers here move quickly, the oysters are fat and salty, and the place has the ambiance of a typical, slightly unkempt, local oyster house. **$$**

Bozo's. 3117 21st St. (at Causeway Blvd.); 831-8666
Fabulous boiled and fried seafood. Everything is cooked to order. **$**

Casamento's Restaurant. 4300 Magazine; 895-9761
Closed June through August. Best fried and raw oysters in the city. The tile-lined walls are immaculate. **$**

Portia's Restaurant No. 2 in 1972. (Michael P. Smith)

Felix's Restaurant and Oyster Bar. 739 Iberville St.; 522-4440
A top-of-the- line, family-style, unpretentious seafood house. The oyster shuckers all seem to be characters worthy of starring roles on a sit-com, and the cooked oyster and crab dishes are home-style. **$$**

Franky & Johnny's. 321 Arabella; 899-9146
Good timin', good drinkin' and good ol' neighborhood-style seafood. The turtle soup and crawfish dishes are terrific. **$**

Sid-Mars. 1824 Orpheum, Bucktown near the lakefront; 831-9541
A meal of boiled crabs on the screen porch in this small fishing enclave is a trip back to a calmer era. **$-$$**

Uglesich Restaurant & Bar. 1238 Baronne; 523-8571
Fried seafood po-boys, plate lunches, real French fries, onion rings, and raw oysters all add to the already pithy ambiance of a hopping, Old World neighborhood eatery. **$**

Meat

Crescent City Steak House. 1001 N. Broad; 821-3271
The 1940s atmosphere and old-style steakhouse booths are the ideal backdrop for butter broiled beef. **$$$**

The Rib Room. Royal Orleans Hotel, 621 St. Louis; 529-7045
The focal point of this elegant dining room is a wall filled with rotisseries where roasts turn on a spit. The rib roast is crusty and succulent, and the chocolate mousse is a must for chocoholics. **$$$$**

Ruth's Chris Steakhouse. 711 N. Broad; 486-0810
Metairie: 3633 Veterans Blvd.; 888-3600
When only a well-aged, prime slab of beef will do, Chris's, that testosterone-affirmative home-away-from-the-car-phone for politicos and sports fans, serves the best steak to be found east of Fort Worth. Favorites include the filet or porterhouse sizzling in butter. Salads, creamed spinach, au gratin vegetables, and thick fried or shoestring potatoes are meals in themselves. Peppermint stick ice cream is the perfect complement for such gustatory decadence. **$$$$**

Grand Bistro

Each year a new crop of trendy eateries makes its debut. First there is a splash, then a buzz, long lines, and fights over who gets a table; then service gets shaky and the crowd shifts to a new spot. The restaurants in this category are those that have kept up with the local crowd for over a year. Reservations are highly recommended.

Bayona. 430 Dauphine St.; 525-4455
Chef Susan Spicer has combined her talent and elegant style to create a terrific menu for her own intimate restaurant. From garlic soup to a black beans and shrimp appetizer, her culinary style is clever, not overbearing. **$$$**

Emeril's. 800 Tchoupitoulas St.; 528-9393
Chef Lagasse wows diners with his own
food laboratory in the Warehouse District using scratch ingredients such as
herbs, cheeses, and fresh produce culled
from his network of farmers. Try ordering six appetizers, finishing off with Creole cream cheese cake. $$$

Gautreau's. 1728 Soniat St.; 899-7397
American-Creole cuisine at its finest.
Dinner only. $$$

Graham's. In the Pelham Hotel, 200 Magazine St.; 524-9678
Chef Kevin Graham, formerly of the
Windsor Court, serves his signature
lump crabmeat cakes, coffee and chicory lacquered duck, and sour lemon tart
at his own sophisticated bistro. The organic salads are noteworthy, as is the
noise level in the stark decor. $$$-$$$$

Grill Room at the Windsor Court. 300
Gravier; 522-1992
Hailed as one of the finest hotel dining
rooms in the country, this is the spot to
hold a perfect knock-your-socks-off
corporate dinner. The food is both innovative and scrumptious. Ingredients
are the best to be found anywhere in
the world. $$$

Mike's on the Avenue. In the Lafayette
Hotel, 628 St. Charles Ave.; 523-1709
In a town known for its own regional
style, Mike's has made quite a hit among
those seeking something different. Here
the culinary styles of the Orient, American Southwest, France, and Italy are all
borrowed, creating a clever, visually appealing fare. $$$

*Uglesich's simplicity contrasts with the elegance of Galatoire's (right)—two
restaurants known for their excellent food.*

'oyal St.; 523-2078
f Commander's
...., jr., has remained fresh and innovative since it opened in 1979. Sample the coconut- and beer-battered shrimp, any of the items from the grill, or pasta jambalaya, followed by killer chocolate cake or a custardy bread pudding. $$$

Nola. 534 St. Louis; 522-6652.
A "Baby Emeril's" sizzling with conversation and lively plates of rich food. $$$-$$$$

Palace Cafe. 605 Canal St.; 523-1661.
The chicken with garlic mashed potatoes, and custardy bread pudding with white chocolate sauce are sinfully delicious. This is another Brennan family restaurant. *(See also* "Jazz Brunch Hotspots.") $$$

Upperline. 1431 Upperline St.; 891-9822
Nestled Uptown is this charming cozy bistro, whose culinary style begins with local products and is elevated with Latin, Anglo-Indian, and classic French cooking techniques. All of the crispy duck dishes are perfection, though the one with ginger peach sauce edges out the others. $$$

Late Night

Camellia Grill. 626 S. Carrollton; 866-9573
The lights are bright enough to elicit a confession and there is often a wait for one of the 29 stools, but the food is worth it. Omelets (especially the potato and onion with chili and cheese on the top), hamburgers, pecan waffles, and pecan pie are all close to the best in the world. The beverage of choice is the mocha freeze. Avoid the coffee, unless you happen to like the coffee in Kansas. Clientele includes university types, ballgoers, and after-rounds physicians. $$

Coop's Place. 1109 Decatur; 525-9053
Back of the Quarter neighborhood bar and pool hall with great omelettes and Cajun specialties. $

House of Blues. 225 Decatur; 529-BLUE
Enjoy jazz and R&B as well as an extensive menu of dolled-up soul food. (See "Jazz Brunch Hotspots," p. 255.) $$

Hummingbird Grill. 804 St. Charles Ave.; 561-9229
In spite of the fact that the "Hummer" is a favorite dingy hang-out for the downtrodden, cops, and patrons with imaginary friends, the food is homestyle and yummy. The breakfasts, the thick slabs of cornbread, and the hamburgers are all good. $

Mardi Gras Truck Stop. 2401 Elysian Fields Ave.; 945-1000
Some of the best grillades and grits in town; the crawfish dishes are also worth a try. $

Maximo's Italian Grill. 1117 Decatur; 586-8883
Innovative northern Italian cuisine in a chic bistro. $$-$$$

Mid-City Lanes Rock'n'Bowl. 4133 S. Carrollton; 482-3133
Great ribs and fried alligator. $

Planet Hollywood. 620 Decatur; 522-7826
Movie star memorabilia and teeny-bop-
per favorite foods. $$

Port of Call. 838 Esplanade Ave.; 523-0120
Hard-core '60s vintage partiers will fit
right into this den of blackness. Serves
fantastic char-grilled hamburgers. $$

Breakfast

Blue Bird Cafe. 7801 Panola; 895-7166
Funky, hippie-chipper service, great
eggs, grits, and pancakes. $

Brennan's. 417 Royal St.; 525-9711
Brunch at Brennan's is one of those
landmark meals to have at least once.
Most famous for their poached egg
dishes, Brennan's claim to sell 750,000
poached eggs a year. Eggs Sardou and
Bananas Foster make a tasty way to frit-
ter away the day. (See "Jazz Brunch
Hotspots," p. 255.) $$$$

Cafe Pontchartrain. 2031 St. Charles Ave.;
524-0581
Eggs Sardou, fresh orange juice, and
other breakfast fare (including biscuits
and blueberry muffins) are served with ·
gracious ease. $$

Columns Hotel. 3811 St. Charles Ave.;
899-9308
Complimentary champagne and live
jazz piano accompany a small, but
pleasant selection of entrees. The infor-
mal atmosphere of dining on an amply
columned front porch is just what the
doctor ordered after one too many elab-
orate meals. (See "Jazz Brunch
Hotspots," p. 255.) $$

Commander's Palace. 1427 Washington
Ave.; 899-8221
The combination of excellent food and
good service keeps the restaurant full
seven days a week with locals and
tourists. Their Eggs de la Salle (served
with crabcakes and wild mushrooms) is
exceptional, as are the coffee and the
dessert selection. On a nice day, request
a table on the patio or in the upstairs
room that overlooks it. (See "Jazz
Brunch Hotspots," p. 255.) $$$$

Dunbar's. 4927 Freret; 899-0734
Uptown soul food breakfast from 7:00
A.M. $

Fiorella's Cafe. 45 French Market Pl.;
528-9566
French Quarter ladies use the front
door and French Market truckers use
the back, on the market side, where the
hours are earlier. Either way, the food
and atmosphere are as real as it gets. $

Foreign Fare

Alberto's Restaurant. 611 Frenchmen;
949-5952
This little second-floor hole-in-the-wall
has the finest cannelloni in town. $

Bangkok Cuisine. 4137 S. Carrollton;
482-3606
Consistently good Thai cuisine. $$

Casablanca. 3030 Severn Ave.; 888-2209
Admirable couscous and Middle East-
ern appetizers. $$

Genghis Khan. 4053 Tulane; 482-4044
Korean food, often accompanied by live
classical music. $$

... **Cuisine.** 539 St. Philip at Chartres; 529-8811/523-4021
Unassuming eatery with terrific Italian food. **$$**

The Little Greek Restaurant. 619 Pink St.; 831-9470 or 837-0636
Greek appetizers, lamb, and fish dishes are a must for fans of Greek food. **$$**

Lola's. 3312 Esplanade; 488-6946
A jumping hole-in-the-wall featuring Spanish/Louisiana-style seafood paella. **$$**

Louisiana Pizza Kitchen. 615 S. Carrollton; 866-5900 (Call for other locations.)
Individual crusty pizzas, fresh from the wood-fired oven. **$$**

Lucky Chang's. 720 St. Louis St.; 529-2045
Asian/Creole cuisine campily served by cross dressers.

Martinique Bistro. 5908 Magazine; 891-8495
Caribbean/Creole food with a French flair and an Uptown style.

Mona Lisa. 1212 Royal St.; 522-6746
Some of the best pizza in the city. **$**

Pie in the Sky. 1818 Magazine St.; 522-6291
Perfect stop while antiquing.

Samurai Sushi. 609 Decatur; 525-9595
Extensive sushi selections and vegetarian entrees make this a hang-out for homesick L.A.-ites. **$$**

Sante Fe. 801 Frenchmen; 944-6854
Southwestern and Tex-Mex style cuisine. **$$**

Camellia Grill, known for its pecan pie.

Shigure. 8115 Jeannette; 866-1119
Japanese home-style cuisine and sushi
bar in an intimate setting. $$

Tandoor. 115 University Pl.; 529-9909
Indian food, with well-prepared Tan-
doori roasted meat dishes. $$

Coffee Houses

Chicorie coffee

Café du Monde. 800 Decatur in the
French Market; 525-4544
Bin Jay pastry
Good Creole café au lait and beignets
without much opportunity to form a
meaningful relationship with fellow
coffee sippers. Open 24 hours, seven
days a week. $ *& Flec market*

Kaldi's Coffee Museum and Coffeehouse.
941 Decatur St.; 586-8989
A vibrant atmosphere fueled by a rich

assortment of music. On a hot day the
Italian cream sodas and the iced coffees
are mighty refreshing. $

P.J.'s. 5432 Magazine; 895-0273/7624
Maple St.; 866-9963/24 McAllister;
865-5705/ 530 Natchez, 529-3658
Uptown housewife types and university students gather for a cup of joe. $

Royal Blend. 623 Royal; 523-2716.
Exceptional selection of coffee drinks in
a courtyard setting. $

Rue de la Course. 1500 Magazine; 529-
1455.
Ideal spot to park grumpy husbands
while antiquing. $

True Brew. 200 Julia St.; 524-8441
This coffeehouse/theater attracts an
artsy, Warehouse District crowd. $

Live music and bowling mix to the beat at Mid-City Bowling Lanes.

Ice Cream, Pastries, and Sandwiches

Angelo Brocato's. 537 St. Ann St.; 525-9676/214 N. Carrollton Ave.; 486-1465
Reminding us of a time when Italian immigrants populated the French Quarter, this quaint sweetshop features traditional Sicilian ice cream, pastries, and candy. Try the cannoli, or a strawberry ice on a sticky summer day.

Central Grocery. 923 Decatur St.; 523-1620

Progress Grocery. 915 Decatur St.; 525-6627
These tiny Italian markets, located almost next door to each other, give any food lover a lot to think about with aisles of olive oil and other gastronomic goodies. Famous for their muffulettas —huge sandwiches filled with ham, salami, mozzarella, and marinated, chopped green olives—that can be ordered in quarters and halves. Word has it that Progress offers a better deal with a larger selection and lower prices.

Croissant D'Or. 617 Ursulines St.; 524-4663
Sweets and sandwiches can be found in this delightful pastry shop, as well as soups, salads, and espresso drinks. A cheery courtyard with a bubbly fountain accommodates both locals and tourists on a sunny day. $

Hansen's Sno-Bliz. 4807 Tchoupitoulas St.; 891-9788
Famous for "snowballs": shaved ice doused with flavored syrups ranging in size from small cups to garbage-can party size. Perfect for beating the heat. $

Johnny's Po-Boys. 511 St. Louis St.; 524-8129
A good, honest po-boy is actually a rare find in the French Quarter, but Johnny's makes up for this disappointment. Choose from New Orleans classics such as roast beef and gravy, fried oysters, shrimp, or ham, sandwiched between crusty French bread. $

La Madeleine. 547 St. Ann St.; 568-9950; 601 S. Carrollton Ave.; 861-8661
This ever-popular French cafe/bakery chain offers quality baguettes and brioches from its wood-burning oven. A selection of tarts, eclairs, and other temptations can serve as finales to a lunch from their kitchen. The lines are long, but move quickly. $

La Marquise. 625 Chartres St.; 524-0420
Intimate and tiny, this is another reliable coffee shop off Jackson Square. Good coffee, croissants, and pastries. $

Napoleon House. 500 Chartres St.; 524-9752
Look beyond the cocktails to partake in this historic spot: the muffulettas, gumbo, and Italian ice cream are worth a try. $

Old Dog, New Trick. 307 Exchange Alley; 522-4569
Innovative vegetarian cuisine and luscious homemade desserts. $

JAZZ BRUNCH HOTSPOTS

The perfect way to spend a weekend afternoon in New Orleans combines the city's favorite pastimes: listening to jazz and eating. Following are restaurants guaranteed to provide a memorable brunch as well as outstanding music, whether traditional New Orleans jazz, gospel, or blues. Price codes refer to the cost of brunch for one, excluding tip and drinks.

Arnaud's. 813 Bienville St.; 523-5433
Rich Creole dishes sizzle to the strains of traditional jazz. $$$

Brennan's. 417 Royal St.; 525-9711
Poached egg dishes and bananas Foster make for tasty accompaniments to traditional New Orleans jazz. $$$

Columns Hotel. 3811 St. Charles Ave.; 899-9308
Champagne and live jazz piano accompany the delightful dishes here. $-$$

Commander's Palace. 1427 Washington Ave.; 899-8221
Crabcakes and traditional jazz: truly a New Orleans experience. $$$

House of Blues. 225 Decatur; 529-BLUE
An extensive buffet and non-stop mimosas accompany arm-waving, Lord-praisin' gospel. $$

Palace Cafe. 605 Canal St.; 523-1661
Updated Creole classics taste all the better with a hearty dose of the blues. But the atmosphere in the bright, two-story bistro will keep you from getting those day-before-Monday blues. $$

Praline Connection II Gospel & Blues Hall. 901-907 S. Peters; 523-3973
A down-home, lively version of the upscale Sunday brunches with a healthy splash of gospel singing. Feed your stomach *and* your soul. $-$$

PRACTICAL INFORMATION

■ AREA CODE

All phone numbers listed in this book, unless otherwise noted, are in the 504 area code. Any number with a (504) in front indicates that the area code must be dialed when calling from New Orleans, even though the area code is the same. These include numbers in Baton Rouge and those across Lake Pontchartrain. The Lafayette area (Cajun country) has a 318 area code, and all of Mississippi has 601.

■ CLIMATE

In the semi-tropical city of New Orleans, there are about 57 days a year when the temperature rises over 90 degrees (33°C). Average temperatures do not take into account that the humidity is about 76 percent, which makes the air thick as a steambath in midsummer. Local weather forecasters report the "heat index," which factors in humidity; for example, when it is 90 degrees (33°C), the heat index may be 104 degrees (40°C).

In the summer most of the public buildings are over air-conditioned. This is undoubtedly why locals are as likely to contract pneumonia in August as they are in January. But some of us actually enjoy the summer heat. We tote fans with us, drink lots of iced tea, eat snowballs, and hold ice on our wrists to cool our blood.

AVERAGE TEMPERATURES (IN DEGREES)

MONTH	FAHRENHEIT		CENTIGRADE	
	HIGH	LOW	HIGH	LOW
January	62	47	17	8
February	65	50	18	10
March	71	55	22	13
April	77	61	25	16
May	83	68	28	20
June	88	74	31	23
July	90	76	32	24
August	90	76	32	24
September	86	73	31	23
October	79	64	26	18
November	70	55	21	13
December	64	48	18	9

When we can, we eat our biggest meal after dark and take naps in the hottest part of the day.

Most of the time, New Orleanians don't turn off their air conditioning until the temperature dips below 68 degrees (20°C). At 50 degrees (10°C) "cold front frenzy" sets in. Of course, raised houses designed to afford maximum cross-ventilation do tend to get a bit brisk inside.

For a daily weather recording, call 465-9212.

Most desirable months: March to May; October to mid-December.

Rainiest months: July average: 7 inches (18 cm), September average: 6 inches (19 cm), March average: 5 inches (13 cm).

Humidity: Mornings often have 100% humidity that wanes toward midday, and rises in the early evening.

Hurricane season: June to November.

Unlike earthquakes, hurricanes do plenty of sword-rattling before they ever come into the Gulf, so there is no excuse for ever being caught off guard. Just be warned—New Orleans is located at the heart of the hurricane target area. It's important to remember that the city is below sea level, is surrounded by water, and is

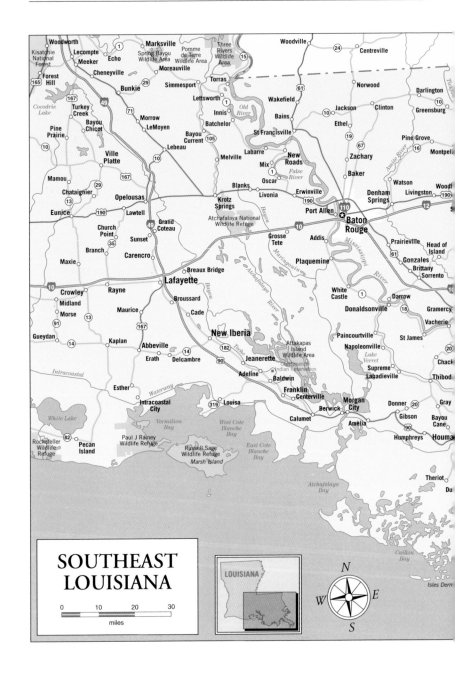

SOUTHEAST
LOUISIANA

0   10   20   30
miles

LOUISIANA

N
W   E
S

a popular target for hurricanes and tropical storms. If a tropical storm is headed into the Gulf, postpone your trip. Even with a tropical storm the city can lose telephone service and power (which means no air conditioning).

■ GETTING AROUND

When navigating the streets of New Orleans, think of Canal Street as the great dividing line. At 171 feet (52 m) wide, it is the widest main thoroughfare and one of the longest streets in the United States. Historically the border between the Creoles and the Americans, today it marks the division between the Central Business District (CBD) and the French Quarter. Where streets cross Canal, those to the north are prefixed "North," likewise those to the south are prefixed "South." Addresses on these streets begin with 100 at Canal and move out to the north and south.

■ AIRPORT TRANSPORTATION

New Orleans International Airport is in Kenner about 14 miles (22 km) northwest of the downtown area. The least expensive way to get to town from the New Orleans International Airport is by **Airport Express** which picks up/lets off on the second level on the far right as you exit, and lets off/picks up at Elk and Tulane near the Public Library. Call 737-9611 for information. The **Airport Shuttle** leaves the airport every 10 minutes for all major hotels and B&B's in the downtown and French Quarter neighborhoods, and for the universities. A ticket booth is inside the airport. Taxis and limos are also available.

■ TRAIN SERVICE

Several Amtrak passenger trains leave from New Orleans weekly, one for Chicago and others for Atlanta, Los Angeles, Miami, and New York.
Amtrak. Union Passenger Terminal (Downtown), 1001 Loyola Ave.; 528-1631/ (800) 872-7245.

■ BUS SERVICE

Greyhound-Trailways Bus Service. Transportation Center, Union Passenger Terminal (Downtown), 1001 Loyola Ave.; 525-6075/(800) 231-2222.

■ LOCAL TRANSIT SERVICE

The city has 499 buses and streetcars. One of the most economical ways to traverse the city is with a VisiTour Pass, a passport to both streetcars and the RTA bus system. A one-day pass is under $5.00; a three-day is $8.00 (the regular one-way fare is $1.10 with a transfer, exact change is required). Subject to change.
Regional Transit Authority (RTA) Timetables and routes available. 569-2700.

■ RECOMMENDED CAR SERVICES

Limousine Livery: 561-8777; Stretch Lincoln, Cadillacs, and sedans. (Most of the chauffeurs are licensed tour guides.)
Touch of Class: 522-7565; Seven Lincolns.
United Cab: 524-9606/522-9771.

■ FERRIES

Ferries offer a lovely short cruise from one side of the Mississippi to the other at Jackson Avenue/Gretna, Canal Street, and Chalmette. They are free for pedestrians and $1.00 for vehicles (collected only on West Bank leg). Usually every 15 minutes. Call to check: 364-8110.

■ DRIVING AND PARKING

Meter maids and towing services work extremely efficiently in New Orleans. The number of drunk-driving arrests is one of the highest in the country. When it rains hard, the streets flood. If these facts aren't a deterrent from driving around, then try to stay in a hotel with valet parking. The Royal Orleans Garage on Chartres Street and the parking area behind the levee (entrance at Jax Brewery) are good, but tend to fill up fast.

(following pages) Blue Plate mayonnaise, a popular New Orleans condiment.

ACCOMMODATIONS

As in many an Old World city, New Orleans has a plethora of places to sleep, from America's top hotels and most gracious European-style guest houses to motels so seedy that the cockroaches complain. In between are the ubiquitous tourist hotels that might as well be located in Detroit or Pittsburgh, spare bedrooms owned by clever homemakers who turn a few bucks in their Sears and Robuckian specials, and some musty-smelling monoliths that haven't had a good cleaning since Eisenhower was President.

More than 45 hotels, motels, inns, and guest houses representing over 4,000 rooms can be found within the 96 blocks in the French Quarter. What follows is a list, by category, of some of the finest accommodations that the city has to offer. A few words to the wise: staying in the suburbs and commuting may be cheaper, but it will entail parking costs and the hassle of fighting traffic. By the same token, there are chain hotels advertised as being "close to downtown" or "10 minutes from the French Quarter." Often they are in neighborhoods in which it is unsafe to walk.

Note: Many hotels have summer specials and packages with rates lower than those the rest of the year.

——— ⚜ ———

Prices

(per person, based on double occupancy):
$ = under $90; $$ = $90-130); $$$ = $130-175; $$$$ = over $175
*(S)= Safer area, although caution is always advised.

——— ⚜ ———

Old World Amenities

The Pontchartrain Grand Heritage Hotel.
2031 St. Charles, 70140; 524-0581/
(800) 777-6193/(800) 952-8092 *(S)
$$$-$$$$
The 18 luxurious grand suites are the prize of this quiet 100-room hotel, which was built in 1927 as a residential hotel. Few private homes in the city can rival the Pontchartrain's elegance. Personal touches give the illusion of private apartments. In the summer the grand suites rent for less than half their usual price.

The Windsor Court Hotel. 300 Gravier St., 70140-1035; 523-6000/(800) 262-2662 *(S) $$$$

Ranked No. 1 in the United States by *Zagat's* (no doubt for its luxuriant courtliness, its exceptional five-star restaurant, grand swimming pool, and health club), the hotel identifies so closely with its British namesake that by eerie coincidence a painting of Windsor Castle was destroyed by fire in one of the banquet rooms the second day of the fire at the Castle. Nicest views are on floors 13 through 22.

High-Rise Hotels

The Hotel Inter-Continental New Orleans. 444 St. Charles Ave., 70140; 525-5566/(800) 445-6563 $$$-$$$$
Located in the heart of the city's financial district and only three blocks from the French Quarter. Request numbers 02-08, 52-28 on each floor. The hotel is topped by a pool on the fifteenth floor.

Le Meridien New Orleans. 614 Canal St. (across the street from the French Quarter), 70130; 525-6500/(800) 543-4300 $$$-$$$$
A first-class French-owned and operated hotel. The Jazz Meridien Lounge features the best of classic jazz bands. Rooms that overlook the river are numbers 17-23 on each floor. The quietest rooms per floor are 10, 11, 12, 24, and 25, which view both the river and city. The Health Club on the eighth floor is newly renovated and has an outdoor heated pool and sauna.

The Omni Royal Orleans. 621 St. Louis St., 70140; 529-5333/(800) THE-OMNI $$$-$$$$
Tops for French Quarter location and New Orleans hospitality. The hotel was built in 1960 as a replica of the palatial St. Louis hotel of the nineteenth century. The view from the rooftop pool on the seventh floor is one of the loveliest in the city. The rooms with the balconies across the front of the hotel on St. Louis Street are the most expensive. Those balconies that overlook Royal Street provide an ideal vantage point during Carnival to view the decadence below. Inside rooms are smaller and quieter and the nicest view is from those that overlook the Royal Garden Terrace.

The Westin Canal Place. 100 Iberville, 70130; 566-7006/(800) 228-3000 *(S) $$$-$$$$
A 438-unit hotel that tops the tower which houses the Canal Place shopping complex. Breathtaking views of the river and the city.

Conventional Frugality

New Orleans is one of the most popular convention destinations in the country. With both the convention center and the proposed gambling casino on the riverfront, hotels within a 10-minute radius are prized locations for the conventioneer who will mostly be using the room as a place to shower and sleep.

The Hampton Inn. 226 Carondelet, 70130; 529-9990 **$$**
Located in a former Central Business District office building. The 186 rooms have sophisticated modern decor.

Le Pavillon Hotel. 833 Poydras, 70140; 581-3111/(800) 535-9095 **$$-$$$**
A once grand turn-of-the-century hotel which has since taken on a slightly *Las Vegasante* patina. A popular stopover for out-of-town attorneys involved in local cases.

Elegantly Romantic

The Josephine. 1450 Josephine St., 70130 (one block from the Ponchartrain Hotel, near St. Charles Ave.); 524-6361/(800) 779-6361 **$-$$-$$$**
Set off from the others at the fringe of the Garden District, near Jackson Avenue, is an Italianate 1870s mansion with fluted Doric and Corinthian columns. The rooms in the main house have 13-foot ceilings and are resplendent with their "Creole Baroque" decor. Room 1 at the front has a magnificent bed with ivory inlay.

The La Mothe House. 621 Esplanade Ave., 70116; 947-1161/(800) 367-5858 **$$-$$$-$$$$**
With 11 rooms and nine suites, the house is located one block from the French Quarter on oak-lined Esplanade Avenue in a white-columned antebellum mansion. All the rooms are furnished in lovely antiques and give the appearance of being rooms in a private home. In the early evenings, guests often congregate around the fish pond on the quiet patio overgrown with banana trees. The guest house's summer rates are among the best buys in town.

The Maison de Ville. 727 Toulouse; 528-9206/(800) 634-1600 *(S) **$$$-$$$$**
A far cry from the hubbub of the twentieth century. The hotel is concealed behind wrought iron gates and semitropical plants in an eighteenth-century French Quarter mansion. Each of its 14 rooms, two suites, and seven "Audubon Cottages" are furnished with nineteenth-century antiques. The rates include a continental breakfast served in the room, and sherry, port, iced tea, and coffee on the patio in the evening. Parking is $15.00 a night. The outdoor pool is near the Audubon Cottages where Audubon lived in 1821 and Tennessee Williams lived while he was working on *A Streetcar Named Desire.*

Melrose Mansion Hotel. 937 Esplanade Ave., 70116; 944-2255 **$$$-$$$$**
The newest of the luxury guest houses is better on service and amenities than decor. The four suites (all with whirlpool baths) and four rooms are located in a mansion built in 1884 as a single-family residence. There's a large heated pool, stretch limo relay from airport, and lavish Southern breakfasts, as well as an open bar and hors d'oeuvres in the evenings.

A private garden in the Uptown District.

The Soniat House. 1133 Chartres St., 70116; 522-0570/(800) 544-8808 $$$-$$$$
This spot brims with a combination of effortless good taste, elegance, and comfort through the sort of planning that would put the Normandy invasion to shame. The owners' care shows in every detail from their restoration of the Creole mansion to the crisp linen on the breakfast tray.

Local Color

Casa de Marigny Creole Guest Cottages. 818 Frenchmen St., 70116; 948-3875 $-$$-$$$
Five cozy European-style cottages in separate 1830-1880 weekend houses, all nestled around a pool and Jacuzzi in a tropical garden. Just steps away from the jazz clubs and restaurants along Frenchmen.

Hazel Boyce, Bed & Breakfast, Inc., P.O. Box 52257, N.O. 70152; 488-4640/(800) 729-4640

The Lafitte Guest House. 1003 Bourbon St., 70116; 581-2678/(800) 331-7971 $$-$$$
A four-story French Quarter home that was built in 1849, it became a guest house in the 1920s, and Cole Porter celebrated his birthday there in the 1930s. The 14 rooms are furnished in Victorian antiques. Rates do not include parking. Reservations should be made at least six weeks in advance.

Le Richelieu. 1234 Chartres St.; 529-2492/ (800) 535-9653 $$
Eighty-six Victorian bedrooms in an elegant building in the back of the Quarter. Free parking.

New Orleans Bed & Breakfast. P.O. Box 8163, 70182; 838-0071
Prices for accommodations in well-maintained private homes begin at $70.00. Reductions in summer months.

Provincial Hotel. 1024 Chartres St., 70116; 581-4995 $$-$$$
This 107-room hotel, popular with music producers and independent filmmakers, is located in a series of French Quarter buildings that date from the 1800s. Parts of the complex served as a Royal Military Hospital, an icehouse, and a feedstore. With a large pool, seven patios, and a restaurant, it offers the convenience of a motel with the atmosphere of a madcap Creole bachelor's guesthouse. Excellent summer rates.

Vieux Carré Rentals. 841 Bourbon St., 70116; 525-3983 $$
Consists of three suites with kitchen facilities carved out of an 1830 Creole mansion. Mainly serving a corporate clientele, the inn is run by a no-nonsense French Quarter woman.

Velveteen Rabbit Ambiance

Bourgoyne Guest House. 839 Rue Bourbon, 70116 (in the middle of the French Quarter near the heart of the gay section); 524-3621/525-3983 $$-$$$

Located in an 1830 Creole house, this inn has been operated by a newspaper columnist since the early 1970s. There are three studios and two suites, all with a mixture of antique and contemporary furnishings and all overlooking an ancient courtyard. Kitchen facilities and private baths in all rooms.

Columns Hotel. 3811 St. Charles, 70115; 899-9308/(800) 445-9308
Rooms with private baths: $$-$$$
Shared bath in common hallway: $$
The large rooms are reminiscent of those romantic, funky hotels straight out of Tennessee Williams. The interior shots in the movie *Pretty Baby* were filmed here. The 19 guest rooms (nine with private baths) are air-conditioned, and some bathrooms feature double bathtubs. Pleasant cocktail lounge. Continental breakfast from 7:00 until 10:00 and Sunday champagne brunch.

The Dusty Mansion. 2231 Gen. Pershing, 70115; 895-4576 $
Four nicely furnished bedrooms in a Gay Nineties Uptown mansion. Off-street parking, sundeck, and hot tub.

Olivier House. 828 Toulouse, 70112; 525-8456 $$-$$$-$$$$
Converted from an 1836 French Quarter mansion into a 42-room guest house in the 1970s. While the majority of the rooms are unpretentious, the hotel has forged a clientele of celebrity chefs, actors, and talent agents who favor the anonymity that this spot offers.

Parkview Guest House. 7004 St. Charles Ave., 70118; 861-7564 $$-$$$
Built in 1884, this inn offers 15 rooms with private baths, seven with shared baths. Continental breakfast served daily. Rooms on the east side overlook the oak-lined park, have ceiling fans and brass beds; those without the view have nicer decor.

St. Vincent's. 1507 Magazine. Check in at 1415 Prytania; 566-1515 $
This nineteenth-century brick orphanage has been converted into a guest house of 31 fresh, cheerfully appointed rooms with private baths and phones. A nice breakfast costs only a few dollars.

Backpacker Specials

Loyola University. Write to Conference Director, Office of Student Affairs, P. O. Box 126, Loyola University, 70118, to make reservations, or call 865-3735/ 865-3622 *(S) $
Located Uptown, the school offers 150 dormitory spaces available to anyone from June 1 through August 1.

St. Charles Guest House. 1748 Prytania, 70130; 523-6556 *(S) $
Six backpacker rooms all share one bath, but there's a pool to cool off in. Near Felicity Parish.

Tulane University. Office of Housing and Residence Life, Tulane University, 27 McAllister Dr., 70118; 865-5724 *(S) $
Offers a great deal year-round for the public in two different facilities with

suites and apartments under $50.00. Make reservations as early as possible.

YMCA Hotel. 920 St. Charles Ave., 70130; 568-9622 $

Fifty institutional, spartan rooms. Each of the two floors has a female and male shower and bath facilities. Close to the streetcar; access to the Y pool and health club facilities. Try to book a month in advance.

■ FESTIVALS

For further information about individual festivals, write the Louisiana Office of Tourism, P.O. Box 94291, Baton Rouge, LA 70804-9291; (504) 342-8119. For general information packets on the state, call (800) 33-GUMBO (334-8626).

J A N U A R Y
Battle of New Orleans Celebration.
Chalmette Battlefield, St. Bernard. Weekend closest to January 8.

F E B R U A R Y
Lundi Gras.
Spanish Plaza by the Riverwalk, New Orleans; 522-1555.

Mardi Gras.
City of New Orleans; 566-5055. Mid-February to early March:
February 20, 1996
February 11, 1997
February 24, 1998
February 16, 1999
March 7, 2000
February 27, 2001
February 12, 2002

M A R C H
Black Heritage Festival.
Audubon Zoo, the Riverwalk, and the Louisiana State Museum, New Orleans; 827-5771. Second weekend in March.

St. Patrick's Day Parades.
French Quarter, Irish Channel, Veteran's Blvd., New Orleans; 525-5169. On or around March 17.

St. Joseph's Day Festivities.
Piazza D'Italia, New Orleans; 522-7294. On or around March 19.

Crescent City Classic.
New Orleans; 861-8686. 10k run. Mid-March to late April.

Earth Fest.
Audubon Zoo, New Orleans; 861-2537. Third weekend.

Oak Alley Plantation Annual Arts & Crafts Festival.
Oak Alley Plantation, Vacherie. Late March.

Piney Woods Opry.
Abita Springs Town Hall, Abita Springs. Fourth Saturdays of March, April, and May.

Tennessee Williams Literary Festival.
Various locations, New Orleans; 286-6680. Last weekend.

APRIL

Freeport-McMoran Golf Classic.
English Turn Country Club, New Orleans; 831-4653. First weekend.

Spring Fiesta.
French Quarter, New Orleans; 581-1367. Begins Friday night after Easter, and continues for five days.

French Quarter Festival.
French Quarter, New Orleans; 522-5730. Second weekend.

New Orleans Jazz & Heritage Festival.
Fairgrounds Racetrack, New Orleans; 522-4786. Last weekend in April to first weekend in May.

MAY

Art in Bloom.
New Orleans Museum of Art, New Orleans. Early to mid-May.

Grand Prix du Mardi Gras.
Central Business District, New Orleans. Mid-May to mid-June.

Calumet Powwow.
Louisiana Nature & Science Center, New Orleans. Mid-May.

Greek Festival.
Hellenic Cultural Center, New Orleans; 282-0259. Weekend before Memorial Day weekend.

Zoo-to-Do.
Audubon Zoo New Orleans; 861-2537. The largest single-night fundraiser in the country. Gorgeous dance under the stars among the animals at the zoo.

JUNE

Tomato Festival in the French Quarter.
Dutch Alley and Farmer's Market, New Orleans; 522-2621. Usually the first weekend.

Reggae Riddums Festival.
Marconi Meadows, City Park, New Orleans; 367-1313/(800) 367-1317. Some of the world's best reggae and calypso musicians perform. Second weekend.

Carnival Latino.
Along the riverfront, New Orleans. The Gulf South's largest celebration of Hispanic heritage. Last weekend.

JULY

Go Fourth on the River.
Along the riverfront, New Orleans; 528-9994. Fourth of July.

AUGUST

African Heritage Festival International.
New Orleans; 949-5610. The music and heritage of the local African American community. Late August and early September.

SEPTEMBER

Honduran Independence Day Festival.
French Market, New Orleans. Second weekend.

Louisiana Swamp Festival.
Audubon Zoo and Woldenberg Riverfront Park, New Orleans; 861-2537. Cajun food, music, and crafts. Two weekends, late September and early October.

3 E R

Oktoberfest.
Deutsches Haus, 200 Galvez St., New Orleans; 522-8014. All month.

New Orleans Film & Video Festival.
Canal Place Landmark Theatre, New Orleans. Early to mid-October.

Festa D'Italia.
Poydras near the river, New Orleans; 522-7294.

Louisiana Heritage Festival.
Rivertown, Kenner. Last weekend.

Witches' Moonlight Run.
Central Business District, New Orleans; 566-5055. Halloween.

N O V E M B E R

Settlers Day, Louisiana Nature & Science Center.
New Orleans. Mid-November.

Thanksgiving Day Race.
New Orleans. Five miles. Thanksgiving.

Bayou Classic.
Louisiana Superdome, New Orleans; 523-5652. Last weekend. Game between Grambling and Southern.

Celebration in the Oaks.
City Park, New Orleans; 482-4888. End of the month through early January. Gorgeous Christmas lights in the park. Take a carriage tour.

D E C E M B E R

Creole Christmas.
French Quarter, New Orleans; 522-5730. Candlelight caroling, madrigal dinners, historic homes dressed for Christmas. All month.

Festival of Bonfires.
Luther Gramercy. Early to mid-December.

Countdown (to New Year's). Jackson Square, New Orleans; 566-5055. New Year's Eve.

■ MUSEUMS

K = *Museums that kids might enjoy*

A Gallery for Fine Photography. 322 Royal St.; 568-1313
Rare photographs and books for sale by artists. Regular shows and book signings with well-known artists and authors.

Archbishop Antoine Blanc Memorial. 100 Chartres St.; 529-3040
This museum complex includes the Old Ursuline Convent, the oldest building in the Mississippi Valley.

Aquarium of the Americas. Foot of Canal St.; 861-2538 K
More than 7,000 different creatures swim in 60 separate displays. A 16-acre park surrounds the aquarium.

Blaine Kern's Mardi Gras World. 233 Newton; 361-7821 K
Ride on the ferry to the historic district of Old Algiers and walk through warehouses where parade floats are made.

Confederate Museum. 929 Camp St.; 523-4522
Louisiana's oldest museum, containing Civil War memorabilia, including uniforms, weapons, flags, and personal effects of Southern leaders.

Historic New Orleans Collection. 533 Royal St.; 523-4662
A tour through the Williams Residence, a nineteenth-century townhouse, and the Louisiana Historic Galleries in the 1792 Merieult house provide a vivid trip into New Orleans's past.

Jackson Barracks Military Museum. 6400 St. Claude Ave.; 278-6242 **K**
An old powder magazine contains a museum of all military engagements from earliest American history. Free.

Louisiana Children's Museum. 420 Julia St., 2nd Floor; 523-1357 **K**
From a do-it-yourself newsroom to a child-sized supermarket, the museum is geared towards stimulation for the very young. All exhibits are interactive.

Louisiana Nature and Science Center. 11000 Lake Forest Blvd. (Eastern New Orleans); 246-5672 **K**
The center offers special education programs, a science resource center with a bird-feeding window, hummingbird and butterfly gardens, forest and wetland trails, and a planetarium.

Louisiana State Museum. Jackson Square in French Quarter; 568-6968
The largest museum in Louisiana, and one of the finest historical museums in the United States.

Louisiana Toy Train Museum. 519 Williams Blvd. (Kenner); 468-7223 **K**
Train aficionados are in seventh heaven here, surrounded by seven working miniature train layouts, trolleys, and a toy carousel. The collection is comprised of 17,000 pieces, many of them one of a kind. An 1890s toy train is the featured attraction.

Louisiana Wildlife and Fisheries Museum and Aquarium. 303 Williams Blvd. (Kenner); 468-7232 **K**
Operated by the Louisiana Nature and Science Center, the museum features a 15,000-gallon aquarium stocked with native species and many hands-on exhibits.

Musee Conti. 917 Conti St.; 525-2605 **K**
The Wax Museum of Louisiana Legends features displays of costumes from the Knights of Sparta ball, to a miniature recreation of the 400 block of Royal during an early parade.

New Orleans Historic Voodoo Museum. 724 Dumaine St.; 523-7685
Tourists can glimpse voodoo as it is practiced in New Orleans at this unique attraction. The museum includes a working altar and offers ritual tours and voodoo walking tours of the French Quarter.

New Orleans Museum of Art. 1 Collins Diboll Circle; 488-2631
Of particular note is the Mathilda Geddings Gray Foundation Fabergé Collection as well as one of the finest photography collections in the South.

New Orleans Pharmacy Museum. 514 Chartres St.; 565-8027
The building that houses this museum was built in 1823 for America's first licensed pharmacist.

Ursuline Museum. 2635 State; 866-1472

By appointment, some of the state's greatest treasures can be viewed at the nation's earliest girls' school including letters from Thomas Jefferson, documents from the king of France, and magnificent religious artifacts.

■ GALLERIES

Today, the center of New Orleans' art community is located along Julia Street and Baronne Street, in the Warehouse District, where there are 16 thriving modern art galleries. Some worth checking out are **Arthur Roger** (432 Julia St.; 522-1999), **Chris Maier** (329 Julia St.; 586-9079), and **Simone Stern** (518 Julia St.; 529-1118). Nearby, **The Contemporary Arts Center,** at 900 Camp, is also a place to view contemporary artwork. It contains three exhibition spaces, with work by local artists as well as traveling exhibitions. If this doesn't satisfy, you'll find galleries located along Royal Street in the French Quarter and on Magazine Street as well.

■ ANTIQUES

New Orleans has been a shopping mecca ever since the days when pirate Jean Lafitte and his brothers sold contraband out of a shop in the French Quarter. These days antique shops have been clustered in two major areas—the Charters/Royal Street area of the French Quarter and Magazine Street in the Garden District/Uptown Area. The Royal Street Guild and the Chartres Street Association both have free brochures which list shops, addresses, and hours which may be obtained from stores on the street. Days can be spent combing the nooks and crannies of the shops, their warehouses and attics.

At the **French Antique Shop Inc.** (225 Royal St.; 524-9861), patrons can climb over a collection of French furniture and chandeliers that appear as if they had been hidden away after the Revolution. Other more conventionally elegant displays of European treasures can be viewed at **Keil's** (325 Royal St.; 522-4552), and **Royal Antiques, Ltd.** (307-309 Royal St.; 524-7033/7035). At **Lucullus** (610 Chartres St.; 528-9620), fine culinary objects from furniture to porcelains are displayed with the grace of a still-life painting. Those with tastes toward the exotic won't be disappointed by **Whisnant** (222 Chartres St.; 524-9766). **Peter Patout** (922 Royal St.; 522-0582), specializes in Louisiana and American furniture.

Decatur Street, at the far edge of the Quarter, is definitely the street for funk and junk. Start at the Esplanade end, pass by the kids with pierced eyebrows and tattoos of daggers, and head for the flea market in the French Market. Strung along the street are vintage clothing and record emporiums, as well as shops with the latest punk paraphernalia.

The auction houses in New Orleans often have great buys on sets of china and silver and Victorian furniture. Before planning a trip, try to get on the mailing lists of the auction houses. These include **Morton Goldberg Auction Galleries, Inc.** (547 Baronne St., 70113; 592-2300); **Neal Auction Company** (4038 Magazine St., 70115; 899-5329), and **New Orleans Auction Galleries Inc.** (801 Magazine St., 70130; 566-1849).

For the literary, hours can be spent browsing through the antiquarian book stores of the French Quarter. One man from London recently was able to purchase a rare English children's book for $4.50. He returned to England and sold the book at an auction for enough to cover his round-trip airfare. Several of the nicest collections can be viewed at **Faulkner House Books** (624 Pirate's Alley; 524-2940), **The Antique Book Gallery** (811 Royal St.; 524-6918), **Beckham's Book Shop** (228 Decatur St.; 522-9875), and the **Librairie Book Shop** (823 Chartres St.; 525-4837).

The Quarter is also a terrific place to find those accessories that add sparkle to your wardrobe. At a tiny little hole in the wall at 503 Royal St. (588-1194), designer **Ray Cole** sells his hand-painted silk creations. **Rumor's** (513 Royal St.; 525-0292), and **Rumor's Too** (319 Royal St.; 523-0011), dispense a wide array of earrings and masks.

For Magazine Street there's a free brochure that lists all the shops along the street which can be obtained by writing **The Magazine Merchants Association,** P.O. Box 15028, N.O. 70175, or by calling (800) 828-2311. The shops in the area seem to become more gentrified each year, though some terrific bargains can still be had. The street also serves as home to over a dozen contemporary and ethnic art galleries. There you will find everything from museum-quality African art at the **Davis Gallery** (3964 Magazine St.; 897-0780) to fantastic buys on silver at

As You Like It (3025 Magazine St.; 897-6915). Here too one can find an equally fine, yet less pretentious array of fine furniture and decorative objects. It is here that internationally known designer **Mario Villa** has his main studio at 3717 Magazine St. (895-8731). There is French Provincial furniture at **Wirthmore** (3900 Magazine St.; 899-8811 and 5723 Magazine St.; 897-9727), and American pieces at **Didier Inc.** (3439 Magazine St.; 899-7749). For antique beds and vintage linens, don't miss **Bush Antiques** (2109 Magazine St.; 581-3518), and for reasonably priced English and French antiques try **Sixpence** (4904 Magazine St.; 895-1267).

Another great resource that New Orleans has to offer is a treasure trove of architectural building materials. For French doors, beveled glass windows, hardware, mantels, shutters, columns, staircases, etc., there are several wrecking/salvage yards that are worth a trip: **Ricca's Architectural Sales** (511 N. Solomon St.; 488-5524), **Addco** (2601 Chartres St.; 945-4879), **The Bank** (1824 Felicity St.; 523-2702). A good bet for finding picturesque antique and reproduction iron garden ornaments is the **White Pillars Repair Co.** (8522 Oak St.; 866-0203), located a few blocks from the streetcar on South Carrollton. And for that prime eighteenth-century decorative ornament at sirloin prices there is **MacMaison** (3963 Magazine St.; 891-2863).

■ GARDENS

American Aquatic Gardens. 621 Elysian Fields; 944-0410. A nursery specializing in water plants such as water lilies and native grasses.

Audubon Zoological Gardens. 6500 Magazine St.; 861-2537. The Leon Heymann Conservatory has both native and exotic species of plants.

Beauregard-Keyes House. 1113 Chartres; 523-7257. Parterre and herb garden in 1830s style.

City Park. End of Esplanade Ave.; 482-4888. Free. A 1500-acre, oak-lined park full of traditional, native plant life.

Gallier House Museum. 1118-32 Royal St.; 523-6722. Courtyard garden kept in its 1857 style.

Hermann-Grima House and Courtyard. 820 St. Louis St.; 525-5661. Vieux Carré garden in its 1860 style.

Jean Lafitte National Historic Park. Barataria Unit; 589-2330. Nature trails and guided canoe trips, especially nice in the early spring when the native iris are in bloom.

Longue Vue House and Gardens. 7 Bamboo Rd.; 488-5488. Extensive, well-maintained formal gardens.

New Orleans Botanical Garden. Victory Ave., City Park; 483-9386. Lovely rose garden and regular series of gardening lectures.

■ PLANTATIONS AND FINE COUNTRY HOMES

Each neighborhood in New Orleans has its own grand scale exhibitions of architectural whimsy. One of the most unique is the pair of identical **"Steamboat Houses"** on Egania Street (in the vicinity of the Chalmette Battlefield) which sit beside the levee. They were erected in 1905 by Captain Milton Doullut, a steamboat captain, who brought his love of boats with him to dry land.

It is outside of the city that men of means dotted the landscape with their full-blown, mini-Parthenons among the bull frogs. It is a sad fact that the economy along the riverfront has changed greatly over the past 50 years. Many of the plantation houses once were part of vast plantations and now sit on postage-stamp-sized plots on commercially zoned land.

The fortunes that were made in rural Louisiana from indigo and sugar gave rise to a lifestyle bent on great monuments. By the 1840s vast plantations staffed by communities of slave labor appeared. The benefits reaped by the planters were used to build architectural monuments. Their homes were palaces inspired by classical style, sometimes ornamented with Gothic and Italianate flourishes.

Along the backroads, one sees once-great plantation houses in virtual ruins. One example of a house fighting for life is **Ashland/Belle Helène,** a mansion surrounded by 30-foot (9 m)-tall columns. The home was thought to have been designed by James Gallier, Sr. and completed in 1841 near a cypress swamp (504-473-1328/504-473-1207) five miles (8 km) north of Darrow.

To understand the working life of the plantations, it is necessary to visit the **Rural Life Museum** (504-765-2437) where the slave cabins, Cajun cottages, and sharecroppers houses have been saved from the wrecker's ball.

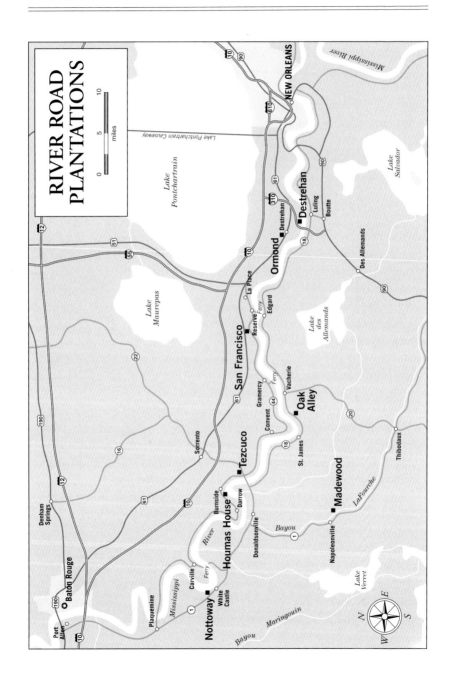

RIVER ROAD PLANTATIONS

HOUSES OF NOTE

Asphodel Village & Plantation. (504) 654-6868. Built in 1820 as a three-story Doric-columned Greek Revival residence that served as the seat of a plantation with more than 400 slaves. It was the setting for the Paul Newman and Joanne Woodward movie, *The Long Hot Summer.* It is located in Jackson, Louisiana, near Baton Rouge and is now operated as an inn.

Destrehan Plantation. (504) 764-9315. Built in 1787, it is the oldest plantation home still intact in the lower Mississippi Valley. Destrehan, a sprawling West Indies mansion with eight mammoth columns across its front, is about half an hour from downtown New Orleans.

Houmas House. (504) 473-7841. Sitting cool and dignified between Baton Rouge and New Orleans in Darrow, near Burnside, this home was built in 1840 by the daughter of General Wade Hampton of Revolutionary War fame, and later served as the setting of *Hush, Hush, Sweet Charlotte* with Bette Davis and Olivia DeHavilland.

Madewood Plantation. (800) 375-7151. A 21-room palatial Greek Revival plantation house designed by Henry Howard and constructed between 1840 and 1848. It is also operated as a bed-and-breakfast, and is located in Napoleonville on the other side of the river from Baton Rouge.

Magnolia Mound. (504) 343-4955. A former indigo plantation built in the 1790s in Baton Rouge. The vegetable garden and kitchen are also worth a visit.

Myrtles Plantation. (504) 635-6277. Built in 1796, the mansion is billed as "America's Most Haunted House" and is located in St. Francisville on the road to Natchez, Mississippi.

Nottoway Plantation. (504) 545-2409. This "White Castle" was an Italianate/Greek Revival palace designed by Henry Howard. Built in 1859 with 64 rooms and 53,000 square feet, it holds the distinction of being the largest antebellum plantation house in the South. Located near White Castle on the way to Baton Rouge, it serves both meals and functions as a bed-and-breakfast.

Oak Alley in Vacherie. (504) 265-2151. Six miles (9.6 km) upriver from the Gramercy Ferry, 60 miles (96 km) upriver from New Orleans. Built in 1839 and named for the alley of 28 evenly spaced monumental live oak trees that are thought to have pre-dated the home by a hundred years, this Greek Revival home, originally called *Bon Sejour* (Good Rest) is a bit more romantic from a distance than it is up close. It was here that the first scientific cultivation of pecans in Louisiana took place.

Ormond Plantation. 764-8544/764-0691. Louisiana Colonial style home built before 1790.

Parlange Plantation. A classic two-story raised cottage near New Rhodes, this home has been in the same family since it was constructed in 1750.

Rosedown Plantation. (504) 265-2151. One of the loveliest homes in St. Francisville. This 16-room antebellum mansion was built in 1835 and is surrounded by 200-year-old oaks and 28 acres of formal gardens modeled after those at Versailles.

St. Francisville is one of the most picturesque and oldest towns in the state. Named after St. Francis of Assisi, the community was established in 1785 on land granted to the Capuchine friars by the Spanish crown. Other sites of interest include Grace Episcopal Church, Barrow House, Oakley, Catalpa Plantation, Afton Villa Gardens, The Cottage, and Greenwood Plantation. For further information contact The West Feliciana Historical Society at 364 Ferdinand Street by writing Box 338, St. Francisville, 70775, or call (504) 635-6330. Attending the "Audubon Pilgrimage" the third week in March or "Christmas in the Country" in December are nice ways to capture some of the essence of the town.

San Francisco Plantation. (504) 535-2341. This 1856 home's original name *Sans Frusquin* is French slang for "without a penny." The exuberantly painted "Steamboat Gothic" mansion was commissioned by a man who thought the Greek Revival mansions of his friends to be dull. A belvedere similar to a ship's crow's nest caps the third-floor ballroom.

Tezcuco Plantation. (504) 562-3929. The raised cottage, fronted by six square columns joined by wrought-iron railings, was completed in 1855. It is seven miles (10 km) above the Sunshine Bridge and has guest cottages and an antique shop.

■ SWAMP AND BAYOU TOURS

Bayou Segnette Swamp Tours. 561-8244/(800) 633-0503. A picturesque swamp tour which focuses on the life of the Cajuns.

Honey Island Swamp Tours. 242-5877/(504) 641-1769. The 250-square-mile (650-square-km) wetland area on the Pearl River is explored with ecologist Dr. Paul Wagner and native guides.

Jean Lafitte National Historic Park. Barataria Unit; 589-2330. Nature trails and guided canoe trips, especially nice in the early spring when the native iris are in bloom.

Southern Seaplane. 394-5633. Air tour of the marsh environs and the city.

Tours by Isabelle. 391-3344. Cajun alligator hunters give guided tours in isolated cypress swamps.

■ NEW ORLEANS TOURS

There are literally dozens of tours advertised in the tourist literature. To determine the best we asked various concierge and museum house operators for their recommendations. Because of new zoning regulations in the historic neighborhoods, the large buses cannot wind through many of the streets in the older neighborhoods. For this reason, the smaller companies' mini-vans are best for viewing architecture.

■ SELF-GUIDED TOURS

New Orleans Self-Guided Walking and Driving Tours. 566-5068. A 1990 publication of the Greater New Orleans Tourist & Convention Commission. Free.

René Beaujolais's French Quarter Extraordinary Guide. An inexpensive, jumbo-brochure-sized walking tour for sale in many of the shops in the French Quarter which offers an overview of the important sites of the Quarter and contains an easy-to-follow double-page color map.

Your Sound Promenade. 8018 Trout Rd., N.O. 70126; 243-1098. These two 90-minute cassettes can be purchased at Quarter Stitch in the Pontalba Building. The author grew up in French Quarter in 1930s and his reminiscences include his boyhood talks with the children of Civil War veterans who lived in the French Quarter. The tapes are filled with legends and the sounds of the city.

■ RECOMMENDED CITY TOURS

Gray Line of New Orleans. 587-0861/(800) 535-7786. This full tour service of New Orleans and surrounding area is thorough and slightly institutional. Eight tours daily depart from behind Jax Brewery.

Helicopters Su West Airways Inc. 242-4883. Pilot's eye view of the city; trips from one-half to two hours from the downtown heliport by the Superdome or the lakefront.

Limousine Livery. 561-8777/561-1000. Many drivers of the stretch Lincolns, Cadillacs, and Sedans are licensed tour guides and they charge no more for the service. When price is no object, the family-operated company can structure a half or full day of activities to the needs of the client. Priced by the hour (minimum three hours), some cars will accommodate 10 people. So the larger the party, the more affordable.

Tours by Inez. 486-1123. Two friendly, fun, and informative tours daily, departing from 339 Chartres, the courtyard of the Hotel de la Poste. Tours must be booked ahead. There is an eight person minimum, 20 person maximum. Tours of houses and gardens on request. (Seven languages spoken.)

Tours by Isabelle. 391-3544. The Combo Tour, a personalized four-hour afternoon city tour and visit to the house and garden at Longue Vue given by this specialized company is one of the best buys going for the discerning traveler.

U.S.A. Convention Planners & Heritage Tours. 592-0560. "Roots of New Orleans," four-hour historical tours focusing on black history with visits to the Quadroon Ballroom and the Amistad Research Center. The morning tours include lunch at a soul food restaurant.

■ FRENCH QUARTER TOURS

Friends of the Cabildo. 523-3939. The informative two-hour walking tours begin at the Friends of the Cabildo Store at 523 St. Ann on Jackson Square, and generally take place twice a day. No reservations necessary.

Gay '90s Carriage. 943-8820. Mule-drawn carriage tour of the French Quarter. The great benefit is the vantage point for viewing the architecture.

Jean Lafitte National Historic Park and Preserve. French Quarter Unit, 916 N. Peters St., 70116; (504) 589-2636/3840. Three tours a day. First come, first serve. All tours are 90 minutes, and vary depending on the time of day.

Tours by Inez. 486-1123. Inez and her 26 guides offer insiders' tips on everything from happy hours to cheap music. Inez gives an overview, heading visitors in the direction of their interest, nipping into private courtyards for a history lesson. Every day, morning and afternoon. By reservation only. Around two hours.

◊ **Voodoo Walking Tour.** 523-7685. See the folklore of the French Quarter including Marie Lauveau's tomb, the Pharmacy Museum, Congo Square, and the exterior of the haunted house. Every afternoon. Two and a half hours.

■ GARDEN DISTRICT TOURS

Jean Lafitte National Historic Park and Preserve. Garden District Tour, 916 N. Peters St., 70116; 589-2636. "Faubourg Promenade" is a one-mile (1.6-km), hour-and-a-half, park ranger–guided stroll through the historic area each afternoon. Reservations can be made by phone or letter up to three months in advance. The meeting place for those with reservations is the corner of First and St. Charles. Free.

■ RIVER TOURS

Creole Queen Paddlewheeler. 27 Poydras St.; 529-4567/(800) 445-4109. Narrated cruises on the Mississippi River on a replica of a nineteenth-century paddlewheeler. Tours to the Chalmette Battlefield.

New Orleans Steamboat Company. Natchez/Cotton Blossom, behind Jax Brewery; (504) 586-8777/(800) 233-BOAT (2628). Narrated bayou and harbor cruises; dance and dinner cruises; and the "Zoo Cruise" between the Aquarium of the Americas and the Audubon Zoo.

■ PLANTATION TOURS

Gray Line. 587-0861. A six-hour guided coach tour along the river road.

Tours by Isabelle. 391-3544. A personalized seven-hour trip through three antebellum mansions with lunch at Madewood in the formal dining room.

■ MILITARY SITE TOURS

Fort Pike State Commemorative Area. 662-5703. Tour of the fort built after the War of 1812 to defend New Orleans waterways.

Jackson Barracks Military Museum. 278-6242. Guns, guts, and glory from the Revolutionary War to Desert Storm, tours by appointment.

Jean Lafitte National Historic Park. Chalmette Unit. 589-4428; 589-4573. The site of the 1815 Battle of New Orleans. There is a 30-minute movie shown on request and four talks daily on the battlefield. Free.

Tours by Inez. 486-1123. By request to the Steamboat House, Jackson Barracks, and battlefields. One-half day.

■ SPECIAL INTEREST

Accent Companions for Kids. 938 Lafayette, Suite 201, N.O. 70130; 524-1227. Professional escorts design special tours for the individual child or teenager from 6 to 18. Far more than babysitting, these tours allow children to see sites and learn history and culture with their own specially trained adult companions.

Architectural Tours. 604 Julia St., N.O. 70130; 581-7032. The Preservation Resource Center can arrange an in-depth tour of the historic neighborhoods with an emphasis on the architecture. Forty-eight hours notice required.

Jean Lafitte National Historic Park and Preserve. Islenos Unit, 1357 Bayou Rd., St. Bernard; 682-0862. The Islenos Unit is a museum dedicated to the Islenos people of St. Bernard Parish, whose ancestors settled in Louisiana during Spanish Colonial rule. Free.

Let's Go Antiquing. 899-3027. Macon Riddle and her associates, antique aficionados one and all, offer half- and full-day specialized "hunting" expeditions designed for the needs of the specific client.

Litera-Tour! 6123 Loyola St., N.O. 70118; 861-8158. A two-and-a-half-hour French Quarter walking tour through local literary history and lore with author Carolyn Kolb.

Louisiana Superdome. Sugar Bowl Dr.; 587-3885. Daily tours will thrill sports fans.

■ CEMETERY TOURS

Lakelawn Metairie Cemetery. 5100 Pontchartrain Blvd.; 486-6331. Cassette and map for walking tour are available at the funeral homes of the palatial 1872 cemetery park. Free.

Save Our Cemeteries. 588-9357. This non-profit group offers a fascinating tour of St. Louis No. 1 given by dedicated volunteer guides each Sunday morning. The price of the hour-and-a-half tour includes the protection of a New Orleans police officer. Three tours a week in the morning of Lafayette Cemetery No. 1 in the Garden District, 1400 Washington. Reservations are a must.

■ B I L I N G U A L   T O U R S
Tours by Inez. 486-1123. German, French, Italian, Russian, Japanese, and Spanish.
Tours by Isabelle. 391-3544. French and English free. All other languages including Swedish, Dutch, Japanese, and Chinese are a few dollars extra per person.

■ S P E C I A L   E V E N T S
Historic Homes Christmas Tours. The Preservation Resource Center, 581-7032, gives holiday tours to seven or eight private historic homes over the first weekend in December.
Spring Fiesta. 581-1367/945-2744. In early to late April, this group sponsors tours of private homes in the French Quarter and several other historic districts.

■ TELEVISION AND RADIO

■ T E L E V I S I O N
Local nightly news appears at 5 P.M., 6 P.M., and 10 P.M. on weeknights. National news is broadcast at 5:30 P.M. The daily *Times-Picayune* has a weekly programs listing as a supplement to the Sunday paper and offers daily television listings in the "Living" section of the paper.

ABC, Channel 8, WVUE, 486-6161.

CBS, Channel 4, WWL, 529-4444.

NBC, Channel 6, WDSU, 527-0666.

PBS programming can be seen on WYES, Channel 12, and WNOL, Channel 32.

FOX programming appears on Channel 38, the local independent channel owned by Quincy Jones. WGNO, Channel 26, is the other independent channel.

■ R A D I O

The local airwaves of late have become rather rife with surprises as programmers, on-air personalities, formats, and owners remain in a constant state of flux.

WWNO, 89.9 FM broadcasts classical music and National Public Radio (NPR) twice daily—once in the early morning and once in the early evening.

WWOZ, 90.7 FM is owned by the New Orleans Jazz & Heritage Foundation and is staffed with volunteer local music aficionados. Twenty-four hours a day the local airwaves are alive with the sounds of traditional jazz, gospel, vintage country and R&B as well as a variety of programs on Caribbean, African, bluegrass, and Irish music.

WYLD, 98.5 FM is a black-owned and operated station that often plays exceptional classic tunes from Smokey Robinson; Earth, Wind and Fire; and Grover Washington, Jr. The station is geared to the urban contemporary audience.

WNOE, 101.1 FM has carved a niche for itself with a rip-roaring country format aimed at the urban audience on a first-name basis with Reba and Travis.

WRBH, 88.3 FM features books and newspapers read for the print-impaired, including wonderful bedtime stories for kids and late-night erotica for grownups.

■ SPORTS

Baseball. Although New Orleans has no major league teams, Tulane University and the University of New Orleans host top collegiate games in the spring which are well worth attending. There is, however, one minor league team, the Zephyrs. For information and tickets, call 282-6777.

Basketball. The Superdome is the site of both the NCAA Final Four when played in New Orleans, and of the Sugar Bowl Basketball Tournament played the week preceding the annual football classic.

Football. The New Orleans Saints of the NFL play Sundays at the Superdome, where cries of "Who dat say say they gonna beat them Saints?" fill the stands. Tulane plays Saturday afternoons. On New Year's Day each year the Superdome hosts the Sugar Bowl, and every four years hosts the Super Bowl. For Saints tickets, call 522-2600; for Tulane tickets, call 861-3661.

■ IMPORTANT PHONE NUMBERS AND ADDRESSES

Directory Information: 411
Emergency: 911
New Orleans Police: 821-2222
Louisiana State Police: 483-4830
New Orleans Fire Department: 581-3473
Orleans Parish Medical Society: 523-2474
New Orleans Dental Association: 834-6449
Travelers Aid Society: 525-8726
Weather Recording: 465-9212
Events Information: 566-5055
Chamber of Commerce/New Orleans and the River Region: 301 Camp St., New Orleans, 70130; 527-6900.
Downtown Development District: 301 Camp St., N.O. 70130; 561-8927.
Greater New Orleans Tourist & Convention Commission: 1520 Sugar Bowl Dr. at the Superdome, N.O. 70112; (504) 566-5011.
Jefferson Parish Information Center: 300 Veterans Blvd., Kenner 70062; 468-7527.
Kenner Office of Tourism: 2100 Third St., Unit 10, Kenner, 70062; 468-7527.
Louisiana State Office of Tourism: 568-5661/(800) 33-GUMBO (334-8626).

RECOMMENDED READING

■ FICTION

Bosworth, Sheila. *Almost Innocent.* New York: Simon & Schuster, 1984. The dark side of a proper Catholic girls' school upbringing. *Slow Poison.* New York: Alfred A. Knopf, 1992.

Bradford, Roark. *Old Adam and His Children.* New York: Harper & Row, c. 1928. *Kingdom Coming.* New York: Harper, 1933. Voodoo during the Civil War and Reconstruction.

Brite, Poppy Z. *Lost Souls.* New York: Bantam, 1993. *Drawing Blood.* New York: Delacorte, 1993. Local color with a liberal dose of horror.

Butler, Robert Olen. *A Good Scent from Strange Mountain.* New York: Henry Holt, 1992. Compelling 1992 Pulitzer Prize-winning short stories set in the local Vietnamese community.

Cable, George Washington. *Old Creole Days.* New York: Scribner, 1879. Pithy portraits of nineteenth-century Creoles.

Capote, Truman. *Music for Chameleons.* New York: Random House, 1975. A young boy's experience of New Orleans.

Chopin, Kate. *The Awakening.* Chicago: H. S. Stone & Co., 1899. A poignant tale of a nineteenth-century Creole wife who must come to grips with her own sexuality.

Faulkner, William. *Mosquitoes.* New York: Liveright, 1955. The swinging set of the 1920s.

Friedman, Patty. *The Exact Image Of Mother.* New York: Viking Press, 1991. A black comedy about life inside the sophisticated Jewish community of the city.

Gilchrist, Ellen. *In the Land of Dreamy Dreams.* Fayetteville: University of Arkansas Press, 1985. An anthology of short stories with recurring characters. They provide one of the strongest portraits of contemporary Uptown/old-line society.

Grau, Shirley Ann. *Keepers of the House.* New York: Knopf, 1964. *House on Coliseum Street.* New York: Avon Books, 1961.

Hellman, Lillian. *Pentimento.* Boston: Little, Brown, 1973. The author's autobiography written in exquisite prose.

Keyes, Francis Parkinson. *Dinner at Antoine's.* New York: Julian Messner, Inc., 1948. An Agatha Christie-style murder mystery set in the famed eatery. *Madame Castel's Lodger.* New York: Farrar, Strauss, & Cudahy, 1962. A story set in the years when General Beauregard was a lodger in the house which the author later bought.

King, Grace. *The Pleasant Ways of St. Medard.* New York: Henry Holt, 1916. The Creole apologist strikes a literary blow for Creole dignity.

Leonard, Elmore. *Bandits.* New York: Arbor House, 1988. A contemporary adventure that crosses all social lines.

Martin, Valerie. *A Recent Martyr.* Boston: Houghton-Mifflin, 1987. The New Orleans Catholic culture of the future. *Great Divorce.* New York: Bantam, 1995. Audubon Zoo and the Uptown university scene provide a backdrop for adultery and the return of the Cat Woman.

Percy, Walker. *The Moviegoer.* New York: Knopf, 1960. A suburban stockbroker uses Mardi Gras as a metaphor for finding meaning in life.

Rice, Anne. *The Feast of All Saints.* New York: Simon & Schuster, 1979. A tale of some of the free people of color before the Civil War. *Interview with a Vampire.* New York: Ballantine Books, 1976. *The Vampire Lestat.* New York: Knopf, 1976. *The Queen of the Damned.* New York: Knopf, 1988. *Witching Hour.* New York: Knopf, 1990. *Lasher.* New York: Random House, 1993. The poetry and witchcraft of four generations of one family. The story is set in the author's own Garden District mansion. *Memnoch, the Devil.* New York: Random House, 1995. Fifth and last Vampire Lestat book.

Robbins, Tom. *Jitterbug Perfume.* New York: Bantam Books, 1984.

Sallis, James. *Long-legged Fly.* New York: Carrol and Graf, 1992. *Moth.* New York: Carrol and Graf, 1993. *Black Hornet.* New York: Carrol and Graf, 1994. New Orleans through the eyes of a black detective.

Sancton, Tommy. *Count Rollerskate.* New York: Doubleday, 1956. A Felliniesque look at the carnies who come to New Orleans for Mardi Gras.

Saxon, Lyle. *Fabulous New Orleans.* New York: Appleton-Century, 1928. Mardi Gras through the eyes of a boy and other episodes involving voodoo and plagues. *LaFitte the Pirate.* New York: The Century Co., 1930. A romantic folktale of the glamorous rogue.

Smith, Julie. *New Orleans Mourning.* New York: Ballantine, 1990. The Edgar Award-winning murder mystery that takes place in the world of the Boston Club and the Rex parade. *Jazz Funeral.* New York: Fawcett Columbine, 1993. The producer of Jazz Fest is murdered in this compelling mystery set within the inner circle of the spring festival. *New Orleans Beat.* New York: Fawcett Columbine, 1994. Computer hacker intrigue in Uptown New Orleans. *House of Blues.* New York: Ballantine Fawcett, 1995. The underbelly of the local casino and restaurant business.

Toole, John Kennedy. *A Confederacy of Dunces.* New York: Grove Press, 1980. Winner of Pulitzer Prize. Contemporary New Orleans at its funky best.

Miller, John, and Genevieve Anderson, Ed. *New Orleans Stories.* San Francisco: Chronicle Books, 1992. A collection of comments and descriptions of the city by a few dozen of America's finest writers.

Williams, Tennessee. *A Streetcar Named Desire.* Copyright 1947 by Tennessee Williams, reprinted by New Directions. The well-known play portraying a less-than-happy couple dealing with the wife's bizarre sister.

Wiltz, Chris. *The Killing Circle.* New York: Macmillan, 1981. *A Diamond Before You Die.* New York: Mysterious Press, 1987. *The Emerald Lizard.* New York: Dutton, 1991. The same Irish Channel detective makes his way through the French Quarter, Lakeview, the West Bank, and Uptown as he unravels a series of mysteries. *Glass House.* Baton Rouge: Louisiana State University Press, 1994. The complexity of racial friendships and fear in the Garden District.

■ HOME & GARDEN

The seven-volume *New Orleans Architecture Series* is the definitive record of the architectural treasures of the city. The books were written in the 1970s and '80s by well-known architects and preservationists. They are available through Pelican Publishing in Gretna; 368-1175.

Seidenberg, Charlotte. *The New Orleans Garden*. New Orleans: Silkmont & Count, 1990. Beautiful prose written by a knowledgeable naturalist.

Sexton, Richard, and Randolf Delehanty. *Elegance and Decadence*. San Francisco: Chronicle Books, 1993. The essence of New Orleans style told with distinctive voice and vision.

Starr, Frederick. *Southern Comfort: The Garden District of New Orleans, 1800-1900*. Cambridge, MA: M.I.T. Press, 1989. Family lore and architecture are discussed in a readable format.

CREOLE HOME WEDDINGS

*T*he weddings are also made at night, altho' I must say that at present a few weddings are blessed in church, but most of them have the blessing and the ceremony in the homes. What brought about this custom and this kindness from the priest is that scarcely thirty years ago, the city was a pool of mud after heavy rains. The streets were not paved, there was no way of getting a public carriage or means of transportation. One old lady, belonging to the best Creole society told me that when she was a young girl, in order to attend the balls and receptions, she was obliged to take off her shoes and walk barefooted in the mud, up to the house where she was invited. Several young girls would make a party and walk in the mud barefooted. In the back walking close by were three women slaves carrying the dainty ball slippers, and all necessary articles to clean and wash the feet when the guests arrived at the home where the ball was given. It is then not surprising that to avoid this inconvenience to a whole wedding party and the bride and groom, the priests had the kindness to make the ceremony in the home of the bride. Torrential rains made the roads and the streets lakes and pools of mud, and naturally it was impossible to request the entire wedding party to cross the city under such conditions.

—Helen d'Aquin Allain,
memoir describing New Orleans c. 1830s

■ HISTORY

Kemp, John R. *New Orleans*. Woodland Hills, CA: Windsor Publications, Inc., 1981. A thorough and entertaining history of the city.

■ CHILDREN'S BOOKS

Fontenont, Mary Alice. The *Clovis the Crawfish* Series. Gretna: Pelican. The 11-book series uses Cajun folk wisdom to help a crawfish handle life's problems.

■ LOUISIANA COOKING

Chase, Leah. *The Dooky Chase Cookbook*. Gretna: Pelican, 1991. Creole-of-color heritage, history, and recipes by one of the city's premier chefs.

Folse, John. *The Encyclopedia of Cajun & Creole Cuisine*. Donaldsonville: The Encyclopedia Cookbook Committee, Inc., 1983. Easy to follow recipes that cross Creole and Cajun lines.

The Junior League of Baton Rouge. *River Road Recipes*. Baton Rouge: Junior League, 1959. Louisiana home cooking at its finest in this granddaddy of all charity cookbooks in America.

The Junior League of New Orleans. *The Plantation Cookbook*. New Orleans: B. E. Trice Publishing, Inc., 1989. Since the book first came out in the 1970s, it has become a staple for local cooks.

■ MUSIC

Armstrong, Louis. *Satchmo: My Life in New Orleans*. New York: Da Capo Press, 1986. The jazz legend's own candid story.

Bechet, Sidney. *Treat It Gentle*. New York: Da Capo Press, 1960. The fascinating autobiography of one of New Orleans's jazz greats.

Berry, Jason, Jonathan Foose, and Tad Jones. *Up From The Cradle of Jazz: New Orleans Music Since World War II*. Athens: The University of Georgia, 1986. The behind-the-scenes look at the Dew Drop Inn and the early careers of such legends as Fats Domino and the Neville Brothers.

Carter, William. *Preservation Hall: Music from the Heart.* New York: W. W. Norton, 1991. Traditional jazz revealed with interviews and compassion.

Friedlander, Lee. *The Jazz People of New Orleans.* New York: Pantheon, 1992. Photographs of the city's jazz legends and marching bands, with a personal afterword on the jazz mecca by expert Whitney Balliett.

Rose, Al. *Storyville, New Orleans.* Tuscaloosa: University of Alabama, 1967. The music and life of this district are described by a well-known authority on jazz.

Smith, Michael P. *A Joyful Noise: A Celebration of New Orleans Music.* Dallas: Taylor, 1990. Smith's black and white photographs pay homage to the music culture of the streets of New Orleans.

■ SPIRITUALISM AND VOODOO

Dreyer, Edward, Lyle Saxon, and Robert Tallant. *Gumbo Ya Ya: The Folklore of Louisiana.* Gretna: Pelican, 1945. Folktales and history reveal as much about the authors as about their subjects.

Smith, Michael P. *Spirit World.* Gretna: Pelican, 1984. The rituals of the Spiritual churches are revealed in Smith's brilliant black and white images.

■ GUIDEBOOKS

Fodor's New Orleans. New York, Fodor's Travel Publications, 1996.

Fonseca, Mary. *Weekend Getaways in Louisiana and Mississippi.* Gretna: Pelican, 1993. Well researched, even giving advice on which hotel rooms to choose.

Griffin, Thomas. *The Pelican Guide to New Orleans.* Gretna: Pelican, 1991.

Naylor, Honey, ed. *Insight City Guides' New Orleans.* New York, APA Publications, 1992.

Odom, Keith. *Only in Louisiana.* Baton Rouge: Quail Ridge Press, 1994.

I N D E X

COMPASS AMERICAN GUIDES

Critics, Booksellers, and Travelers All Agree You're Lost Without a Compass.

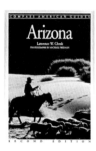

Arizona (3rd Edition)
1-878-86772-5
$17.95 ($25.00 Can)

Chicago (1st Edition)
1-878-86728-8
$16.95 ($21.50 Can)

Colorado (2nd Edition)
1-878-86735-0
$16.95 ($21.50 can)

Hawaii (2nd Edition)
1-878-86769-5
$17.95 ($25.00 Can)

"Exactly the sort of historical and cultural detail about North American destinations that curious-minded travelers need."
— *Washington Post*

"Use them not only to plan your trip, but to savor the memories once you're back home."
— *Mademoiselle*

"Highly evocative... the chapter on food forced me to stop reading and go eat."
—*New York Times*

"Compass Guides capture the true spirit of a place from its early settler days to modern times."
— *America Online*

Montana (2nd Edition)
1-878-86743-1
$17.95 ($25.95 Can)

New Mexico (1st Edition)
1-878-86706-7
$15.95 ($19.95 Can)

New Orleans (2nd Edition)
1-878-86786-5
$17.95 ($25.00 Can)

South Dakota (1st Edition)
1-878-86726-1
$16.95 ($22.95 Can)

Texas (1st Edition)
1-878-86764-4
$17.95 ($25.00 Can)

Utah (3rd Edition)
1-878-86773-3
$17.95 ($25.00 Can)

To order a Compass Guide, call Random House at (800) 733-3000.

Hollywood (2nd Edition)
1-878-86771-7
$16.95 ($23.50 Can)

Las Vegas (4th Edition)
1-878-86782-2
$17.95 ($25.00 Can)

Maine (1st Edition)
1-878-86751-2
$16.95 ($22.95 Can)

Manhattan (1st Edition)
1-878-86737-7
$17.95 ($25.00 Can)

Oregon (1st Edition)
1-878-86733-4
$16.95 ($21.50 Can)

San Francisco (3rd Edition)
1-878-86770-9
$16.95 ($23.50 Can)

Santa Fe (1st Edition)
1-878-86775-X
$17.95 ($25.95 Can)

South Carolina (1st Edition)
1-878-86766-0
$16.95 ($23.50 Can)

Virginia (1st Edition)
1-878-86741-5
$16.95 ($22.95 Can)

Washington (1st Edition)
1-878-86758-X
$17.95 ($25.00 Can)

Wisconsin (1st Edition)
1-878-86744-X
$16.95 ($22.95 Can)

Wyoming (2nd Edition)
1-878-86750-4
$17.95 ($25.00 Can)

ROSEMARY CARROLL BUTLER

■ ABOUT THE AUTHOR

Bethany Ewald Bultman has never ceased being an enthusiastic tourist in New Orleans. She first fell in love with the city as a child when she started making monthly trips from her home in Natchez, Mississippi with her parents. After attending college at Tulane, she made it her permanent home. Her articles on food, design, travel, architecture, and ethnic culture have appeared in such publications as *Town & Country, Elle Decor, American Heritage, House Beautiful, Travel & Leisure,* and *Travel Holiday.* She has served as a contributing editor for *House & Garden* since 1975, and has written two previous books, *The Joys of Entertaining* which she co-authored with Bev Church (Abbeville Press, 1987) and *Reflections of the South* (Gallery Books, 1991).

Now she has turned her full attention back to her favorite passions and pastimes—the food, the music and the socio-economic complexities of New Orleans, where she lives in a historic home in the Garden District with her husband and two sons.

■ ABOUT THE PHOTOGRAPHER

Richard Sexton lives in an 1860s shotgun cottage in Uptown New Orleans with his wife Rives and daughters, Adrianne and Claire.

Sexton's images of architecture, interiors, and gardens have appeared in *Abitare, Home, Interiors,* the *Los Angeles Times Magazine,* the *New York Times, Southern Accents,* and *Smithsonian,* among others. He is the author and photographer of *The Cottage Book* (1989), *In the Victorian Style* (1991) and *New Orleans: Elegance and Decadence* (1993), all published by Chronicle Books. His most recent book, *Parallel Utopias,* was published by Chronicle in 1995.